En Punto

Arriving at *THERE*: a study in spiritual exactness.

C.R. Oliver

EN PUNTO

DR. C. R. OLIVER

© 2002, C.R. Oliver

ISBN 1-931898-00-6

Zadok Publications Inc.
Subsidiary of OEA Intl.
P.O. Box 971
MONTGOMERY, TEXAS 77356
www.zadokpublications.org
E-Mail: zadok8@yahoo.com
zadok@wt.net

Printed in Colombia

Dedication

En Punto is dedicated to all those who have been brought into my life through the Holy Spirit. Seemingly they fall into two categories: those who have crossed my path physically and those who have invaded my thinking through their works. Most are in both categories. The names mentioned here are but a token of the vast array of those foreign and domestic who are on my heart and emblazoned in my spiritual history. I shall simply name them as they come to mind:

Rev. James Cass Oliver, Great Uncle, who dedicated me to the work of the Kingdom

Dr. Porter M. Bailes, Sr., Pastor and friend who dared to lay on hands of anointing

Dr. J. C. Chadwick, Fellow minister who saw potential beyond the flesh and into the spirit

Dr. Leonard Ravenhill, whose books and personal friendship still mount up on eagles' wing

Rev. Frank C. Sisson, a friend for 48 years, who always held me before the throne of God

Clayt Sonmore, a Prince in the kingdom whose fierce consistency has overcome

Russell Stendal, Missionary to Colombia, whose work ever increases in fruit for Jesus

Rev. Kenneth Copeland and his son-in-law, Rev. George Pearsons for ministry to my spirit

Rev. Keith Moore and his mentor, Rev. Kenneth Hagin, whose teachings on faith prevail

Rev. John G. Lake, who left this world when I entered it, whose life and writings live on

Rev. Billy Sunday, whose dynamic message indelibly marked my inner man

Rev. C.B. Jackson, evangelist, whose messages still ring in my heart after 50 years

Dr. Cassius Elijah Autry, whose fiery Elijah-Spirit never ceases to challenge

Aunt Kate Lindsey, whose nurturing faith that "the Lord makes a way where there is none" found fertile ground in my young heart and sustained me for many a year.

Dr. M. B. Wade, Prof. emeritus, mentor and friend

The Oliver and Floyd families that comprise my extended family, who came to this country for religious freedom and found it.

To my father and my mother who loved their son dearly and who found that love returned.

To a vast number of missionaries by whose side I have worked and who labor under great travail, many who have loved not their lives to the death

To great men and women of God who have not known a pulpit, only a prayer closet and used it to hold up the arms of the servant of God—Furman Barber, Veatrice Spraggins, Willard Propst, Glenn and Liz Manning, and Mattie Pearson to name a few.

To all these dignitaries, I dedicate this text, only the Spirit could have caused our paths to cross.

Preface

*A*t least one indispensable prerequisite exists for those who aspire to engage in what is described in this book. The practice of *En Punto* requires a pure heart that can only be the result of coming into covenant with God on God's terms. Man's schools, discipline and training can provide certain theological formation but only a direct and sustained encounter with the presence of God will result in transformation.

To attempt *En Punto* with a heart that is less than pure will undoubtedly lead to deception, betrayal and defeat. This is one of the main reasons that most established Christian groups set up some form of human "covering" in a futile attempt to protect their directives, order and reputation. Who are you submitted to? Where do you congregate? What group are you licensed by? Questions like these have become the order of the day as well meaning Christians attempt to isolate themselves from the contamination and compromise that have become all too prevalent among those who name the name of Christ.

Unfortunately, when the directives of the Spirit are submitted to the bureaucracy of man for confirmation and approval, the exact timing and precision necessary for success is often lost in the shuffle. *En Punto* goes beyond the gifts and callings of ministry that are known to the age of Pentecost. Those like myself, who have been walking in the wonderful realm of *En Punto* for years in difficult areas such as the war zone of eastern Colombia, know that many times decisions involving life or death have to be made in a split second without even the time to offer a formal prayer for guidance. Only the instantaneous response of the Holy Spirit through a heart that is clean and pure will suffice. Jesus' ministry was a sequence of such occasions as he walked in perfect agreement and submission linked by the Spirit to the heart of His Father.

Pureness of heart is never the direct product of human instruction or of submission to human ministry, order or directive. It cannot be obtained by years spent in a Bible School or Seminary or by submitting to the leadership of a given religious order, church group or Christian community. True purity of heart comes only by the direct dealings of God in the life of the believer. In his two previous books, C.R. Oliver covers this ground in detail. Therefore, I consider the message contained in *Solomon's Secret* and *The Sons of Zadok* to be of great importance to those who read this book.

Just as the hearts of the disciples burned within them as they walked with Jesus on the road to Emmaus, so will your heart burn with a new intensity and expression of the love of God —if you allow the Lord to correct you as a son and prepare you to represent Him as He desires to be represented. Soon He will begin to guide you to the right people in the right place at the right time with the right word and in the right company. This is the way of life that my friend C.R. Oliver calls *En Punto*. May God bless you as you receive this timely word.

Russell M. Stendal
Editor

Order Solomon's Secret "

Introduction

Within the pages of this book lie principles that were fully explored and utilized by the early church. The book of Acts is really a model in which all bodies of believers should find themselves. One of the deep premises of this text is that somehow through the ages following the early church, the true model for ministry has been lost or changed.

En Punto is about restoring that model. Because of the complexity of the issue, twelve chapters of faithful Biblical study have emerged as the book's foundation. *En Punto* has its place in Christian Literature for one reason, the Spirit brought it forth. Compromising tolerance characterizes the demeanor of the church in the Twenty-first Century. *En Punto* stands as a challenge to this Un-Divine Order. Somewhere in the realm of Christendom, there must arise a clear call to strict obedience to the Holy Spirit. When the new millennium arrived, spiritual history changed forever. *En Punto* declares this new day as important to world history as A.D. was to B.C. The old order is forever done with as the Lord establishes a dominion in the hearts of people unparalleled in spiritual history. He is assembling His Church, one that hears His voice and does only what He instructs.

En Punto is about that body of believers. As the text develops its themes, great streams of understanding will pour into the reader's spirit. En Punto was designed to be a study-not light reading. En Punto was written to be a guide toward its companion volume to be published in 2003, *The Regal Pair*. As the author, I ask that you seek the Lord as you read these pages and repent every time the Spirit shows the need. Read its pages marking the times your spirit soars to new heights of understanding and never cease to pray this prayer—"Lord, I will do what you command."

C.R. Oliver, Spring 2002

Table of Contents

vested authority; Differentiation of man's work and
God's work; Study in Gospel of John of Jesus' use of
spiritual authority; God assigned spiritual authority;
walking in Dominion and Power within the Spirit;
Hosea and *En Punto*; Spiritual authority today.

CHAPTER ONE

En Punto

"A study in spiritual exactness"

INDIA

As Abraham Rao purchased his ticket at the rail station in Northern India, he again quizzed himself about why he was leaving at this specific time and embarking on a twenty-five hundred mile trip south to his native Hyderbad. Hyderbad, Andhra Pradesh, in Southern India was where his father's ministry had been; Samath Nagar Church was his home church. He consoled himself that the Lord had pressed upon him the urgency of returning (he thought) in order to clear up matters related to his late parents' estate. Since they had been dead only a short while, perhaps there was business only his hands could conclude. His own fellowship (a small Mission) understood why he felt he must return, and key believers volunteered to keep his congregation during his absence. Still, there was an ingredient almost unexplainable in this trip, a degree of urgency deep within his spirit that he knew was leadership from God—but why now? Why wouldn't the Lord allow him a few more weeks before going, when his financial situation could better afford his traveling? Oh, no! Every time he had contemplated such action, his inner man would press upon him the necessity of "now." (Such is the leadership of the Holy Spirit upon the likes of man.) He knew his commitment to follow the Spirit's leadership in every aspect of his life was being tested in this matter. He would go; he would stay as long as the Lord wanted him to stay and do whatever the Lord prompted. Besides, his fiance was there.

He gathered his bags and spoke to his companion, one of the new converts from the work he pioneered. The young man was so grateful for Abraham that he could not do enough to show him. Being single, he tended Pastor Rao like an indentured servant. His devotion did not rise from a form of penance but from the knowledge that the Lord had ordered it. Joy surrounded both of them, and they were more true brothers to each other than if they had been blood brothers.

The Journey South

Abraham's companion hoisted their belongings aboard the train, planning to make the best of this test of patience and endurance. Rail travel in India is a unique blend of the exotic and the exhaustive. It is sometimes compared to a cattle car with bench seats. Twenty-five hundred miles would require days of stopping and starting, hours of waiting at intermediate stations as goods and passengers entered and exited all hours of the day and night. Luxury is an unheard of commodity in such travel, as is privacy and accommodation. They had taken the slow train.

The slow train is for those who do not have a lot of money, who live as conservatively as possible, and who understand India. On these trains there are those who take the family goat with them in order to supply multiple children with fresh milk. Huge boxes tied with ropes often substitute for luggage. Passengers wear varying dress, which could range from a beautiful sari to a gauze wrapped loin cloth. India has its Western influences, but in rural India, Abraham's jeans and shirt tended to set him apart. There were plenty of opportunities to witness about Jesus on such a journey, and he convinced himself that this alone might have occasioned the trip. He would soon discover such was not the case.

Convergence From the West

As the two were boarding the train and dreading the trip south, far to the west, members of a different group were making last minute preparations for a mission trip to Hyderbad. Briefings had taken place and assignments were solidified. In a few days, a plane would land these Americans in Deli, and they would be wending south. Cartage had been arranged by a mission board. Their orientation had already cautioned them that Hyderbad was religiously divided between long standing Muslim populations and their rival Hindu counterparts. Pictures of the famous Hindu Temple covered all the travel guides. Fortunately, many Christians resided there also, as testimony to the witness of Thomas who ministered in Madras further south. It seemed beyond belief that one who had been invited to reach inside the wounded body of Jesus would have traveled so far, but he followed the same Spirit each one of them followed.

Reality Test—The First Shock

No one in the group was prepared for the shock which would be encountered upon arrival. Not yet refreshed from a long initial flight, followed by travel south in what might better be described as an ancient school bus, the group was not prepared for the news that came to them shortly after checking into their modest hotel rooms.

Arriving on Saturday afternoon to discover that the Samath Nagar Church pastor had died some forty-five days previously and that no one in the congregation even knew that a mission team was coming, sent the entire group to immediate prayer. "How, Lord, could You direct us to this place, allow us to travel this distance, cause us to be assigned to this congregation in a different culture, and have us face a situation over which we have no control and no one to assist us?" This was not a prayer of faith. It was, however, the opening words to an extended prayer meeting from four devastated missionaries. Faith grew as scriptures were read; the promises of God began taking hold of astonished hearts. Each was forced to review the leadership of the Spirit in his or her separate life, all were convinced it was the Lord who had called them. The primary musician, a retired piano store owner, declared that God knew from the beginning what was to be done. Hearing that elder statesman declare victory encouraged everyone present. One by one, each person came to a similar conclusion. Slowly, God's Spirit Plan was brought into action. The group hired a car and went to the church grounds and there prayed, interceded, and believed, until God showed them He had already answered their prayers.

No Time to Delay

Their prayers were answered twenty-five hundred miles and several days before. The moment Abraham Rao heard the Lord tell him, "Go to Hyderbad," and he boarded the train in obedience—provision was made. Even he did not understand the prohibition of the Spirit when, four hundred miles from his destination, he was tempted to relax a few days in a familiar city. Although his armor-bearer had already taken their luggage to the platform, both of them agreed this was not the will of God. They reboarded and continued without hesitancy, suspicioning the urgency of their mission.

Holy Convergence

The missions group from the U.S. arrived at Samath Nagar church around 5:30 Saturday evening. The church doors were locked; the small gate to the side yard fence was not. They gathered inside the walled area and began praying and thanking the Lord for provision they could not see, knowing that faith would conquer this situation. One of the group went searching at the back of the court and discovered a garage-like area. Since the missions evangelist was the only one tall enough to peer in, he observed two figures asleep, one on a cot and the other on a sitting rug just beyond the place where light struck the floor. Cupping his hands around his eyes and then wiping the dirty windows, he began to tap gently. Finding his tapping met no response, he began a more insistent barrage at which the figure on the cot stirred, but the one sleeping on the rug scrambled to unlock the doors. Sleepily, Abraham Rao and his companion introduced themselves and asked why we were there. After much explanation, his face brightened, and he said in typical Indian fashion, "Not to worry, I now know why the Lord has brought me home, and I also know what I am to do." He then spent the better part of an hour relating their trip, his desire to assist (because he knew all the church members as well as the native language of the area), and his plan of action. The ensuing meeting garnered hundreds of new converts to Christ and included miracles of healing and deliverance. Obedience on the part of two different groups separated by thousands of miles brought God's results.

This was *En Punto* in action.

Each one of the group was beginning to glimpse into the world of *En Punto*, that exact world of provision where thousands of miles make no difference, where circumstances do not reign and where prayers are answered far in advance. When the Lord's leadership is sought and honored, He can maneuver His saints around the globe to assist, testify, encourage, witness. He is able to make provision for His children even if it requires making strange trips of twenty-five hundred miles and beyond. Such is the world of "En Punto."

EN PUNTO—THE MEANING:

En Punto is a Spanish phrase used as the title for this book to relate the exactness by which God can prompt, place, or cause His children to be anywhere, at any time, at His command. Its meaning in Spanish is varied but primarily it means, "on the dot."

En Punto means Abraham Rao sleeping at the back of the church while a group in faith are praying at the front. It means a thousand configurations in the history of a spiritual kingdom as vast as God: a kingdom most church folk do not know exists. It means that in a world of inexact spiritual turpitude, there exists another world, so exact, so specific, that its "hearers and seers" know with definitive power, "what it is to be in the will of God."

Those who walk by the Spirit, live by the Spirit, and are controlled by the Spirit, live in the wonderful clime called: *En Punto*. The *En Punto* life is drastically different from the sloppy life style exhibited by most Christians. *En Punto* has a cosmos of its own. *En Punto* has its own atmosphere. It has its own reward system, its own method of doing and being, its own standards, weights, and measurements. Its judgments are foreign to its spiritual opposite: the modern church. It hears when no voice is heard, unlike those in ancient days who "supposed they heard it thunder." It sees, when the human eye sees nothing. It weeps, when the world has no concept of "why?" It smiles, when frowns are in order, when turmoil and tribulation rear their defiant head.

En Punto means when God sends one across the street in the middle of a walk, there will be a reason beyond which man's comprehension is tuned. Nonetheless, across the street is the place where God ordained His child to be. Perhaps there is a vantage to see from, a person to encounter, a discovery of one sort or another, or just a testing of obedience. When the Spirit says, "Cross the street," the believer crosses!

En Punto, it will soon be discovered, is a measure based on a mark, a place on the clock, or a calculated distance (such as a road sign). It is not a degree of perfection; it is perfection. It finds its definition in exactness and not in approximation. *En Punto* determines what will be the admissible distance parameters surrounding it. It passes through designated areas without trepidation and determines its own course based on plan rather than occasion, circumstance, or opportunity. It fits where it is designed and assumes the responsibility afforded by the fit.

En Punto has a life of its own. One may participate in that life but only on its terms. To be a part of the *En Punto* family means adopting its attitudes and methods. Just as "be ye holy as I am holy" sets forth a different attitude than "thou shalt not," so *En Punto* establishes its different domain. *En Punto* challenges the mind to rethink its basis for making judgments. It reaches into the inner core of one's being and searches for agreement with God's judgment rather than the pseudo-satisfaction of being "acceptable."

BOGOTA, MAY/JUNE, 2000, EN PUNTO'S BIRTH

En Punto was heavy on my mind with all the aforementioned ramifications as I surveyed the rear door of a gathering place which opened to the streets of Bogota. For five days they had gathered, these tested saints, many of whom had suffered indignities as hostages and/or had their ministries shut down by guerrilla action or by right-wing paramilitary groups. They were seasoned souls. They had assembled to hear a fresh word from God. They would not be disappointed.

The faces of these saints did not often reflect what they had endured, for not all their testimonies were the same. The age-lines of one such "man of God" who generally arrived at the meetings early did not depict the tremendous stand he had made for his Lord.

The missionary, Martin Stendal, had enumerated this man's faithfulness at an earlier time and shared a few of the extraordinary feats of faith which the Lord had accomplished through him. His small frame did not belie the giant of faith living inside. His warm smile and open demeanor foretold the many experiences inlaid in a life-mosaic filled with Christian love. No one could look into his eyes and not see Jesus indeed lived inside him. Though he spoke little English, he communicated more in one glance than some sermons which have taken hours. (I could not forget the parting I shared with him, late on a Thursday evening, when he tugged on the arm of Marina Stendal and asked her to interpret. Speaking past Marina, he said, "Before you came to Colombia, I saw you in a vision and the Lord said, 'give this man sweet candies,' well, I have no money today to purchase sweet candies—so, instead, I offer you my heart.")

BOGOTA GATHERING

As missionaries arrived following a thirty minute ride by private car, it became apparent that most of the crowd had spent many hours aboard public transportation in order to attend. The deep economic depression of Colombia had devastated some budgets and dreams. When 300 people can gather with only five cars arriving, one knows many walked or rode buses to attend. (Their wage scale barely afforded enough for food and shelter.) Services began somewhere between the announced time and when the majority could get there. Services in South America are characterized by people coming and going at all times during the meetings.

En Punto has nothing to do with Latin American time frames, however, for travel time is always a variable. I surveyed the expanding crowd. This gathering was a mixture of persons from all walks and levels of Christian maturity. Some were physicians (The gathering area was provided by a husband and wife dentist team, who were ardent Christians with connections to daily spiritual broadcasts on local radio.); some were housewives with little children. University students mingled with retirees expressing one single motive— to hear from God. Perhaps that is why the Spirit kept painting pictures of *En Punto*.

The message which had been announced on the previous evening was scrapped in order to make way for God's message—a message which eventually would consist of the format for this book. Born from the heart of God, *En Punto's* message was intended to prepare a people to function in the critical period known as the "last days." Their nation was aflame, caught in the crossfire of opposing forces. Now, America has experienced the same.

Deep within me groanings for these people began to arise. Who could know or estimate their future? Reality for them demanded an understanding of how to listen to the Spirit of God. His Spirit, who was speaking from inside them, would carefully execute His word and directions. Accuracy in hearing and carrying out what was heard was of utmost importance. Their lives depended on knowing and operating in spiritual discernment. Just to say, "My sheep know my voice," is easy, but how one determines if the voice one is hearing is truly His, is a matter of spiritual perception. It involves testing spirits (a quality bereft in the modern church).

As these dear children of the Lord poured into a "standing room only" meeting, I thought, "How similar you are to those saints in history who had to rely totally on the Spirit to direct them to places and times of meeting." (China and the old Soviet Union bore testimony of such in their underground church. The underground church depended upon the voice of the Spirit to warn them of impending danger, reveal future events, give the proper words to answer officials of the State, and bring the Word to their remembrance. Such activity is endemic to the promise of the Holy Spirit, who is sovereign to administer these areas.) Daily, the entire world is moving to a time in history when controlled governments will limit the freedom of believers. True believers may not be allowed to openly gather. Public announcements may not be allowed, but Spirit announcements will always make it through.

My mind trembled at the thought of the magnitude of potential persecution which could befall these figures as they embraced each other, greeted their counterparts across the room, and found seats crowded against one another. The "approved from heaven" are swiftly becoming the "unapproved of earth."

My heart raced ahead of them in anticipation of the time appointed for this message. *En Punto* (This was the title of the message God laid upon my heart.) rested upon me like a runner at the starting line; the energy of it precluded all other actions. I thought, "the power of this message must get out, it must be precise, it must capture the soul and rescue the mind of the hearer." Such is the way of the anointing!

A Heightening Service

When the last strains of music faded to conclusion, it was obvious that the songs of worship had been led by the Spirit. He had arranged them to prepare the congregation for what they were about to experience. God uses many venues for drawing His people, but none so effective as the true gift of music (not the breathy melodies of "would be starlets," but an enfolding concert designed by the Spirit, all the while bathed in the smoke of His Presence). With technological wonders at the beck and call of modern musicians, the worship experience in most congregations falls short of that which took place in David's day. Review I Chronicles 25: 2b and 3b:

> *...the sons of Asaph were under the direction of Asaph, who*
> PROPHESIED *according to the order of the king.*
> *...six, under the direction of their father Jeduthun, who*
> PROPHESIED *with a harp to give thanks and to praise*
> *the LORD.*

Then verse 7:

> *So the number of them, with their brethren who were in-*
> *structed in the songs of the Lord, ...*

Where does one go to experience prophesying in song and by instruments? I believe the key to change for the present day musical shortfall is the Holy Spirit. These Bible-men, dedicated to God's service, were chosen in order, rank, and time by the Spirit of God. Their music was different! Later in another Chronicle passage, there is a review of how lots were cast and how they fell. Imagine casting lots to discover who God wanted to play the music for the service. A music school put together under the direction of the Spirit would be worth attending, for there singers would be taught the "Songs of the Lord."

The musician in charge of the Colombian service came very close to prophesying through the songs he wrote for that evening.

Inside me, a prayer began to form, a prayer of intercession and longing, a quest for God to do a Sovereign work of grace. I called for this work to be so amazing even those not having much spiritual understanding would have complete knowledge of all His desire. This prayer was coming forth from my inner man as my voice was giving instructions to the interpreter. I asked him to read the first of the text passages quoted above. (It is strange, but one can speak to an audience while carrying on a non-verbal dialogue with Jesus about another matter. I will never forget such an occasion in Sao Paulo, Brazil, during the service in the Baptist Church in Maua. I was well into the message on the *Song of Solomon,* when the Lord took my spirit aside from my body, and we discussed His will about another matter. He gave me instructions concerning a situation about to take place in another church and instructed me on what to say and do. All this was going on as my body was delivering the message, without missing a point. Supernatural transmission is often accompanied by exhilarating new experience. To know His will, His ways, and His Word affords a dimension of preachment beyond the average pulpit.) Something amazing did happen that evening in Bogota. The Spirit of God took the oil of anointing and swept through that crowd doing works of healing, conviction, and correction. *En Punto* operated in this dimension; the exact crowd that was to hear this exact message responded in surrender to His exact will—it was beautiful. This is Divine Order! The supernatural is integral to *En Punto*.

Supernatural Leadership

En Punto is about supernatural leadership. To hear, "say this..." or "move here"... "look there" is different from a pre-set agenda. Man is not in control, God is!

> (I liken the leadership of the Spirit to a classroom agenda. It was my habit near the beginning of a semester, to instruct my college classes in this manner: "You are going to experience the same kind of thing one experiences in a tour of an art gallery. I will traverse through the halls of this course pointing out this painting, that sculpture, this or that unique quality which will relate to the subject of study. It may not be the same things I pointed to last semester, or last year, but when you have finished, you will know that you have viewed different thoughts, variant patterns of reason, and hold a grasp of the subject matter which will be equal to any in the world and beyond some.")

When preaching by the Spirit, He is the one doing the pointing out. He determines the emphasis; He guides one through the halls of learning with one motive: perfection in Him! His is an exacting course, not to be entered upon without a commitment (a decision to attain His goal). Matriculating from His instruction gives credentials no theology school can award!

Forever changed is the condition of the heart of His disciple, once having entered His sacred halls. The Spirit is a teacher superceding all others. His wit, His charm, His command outweigh any attributes found in mere man. His hand steadily guides experience so that the student is not an observer, but a participant.

A New Science

An advanced learning takes place when one enters into the subject at hand experientially. As one learns to be extremely obedient to the voice of the Spirit, a spiritual science is born. This becomes science on a higher level. By taking what may appear to be a concept and living out its reality changes it to a Law of Life. To grasp this kind of understanding means that nothing in the Spirit curriculum is subject to shaking.

Nothing can shake it from you. The doubts and fears which attend many learning experiences are answered! Their voices are mute in His classroom. His science calls for a greater dimension of faith than the current church walks in. This is the science practiced by Jesus. The Spirit's directing voice actually becomes the basis for all life experience. One experiences Him!

Any attempt to wrest from you what has actually happened in your experience- zone is nigh impossible. An example of such learning in the Bible is found in the life of Peter and John. It caused Peter and John to reveal a principle of faith: Once having touched Him, no man can say it is not possible to touch Him. Once having tasted Him makes doubters of the tasting of no effect. They would not deny their experience-based life.

> *"For we cannot but speak the things which we have seen and heard."*

Acts 4:20 (NKJV)

Examine Paul, the epistle writer. Paul wrote every epistle having freshly come from the learning halls of the Spirit. No man could change his mind, dampen his resolve, or cause fear to turn him back. THAT IS THE LEARNING EXPERIENCE WHICH MUST BE IN THE REPERTOIRE OF EVERY BELIEVER! These are the last days! There is no time for vacillation. There is no space for error. There is no provision for religious tolerance (using a machinist term by which certain tolerance is built into a product by engineers who measure the degree of variance which can be functionally allowed), for in Him there is no "variance of turning." (Religion allows for tolerance levels beyond those allowed by the Spirit. Here is the problem!)

DIVINE ORDER and *En Punto*

In most religious circles, Divine Order is something different than what is referred to in this text. Clarification of the term "Divine Order" is a most necessary study. In traditional churches, such order might refer to Bishops or Prelates dictating to the congregation what they must do, read, or believe. To them, the stage is always set by long histories of precedence and filled with treatises based on compromise and decorum. In less traditional churches, the same type of order exists but under different guises and through more variant channels. Church order may surface as "committee democracy" or "standard church polity," but always as the end product of compromise. "We have all agreed," sounds different than,"the Lord has directed."

Divine Order does not incorporate echelons of authority, does not consider rules of order and propriety, refuses to submit to man's idea of covering, and does not regard man's dimensions of time and place. (It occurs to me the same inference was made by Jesus while moving along with what is known as "the triumphal entry." [If man refused to do the exact will of God, at God's exact time, then rocks would cry out!])

Time and place are to be designated and determined by the Divine. (Jesus said He did not even know the hour of His own return to earth, for instance.) Time and place are ruled by the Spirit. For the Disciples to receive the baptism of the Holy Spirit, they had to remain in a place designated and for a time to be revealed, both determined by the Spirit alone. This means that the first "conditioning-experience" of the church was on the day of Pentecost. Pentecost is not Pentecost without the discipline of being Spirit-controlled. The modern church must condition itself to be exactly where God calls it to be and there to wait for the Spirit's timing. To experience Pentecost, the church must first experience Spirit-timing. Churches of today seek the miracles of the Disciples without their obedience to Divine authority. The expression of the Spirit demands the sovereignty of the Spirit.

Where is the Church in all this?

The church was born in the wind and fire-power of the anointing through the Holy Spirit. Its spokesmen were moved by the Holy Spirit, DAILY. Who, but the Holy Ghost, could have ordered the steps of Peter down certain streets in order for his shadow to fall on those needing healing and deliverance? Angels escorted prayer recipients through closed gates and guarded towers, carrying out the orders of the Most High (in order for them to appear at the proper time and place the following day). Every believer in the early church was accustomed to such words as: "Arise, Go, Cease, Stop, Stay, Watch, Pray." Such leadership required an ear attuned to Divine Orders. The question must be asked: "Who, in the modern church, hears or cares to hear such direction?" Allow me alliterative license in order to prove a point.

Presently, pious prelates prescribe popular potions patented in "Pablumlabs" and poured out as pitiful placebos to impoverished parishioners. Compare this to the power experience of the church in the book of *Acts*, who waited under Divine Order for their exact timing by the Spirit. The disciples in *Acts* lived the *En Punto* life. They did not miss the mark after Pentecost.

If sin is to be described as "missing the mark," and poor laity (crowded in stained glass sanctuaries) are to be constantly reminded of their miserable state in having "missed it," then what will be their sermon to the clergy? If congregations are to experience the awful consequences accompanying their infraction—what is the judgment to be pronounced on the administrators of their churches for missing *En Punto*? God instructs us that sin is sin. Missing God's mark of Divine Order is so large a sin that it must be dealt with FIRST, before any other malady affecting believers can be treated. In order to fully understand this truth, review the current concerns of the church. The problems and concerns of the modern congregation do not approximate those of the early body. What disturbed the disciples does not disturb today's church, for hearts are not under the discipline of the Spirit as was theirs.

Today, the church's energies are spent in arbitration between "what the Word says," and the "realities of life." Such mediation is a subtle form of legalism which aggrandizes man and his institutional religion. It is as if all the error of the Hebrew Temple, during Jesus' day, has suddenly found itself in Christendom.

Just as the temple rulers had no ear to the voice of the Spirit, their deafness is re-occurring today; their sin is repeated in thousands of congregations. Jesus' message to those "temple-ites" is the same as His message to the church today: "It is too late for all this junk" (Paraphrased). A new hour has dawned and there is no time to filter what God is doing through a system that is out of tune with the Spirit. It is too late to re-arrange dead theological functions (and functionaries) to accommodate what God is bringing swiftly on the scene. It is too late to seek to recharge, renovate, renew, or restore man's order. The only message to those in former days was "come out from them my people." The same message is cogent for today! Inspect the congregation which waited patiently in the upper room. Observe the simplicity with which they prayed and fellowshipped, and you will discover the key to their usefulness to God.

In the upper room, there were no five fold ministries, there were no deacons, there was no apostolic succession, there was no hierarchy, no elders, no titled clergy. There was only the body of Christ ministering to one another until Divine Orders arrived. In their several frames, all the ministry attributes that would be later manifested—rested, waiting for the Divine touch, the Divine call, the specific order. Body ministry still must depend upon waiting on the Lord. In the upper room, words like: "Now separate to Me Barnabas and Saul, for the work to which I have called them, (Acts13:2)" had yet to be uttered. These words would come forth in the proper time of Divine Order. These words would not be uttered by some prophetic word or handed down by ordaining counsels; these words were uttered by the Holy Spirit.

Notice the context in which this specific word came to those in attendance...certain prophets and teachers were assembled from the church in Antioch to minister to the Lord. Barnabus, Simeon, Lucius, Manaen and Saul were assembled to minister to the Lord. "AS THEY MINIS-TERED TO THE LORD AND FASTED" ...the Holy Ghost spoke. Many factors are at hand in this setting. The group continued to fast and pray (v.3), that alone is the constant. Then, those not chosen for this ministry "laid hands (of blessing and anointing) on Barnabus and Saul and sent them away." (Having heard directly from the Spirit, there was no question or reason for jealousy. One never heard another say, "We have been faithful longer than Saul...besides, how can we really know this Saul fellow will properly represent us?" The great truth is that their hands did not lay upon these chosen ones as a sign of approval to represent their group; their hands were laid to affirm their blessing on what God directed. It was their "Amen.")

"Being separated" marked the beginning of the missionary ministry of Paul. (So dynamic was this calling, that he disassociated himself from his former image as Saul of Tarsus and became known as Paul, the apostle.)

Look what Paul and Barnabus did after this distinct word from God. They considered this a Divine Appointment. "So, being sent out by the Holy Spirit, they went ...(v. 4)." Divine appointment gives power to carry out Divine Order!

Author's Note: In chapter 10, I will discuss the "sphere's" that came with this appointment.

Paul and Barnabus did not become professional clergy when they heard from God. They did not rise to a position; they went forth as men whom the Holy Spirit separated. This separation was a sovereign act of God. God's people (the true Body) must never again trust ordaining councils, licensing bureaus, and doctors of indoctrination to determine who among them is to occupy the offices of ministry. It is too late in history to rely upon traditional avenues. God has eclipsed this façade of religion and is ordaining anew, through direct words from the Spirit. This is why the call is clear, "Come out from them and be ye separate." *En Punto* requires it!

RELIGIOUS PLURALISM OR SPIRITUAL SCHISM?

Along with the recent move of God comes two distinct processes: The falling away of the old and the generation of the new. In the falling away, there will come consolidation of people, congregations, and resources. Never in the history of man is the church closer to consolidation than today. Unfortunately, it is a consolidation of a system the Lord has forsaken. The Lord is establishing an "invisible body" of believers ("invisible," as being distinct from the visible church with its buildings and its clergy). It is invisible to those of worldly demeanor but highly visible to those with spiritual discernment. This is no different from the underground church founded in totalitarian countries. The "invisible" body is composed of those who are called to usher in the last days in great power. Many of them are like the early disciples who continued to meet in synagogues and the Temple until a distinction between them and the "normal" constituents became evident. The diaspora of their "invisible" church, now made visible, preceded the historical diaspora of the Jewish community.

Inevitably, the true believers had to separate themselves from the established Temple group. Persecution followed. Those who once embraced their families and friends as "brothers" began to castigate and purge them from their midst. Repeats of this scene have been replayed through history. The Protestant reformation began as an attempt to reform the established church while remaining loyal to it; it failed to bring reformation. Seeing that no reform was sufficient, the next step was separation followed by persecution. Many true believers are still mingling with established religious bodies at the beginning of the new millennium, but soon this will change!

A separation is inevitable, as the mainline "in-group" takes exception to those whose thinking is different from their own. As cracks appear in the network of mainline religion over a plethora of relativisitic issues, those who are true believers must distance themselves from the core. Leaving these congregations will be a difficult decision, for often there is no place else to find camaraderie and friendship. Those led by the Spirit will be forced to depart from those who are led by other spirits. With this exodus goes the last vestige of spiritual balance in these congregations, and they will strengthen their worldly devices. Meanwhile, those who have departed will find themselves greatly dependant upon the leadership of the Holy Spirit. Some will find themselves fellow–shipping with strangers (as they are joined with God's elect). In the end, it is this group of "misfits" who will rally around the King, just as in David's day when Saul was yet to be deposed. God is rallying his army around King Jesus; they will receive their orders in spiritual caves, wilderness settings, and solitary treks. Convinced they are alone in their calling and separation, many will go back into the bondage from which they came, while the faithful await the word of the Lord to join the ranks of their compatriots. It is the Lord who will direct them to others, the Lord who will determine the place and time, the Lord who will do with them as Barnabus and Saul.

One unique characteristic surrounds the word "separate" in Acts 13:2; it means "to sever." No longer were Barnabus and Saul to walk in the same circles in which they once felt an integral part; they were separated to "HIM." The words were clear: "Separate to ME." The Holy Spirit wanted to direct them, lead them, talk to them, possess them. The others in that prayer meeting knew the great sacrifice they were about to make: it would mean forever— their group would not be the same. When reports began to return of exploits done by these two (Paul and Barnabus), Lucius, Simeon, and Manaen knew they were reports of the exploits of the Spirit. It is too late in history to hear reports from any other! Those who occupy places of leadership must now be those who are ordained of the Spirit and moved by the Spirit. It is too risky to listen to other voices who receive from sources outside the Spirit. These are the Last Days!

(Perhaps this is a good place to inject what the Spirit has emphasized repeatedly to me in these last days—believers are not only to examine who they listen to, but they must watch also what they read. The fact there are "Christian" Bookstores indicates to the world that religion has a great selling forum. The magnitude of words is amplified by mass media and computer expertise. Which word, which book we are to read is a matter to be determined by the Spirit.)

The book, *En Punto*, is not for everyone, but for those to whom the Lord directs its reading, it will be a "word from God." Like those who gathered in Bogota, the anointing will work a miracle of grace, power, and direction. To embrace *En Punto* is to embrace the redefinition of what it means to be a "child of God." Religion and the church have marred and skewed the tenets of the early church. Meticulous care must be taken in hearing the Spirit, so He can breathe His definitions into our hearts.

(*En Punto*, as this volume will use the term, is defined as "residing on the absolute accurate spot where God appoints one to be at any given moment in time." The following chapters will illustrate the importance and the power of being on that spot!)

CHAPTER TWO

A Study in the Practice of *En Punto*

Philip and the early disciples

OBEDIENT BEGINNING: THE UPPER ROOM

Since *En Punto* is the practice of following the Lord in exactness, then the upper room takes on new value.

The upper room was more than the place where the Holy Spirit individually anointed each attendee. The upper room was a place for <u>conditioning</u> the saints who were to watch in the Spirit and pray in the Spirit. Philip was one such saint. "Watching in the Spirit" for the hand of God was basic for life and ministry in the early church. So, the upper room constituted the first independent responsibility on the part of the early church to carry out the exact command of Jesus on earth. Up to this point, Jesus had always been present physically to monitor and refine their activities. Now, they were put to the test as to their ability to follow His instructions to the letter in His physical absence. Here, they laid aside all other considerations in their personal lives to perform His command. They were to "watch and pray" until they were endued with power. There was another time in which they were instructed to "watch and pray," but on that occasion they failed. This time, they would not fail. Prayerfully, they waited on God's plan, God's timing, which was of prime importance to them.

The Formula

The upper room was a <u>place of conditioning,</u> where those who were present faithfully dedicated themselves to what would be a principle in the early church. This principle simply stated was: No matter how long it took, no matter what personal inconvenience must be endured, no circumstance of life was more important than being exactly where the Lord wanted them to be and to be doing what He wanted done. This formula again is the agenda for true believers if they endure the Last Days.

This chapter will examine how the early church appropriated this formula of prayerfully waiting for the voice and hand of God in all their considerations. One of the prime examples is found in the life and ministry of Philip. By focusing on Philip as an example of a man being sensitive to the moving of the Holy Spirit, the reader will comprehend why such conditioned-responses to God are blessed. The book of Acts is full of similar examples and this chapter will point them out.

PHILIP, SPIRIT LED EVANGELIST

Philip followed the Spirit's direction from earliest times. The book of Acts is a treasure of scriptures focusing upon his obedience. To use these texts as a guide is of utmost importance to the believer who seeks instruction in Divine Order. As one considers these passages, one must review them as proof texts for training in sensitivity to the Spirit's commands. The necessity for such obedience was in direct proportion to the increase of persecution found in the book. The same is true for the modern Christian as the promise of Jesus is fulfilled concerning the last days.

Acts 8:4 makes a little statement about persecution emanating from Saul and the impending result of that persecution: "Therefore those who were scattered went everywhere preaching the word."

This statement is followed by Acts 8:5-6:

> Then Philip went down to the city of Samaria and preached Christ to them.
> And the multitudes with one accord heeded the things spoken by Philip, hearing and seeing the miracles which he did.

> (NKJV)

Demon-possessed people had unclean spirits cast out of them, the paralyzed and the lame were healed, and the city burst open with joy, as the result of persecution which in turn helped bring about the preaching of Philip. Once, Samaria was the home of the Northern Kingdom; now it was a place remonstrated by legalistic Jews as being the home of "half breeds." Samaria responded magnanimously to the gospel. Those in Jerusalem, hearing that Philip was having great response to his preaching (with many men and women showing their true repentance by baptism), sent Peter and John to assist. They began to lay hands upon the Samaritans to receive the Holy Spirit. They felt it was necessary for these new believers to have the leadership of the Spirit in their lives in the same way they did. This meant they taught the Samaritans obedience to the Spirit and revealed the power of His direction as their source of leadership. Peter and John added their testimony to Philip's efforts and then returned to Jerusalem (preaching as they went). The early disciples made no decision without consulting with the Spirit, which leads one to ask about Philip being in Samaria in the first place.

How did Philip determine to go to Samaria? Did he simply decide because of the command of Jesus to begin at Jerusalem, and move to Judea, then to Samaria, and the uttermost parts of the world? Did he decide to separate from the apostles and go out on his own? Did he go to Samaria because the heat of persecution was too great in Jerusalem? These questions are answered in the next few verses. The trailing verses indicated that Philip did nothing apart from the leadership of the Spirit, and that he was conditioned to immediate response to the voice of the Lord. (When the word "conditioning" or "conditioned" is used, it varies from the psychological terminology used in education, or the works of Skinner and Pavlov. The term is used in its highest form, that of a personal decision to respond without hesitancy to the leadership and voice of the Lord. Philip always dropped whatever he was doing and went wherever the Lord directed. His modus operandi was to follow the Lord specifically. This makes him the perfect example of *En Punto*.)

Acts 8:26 begins with a microcosmic experience which is indicative of the macrocosmic manner by which Philip governed his life.

> *Now an angel of the Lord spoke to Philip, saying, 'Arise and go toward the south along the road which goes down from Jerusalem to Gaza.' This is desert.*

When the angel gave His instruction to "arise and go," the next verse glibly reports: "So he arose and went." Many truths are involved in these two verses. First, we are not told the location of Philip when the angel appeared. If we assume that he was back in Jerusalem, having returned with Peter and John and preached along the return route, then he probably was at home. Many details are not given in the scriptures, but inferences can be made about some things. We know that he had a family, for the scriptures indicate that his daughters possessed a special gifting of prophecy. These matters being in place, a number of variables can be perused. The angel did not tell him how far away this assignment was, how long he would be gone, or to what other place he might be obliged to travel. The angel did not relate the specifics of the assignment. Philip did not have any other prompting from the Spirit until he was in view of the Ethiopian. Then, the Spirit said to him, "Go near and overtake this chariot." The angel did not allow time for dalliance. The fact that Philip "arose and went" reveals the depth of his commitment.

In modern parlance, one might assume Philip's wife would have had some questions related to his leaving. Was she so accustomed to this way of life in Philip and the other disciples that she did not question his abrupt departure? Was she not at home at the time of the command? Even the most demure of wives might have questioned how long he would be gone or when she could expect his return. She might have quizzed him about, "Why, at this exact moment, is it necessary to drop everything and leave at a seconds notice?" Surely she cared enough for Philip that she wanted to know if he was going to be in any danger. After all, these were dangerous times for the disciples of Jesus. Her concerns might have run the gamut of questions. She might have queried Philip as to how extensive were the directions to the road in question? His reply might have been, "very general in nature." Following that, she might wish to know who to contact if he did not return in a reasonable season? His answer would have indicated he had not been made aware of the name of the party, the nature of the business, or the extent of his mission. Additionally, she might want to know what she should do with his business while he was gone? What would she tell the children about his absence? What if someone inquired about his being away and what would she answer them in regard to the assignment? (We are not told these facets in the scripture, but life has common threads and wives must be considered.) These considerations are brought to the forefront to show the complexity in making a major decision to listen ONLY to the Spirit and follow His leadership.

One thing we are told; he arose and went immediately. Why should an early believer, an upper room congregant, react differently than a believer in the last days? The answer is simple; the early believers had made a covenant-decision (often called "a quality decision" but Philip's decision went deeper than that) to obey the Spirit without question. Their day and the nature of their assignment to evangelize the world required this kind of commitment. When Jesus spoke these words, things changed for them, "But you are those who have continued with Me in My trials. AND I BESTOW UPON YOU A KINGDOM, JUST AS MY FATHER BE-STOWED UPON ME (Luke 22:28-29 NKJV)." Here lies the difference between those disciples and vast multitudes who name the name of Jesus today. They received that bestowal, and it became their utmost desire to continue operating in that kingdom just like Jesus. The kingdom was in their hearts, and its care made demands upon them just as it did on the life of their Lord. They listened for the Heavenly command and ordered their every waking moment based on that leadership. The bestowal of the king-dom in the heart of the believer is the separating difference among Chris-tians. Few believers have any concept of the kingdom and certainly no idea of anything like a "bestowal." Their casual walk is indicative of a lifestyle void of kingdom principles and demands. When Daniel spoke in Daniel 7:18, "But the saints of the Most High shall receive the kingdom, and possess the kingdom forever, even forever and ever," he was relating a fundamental truth about God's people. They are the ones who have received the "bestowal." Kingdom investiture is absolutely foundational to an understanding of *En Punto*. The kingdom was bestowed upon them, not in a lakeside ministry, not at the Temple, but at the Lord's supper in the upper room. The bestowal came just before His betrayal and was accompanied by a warning to Peter. The bestowal preceded Jesus' return to Mt. Olivet and His words to "watch and pray." Perilous events were taking place, and the time was fast approaching when Jesus would no longer be physically in their midst. He bestowed the kingdom to the group who would have to listen to the voice He listened to and carry out every command in similar manner. Perilous times required a commitment to the kingdom that went beyond the petty rivalry of "who would be the greatest." Perilous times in these last days demand the same commitment, and the believer must receive the "bestowal."

These are similar perilous times which require the same covenant decision between the modern believer and his Lord. The early church had a sense of being co-laborers with Christ, a quality which is missing today. Their concept of sharing in Jesus' ministry came from three years of practice. They knew His ministry required them to be in the right place at the right time in order to be used of God in exactness. There was to be no gap in the hedge (spiritually speaking) and no one absent in the line of duty. Just as the kingdom had invested itself in earth, they were (and we must be also) totally invested in the kingdom. "Thy will be done, Thy kingdom come on earth as it is in heaven," is more than a patterned prayer; it is a commitment to function in the earthly kingdom just as the messengers of God function in the heavenly kingdom. He speaks; it is instantly done!

The disciples knew that no angel would hesitate, question, or fail to execute the slightest command of God. The disciples wanted to bear the kingdom with the same care that Jesus exhibited. His prayer at Gethsemane was living proof that "nevertheless not my will, but thine be done," applied to their lives as well. Colaboring with Jesus meant that all believers had to exhibit in their lives the obedience to the Spirit that their Lord exhibited. No schedule of theirs was set in concrete. Their schedules, their personal agendas were subject to change at a moment's notice. (Not so in the current church, not so among modern Christians.)

The early disciples believed that the upper room was a sealing through the Spirit of this kind of commitment. The flame of the Holy Spirit skipped no one, for each person knew the significance of this sealing. What had cost the Lord Jesus His life, would also claim theirs. They saw Him instantly respond to the Father, so they too instantly responded to the Spirit. There is no other alternative open to the believer. They saw Him operate totally in the Spirit as an example to show them how to heed His words. This is why the word "commandments" is used in these last accounts of Jesus' walk on earth.

> *until the day in which He was taken up, AFTER HE*
> *through the Holy Spirit, had given commandments*
> *to the apostles whom He had chosen...*
>
> Acts 1:2 (NKJV)

One of the commands is noted in scripture. It is the command to stay in the upper room and watch and pray. In answer to a question posed by the disciples, He (v.7) flatly tells them they are not to know certain "times or seasons," for the Father has authority over those matters. The Father would reveal those things at the proper time and when the season was right. Listen, the Father is revealing things to obedient children now; these are the last days! The time is right. Those who are receiving from God are those who have received the "bestowal" and have a covenant commitment to respond in exactly the same obedience to His command as the early disciples. There is no other way to receive! Return to Philip and his journey.

Philip did not question the angel, nor did he hesitate in his response. The Bible did not specify whether or not he knew by Divine revelation the full extent of this venture. He knew only that he was chosen and that "arise" meant "get up," and "go" meant "now!" His response was immediate and enthusiastic. (Compare his response to those of the church today. Compare his ability and the crippled inability displayed repeatedly by the body who, with myriads of technical advances, never is instant in response. Only on an individual basis can this response be made, for the unwieldy church is too encumbered by rule and regulation to make such responses. However, those who are an integral part of an "unwieldy institution" must now condemn it. This must be done by verbal or written challenges and/or by papers of resignation and by similar participational refusals.)

Philip's trip did not depend on congregational approval, some elder's authority, or a meeting of some board. These are the trip agencies normal to modern religion. His sole authority was the command of God—no other was needed or is needed. (Again, these days in the twenty-first century are like the days of the early disciples, who were fresh from the upper room.) God, who eclipsed Temple rulers, has done the same with the modern church. The kingdom was not bestowed on them. Kingdom bestowal is most observed in the area of response. Allow me to insert at this point a personal reference to an event in Mombasa, Kenya.

KENYA

As a case in point, I cite my participation in a campaign in Kenya that was concluded with a great need to build a church edifice in a particular area of East Kenya. The land for the church was only granted by the government for a six month period. Unless a building was built within six months, the land reverted back to the granting government agency. I was told by the resident missionary, a man of great compassion, that it would take longer than six months just to petition his mission board, establish the transfer of funds, and oversee the work. Like an arrow, the word of the Lord came directly to me, "Give him the money you have for your extended trip to South Africa." I distinctly remember asking what the raw materials for building would cost. I was told $7500 US— exactly the amount of money I had set aside. I also remember immediately canceling the trip to South Africa and pledging that amount of money. I pledged to send the money to the proper Kenya accounts within two weeks of that conversation. Upon returning to the U.S., I transferred the money; the church was built. This example is used only to reveal the complexity of the modern church dilemma. Churches in Europe and America have hordes of cash reserves while the cause of Christ suffers with mission boards and passionless prelates. The Catholic Church alone has huge depositories of gold, art works, jewels, and ornaments. Someone has to challenge these hordes against the needs of missionaries around the globe. They have banks and agencies worldwide. With vast land holdings and resources beyond the wildest dreams of an entrepreneur, the Catholic Church hordes billions, while the hounds of hell bark at the doors of most of the world. Evangelical bodies are not to be excused either. Investment vehicles, tax free enterprises, and endowments abound, while a Kenyan ministry (and many other missionary fields) languishes for the lack of a few hundred dollars. God forbid that these entities garner more into their contemptible coffers and continue to be associated with the kingdom of our Lord and His Christ.

PHILIP, THE KINGDOM AGENT

Not knowing where his venture would take him, Philip went to a desert place on the road from Jerusalem to Gaza, exactly as the angel directed. Not knowing what or who he would find there, he blindly obeyed the angel of God. We are not told what coursed his mind, only that he went. He trusted God, he trusted hearing from God, and he trusted the messenger as being from God. (One of the great deficiencies of the modern church is these three elements.) Philip was prepared to remain as long as the Lord deemed it necessary, to drop immediately his own plans and activities, and to engage himself only with the spiritual task at hand. He trusted God for every detail.

Ahead, on the "road of destiny," Philip saw the Ethiopian Eunuch seated in a stilled chariot, reading the book of Isaiah. Fresh from Jerusalem, his interest in religion at its peak, the Eunuch needed some expert assistance. Who better to fill that need than a man who had humbled himself before his Great God and offered his all: spirit, mind and body. The Spirit told Philip to run and catch up to this Eunuch. Philip did not offer an excuse about being out of shape. The Eunuch was reading Isaiah at the same moment Philip's heart was brimming with understanding. Had Philip waited for a call to service before making preparation, He would not have been prepared for the work. To him, it was a daily matter to "study to be approved of God," so he could begin at any scripture and preach Jesus. The Spirit gave him utterance, and he began a dialogue that ended in repentance and a public baptism.

Imagine this scene: the exact scripture concerning a prophecy about Jesus was being read at the exact time of Philip's arrival, which was exactly at the moment of the Eunuch's greatest need for instruction. Imagine the Ethiopian embarking on a long journey, and not far from his starting point, he stops to read the Bible. This man was serious, and the Lord is interested in serious inquiry about His Word. Imagine this man waiting for a divine appointment when He is not aware that there is such a thing as a divine appointment. (There is no such thing in spiritual matters as a "happenstance" occasion. It is impossible to enumerate the number of these divine appointments which have been mine. My wife and I were walking out of a vacuum cleaner repair shop when a lady across the parking lot spoke, "I have to know who you are." She was in her 70's at the time. She said the Spirit told her to approach us and inquire as to who we were. That is why she used the statement, "I HAVE to know who you are." No one on earth could imagine the mutual blessings that have come from the friendship which grew in the ensuing years. Her home was a continual passage to wellness for homeless women, derelict youth, drug addicts, alcoholics, and seekers of faith. To think that she hailed us BY THE SPIRIT is a compliment from heaven. This meeting with Mrs. Veatrice Spraggins is one small example of thousands like it. Believers must walk by the Spirit, live by the Spirit, and talk through the Spirit, just like Jesus in Acts 1:2ff.)

Acts 8:36 says: "Now as they went down the road, they came to water." Ordinarily this reportage would not raise an eyebrow, but two factors stand out too clearly to be ignored. Philip was prepared to ride with this treasurer to Ethiopia and spend the rest of his life preaching there if the Lord willed. Every horse step down that highway was one more in distance from his home. Every wheel turn meant he was nearing a border where, if he crossed, it would put him in enemy territory, for the Jews were not well liked in Egypt. The speed of the driver meant they were determined to be at a resting spot of his choice for the ensuing night. Philip was not in charge. Listen, this is the kind of dedication to the cause of our Lord that is required for these last days. While believers are focused on rapturing out, God is focused on divine appointments with people on desert roads. Like the Ethiopian, there are people waiting to be apprehended by Spirit-led people of God who know answers!

Philip would never have had the joy of leading a NATION to God had he not been willing to follow the exact direction of the Spirit. It is the Spirit who can locate key men in every country. He has a better record than churchmen seeking out those they consider to be key persons. (Remember, the Ethiopians were, until the last two decades, the most Christian and Jewish nation in Africa.) Philip did more in this moment of history than a revival campaign lasting years could have accomplished. What is the difference between the approach of the church today and the day of Philip? Simple, the Eunuch in the modern setting would have had to make an appointment, be interviewed and summarily questioned as to the extent of his Biblical knowledge, then given a regimen of biased literature to assimilate before he could be ushered into an indoctrination class lasting several weeks, and finally be allowed to ask a question in a group setting.

No, really that would not have happened unless he was a commoner, for this Treasurer of a wealthy nation would have had several donation-hungry clergy bidding for the opportunity to have an audience with him. They would be hoping to find favor enough to be invited to minister to the Queen and her staff of advisors and perhaps establish an office for religious purposes in the capitol. Television cameras would have been whirling as this elite member of a foreign country was interviewed in order to increase the offerings.

Think of the profoundness of this event between the Ethiopian and Philip. Spiritual precedence was set on this occasion. Instead of relying upon man's mass meetings and vast media coverage, the Spirit accomplished, in one small setting, a rendezvous which affected an entire nation. Look at the ramifications of this lesson.

There are currently about 150 countries or nations (counting the multiplication of many countries through subdivision due to treaties and wars) in the world. It would take 150 such divine appointments, as experienced by Philip, to bring the world to the throne of God. These kinds of appointments would bring glory to God and to His obedient servants who, like Philip, move within a moment of the command! Divine Order is better than man's order!

Philip began with the Isaiah passage fingered by the Ethiopian and preached Jesus. An amazing thing happened at the exact moment of the Ethiopian's conversion. Remember, the scripture said, "It is a desert."

Somehow, just as Philip was telling about the significance of being baptized as an outward sign of inward true repentance, water appeared on the horizon. God provides everything when His will is being carried out!

However, another main event was also in the making. Just as they came up out of the water, Philip disappeared. Nothing is told about the Ethiopian and what he thought about the disappearance of Philip, but Philip found himself at Azotus, many miles away. (Hundreds of believers would love to travel in the supernatural like Philip. I have heard many people say they would like to experience these supernatural events in their lives. Like Simon the sorcerer, nothing would be more pleasing to their flesh than televising their translation experience in front of millions as they utilize two camera teams in distant places to record every detail—such would be fodder for years of programming.) The Lord is no respecter of persons; what He did for Philip, He can do again. Supernatural living includes supernatural adventure. When a yielded life begins to move according to the Spirit, that life can expect supernatural experiences. (I believe that when the two witnesses lie dead in the street according to Revelation, they will be raised up supernaturally. I believe that these events are so prophesied in order to show that God will re-institute a sovereign move from Him, which will astound the world. The Last Days will produce men like Philip whom God can use and around whom He can embellish miracles, signs, and wonders. The church's feeble displays, in what has been considered miracles, will pale in comparison to true miracles which will take place at the command of God. Such distinction will have similarities to Moses and the court of Pharaoh. The False Prophet will attempt to deceive many through trickery and false miracles, but when God shows up, The Lord will change the definition of "supernatural.")

THE OBEDIENCE OF THE EARLY CHURCH

Philip was absolutely not the first, nor was he the only one in his day, to be "En Punto." By taking a brief overview of the book of Acts, that fact will become real. The balance of this Chapter One will be devoted to one matter of research: discovering those events that are "command events," and seeing how the early church responded. Chosen verses will serve as keys to what must be the norm in these Last Days.

From the time of the upper room forward, the early church did not move without consulting the Spirit. Their decision to elect someone in the place of Judas was prayerfully designed to approximate the electoral methods utilized by the priests in determining service in the Temple (These early churchmen were kings and priests unto their God; therefore, they felt justified in using this method.). The casting of lots was a method of Spirit leadership found in I Chronicles 25:8. Note the words of Acts 1:23-24:

> *And they proposed two: Joseph called Barsabas, who was*
> *surnamed Justus, and Matthias.*
> *And they PRAYED and said, 'YOU, O Lord, who know*
> *the hearts of all, <u>show which</u> of these two YOU have cho-*
> *sen to take part in this ministry and apostleship from which*
> *Judas by transgression fell, that he might go to his own place.'*
> *And they cast their lots, and the lot fell on Matthias.*
> *And he was numbered with the eleven apostles.*

(NKJV)

Every activity of the Disciples' lives revealed dictation by the Spirit of God. (As the review of scriptures in this text excludes activities not under vocal command from the Lord, it in no way should be construed that other activities and events were not so directed.) Men and women who were accustomed to the vocal commands of the Spirit, Angels, and the voice of God were not likely to make choices and order their lives apart from the inner direction of the Holy Spirit. The book of Acts is a record of the rule and principle spoken of in 2Timothy 2:4,5:

> *No one engaged in warfare entangles himself with the af-*
> *fairs of this life that he may please him who enlisted him as*
> *a soldier.*
> *And also if anyone competes in athletics, he is not crowned*
> *unless he competes according to the rules.*

(NKJV)

The rule is simple: follow the Spirit. In the upper room, they spoke "as the Spirit gave them utterance (Acts 2:4)." This was the occasion when men and women from many places heard "them speaking in our (their) own tongues the wonderful works of God." The same Spirit that gave utterance in foreign tongues gave Peter utterance on the day of Pentecost and prompted him in his preaching. Again, the same Spirit filled Peter in Acts 4:8 as he preached to the Sanhedrin. Every message from the upper room forward, no matter the speaker, would somewhere in it say that the deliverer was "filled with the Spirit." This is more than an ecstatic event; they were speaking what the Spirit dictated, nothing more and nothing less. These incredible messages inculcated scriptures from a vast range. No man alone, under duress from an angry crowd, could have delivered such poignant challenges and scripturally correct messages apart from the Spirit. It mattered not if such delivery would mean his death; the faithful soldier pleased the One he served. More than once, these circumstances were repeated where the deliverer lost his life or suffered pain for speaking the exact message of the Spirit. Such will be the scenario of the last days, for the Spirit will have verbal testimony spread upon the earth with "Divine Utterance" being the vehicle for God's righteous judgment.

Jesus, Himself, used this method. The Father spoke through Him with spiritual accuracy as He addressed the Temple system. When judgment fell in 70 A.D., God was justified and righteous in His judgment. They had been warned sufficiently through the Spirit speaking through the mouth of Jesus. God is raising up a host of those to whom one goal is tantamount: They too will speak the words given by the Holy Spirit. Spoken in their entirety, the Righteous Judge will then bring judgment upon the unrepentant hearers. They will have had sufficient words spoken through the lips of righteous servants.

Alas, there is breaking upon the earth, a new message about a Kingdom almost unheard of in the kingdomless systems of religion. This is a Kingdom whose gospel sounds vastly different than the diatribe associated with Sunday services. It is unafraid of the crowd and not based on any criteria short of the glory of God. It is the message from a heart "filled with the Spirit," wielding the "sword of the Spirit."

Notice in the ensuing verses how carefully each participant of the "upper room filling" carried out the verbal commands of the Living God. Acts 4:24 reports, "they raised their voice to God with one accord and said..." (What did they say in that prayer?) Their prayer began with the most basic of foundational truths; it reviewed God's power in creation and His power now!

> *Lord, You are God, who made heaven and earth and the sea, and all that is in them. Who by the mouth of Your servant David have said, 'Why did the nations rage, And the people plot vain things? The kings of the earth took their stand, And the rulers were gathered together Against the Lord and against His Christ.'*
>
> Acts 4:24b-25 (NKJV)

The inclusion of David's prophesy in Psalms 2:1,2, was a vital part of that prayer which they quoted from memory. They stopped short, however, of including verse 3. They did not say: "let us break Their bonds in pieces and cast away Their cords from us (Psalms 2:3)." They refused to give voice to the sorry words of heathen nations. They refused to allow their mouth to quote scripture which went counter to their power in the kingdom. The cords of the kingdom were upon them, and their bond with its King was unbreakable! They knew that those who opposed Him were saying this of them. They knew that Psalms 2:9,10 ,"You shall break them with a rod iron; You shall dash them in pieces like a potter's vessel," meant the "You" who dwelled in them. That is why they cried out for boldness!

> *Now, Lord, look on their threats, and grant to Your servants that with all boldness they may speak Your word, by*

stretching out Your hand to heal, and that signs and won-
ders may be done through the name of Your holy Servant
Jesus.

Acts 5:29-30 (NKJV)

Such a prayer is never heard in cathedral or church hall in the twenty-first century, but will again be heard in prayer meetings across the world as God joins his faithful in prayer. Holy boldness will be the hallmark of those who bear His seal. The result will be the same now as it was then: "And when they had prayed, the place where they were assembled together was shaken; and they were all filled with the Holy Spirit, and they spoke the word of God with boldness." (Is it any wonder they followed these prayer meetings by having all things common? Yes, this "banqueting scene" soon would be dissolved in "come away with me my Love"[Reference to Song of Solomon]). They were dispersed throughout the world and were joined by thousands of others who heard them pray and linked up with them in their prayers for boldness to speak just HIS WORD alone!

PETER AND JOHN

Often they went from street healings to jail, which was the result of their holy boldness and their inerrancy in following the Spirit. God was willing to perform great miracles and wonders for His tenacious saints. Acts 5:19 showed the delivering Angel opening prison doors to them and bringing them out. His words were simple: "Go, stand in the temple and speak to the people all the words of this life." What does the next verse say? "And when they heard that, they entered the temple early in the morning and taught." How much time lapsed between the angelic message and the carrying out of that plan? NONE! Such holy boldness caused Simon to say in the Temple,"We ought to obey God rather than men (Acts 5:29)."

Is this not the crux of the matter? The religious scene has so many filtration systems devised by man, that from the time the message is received until it finds its way out to the pulpit, it has become unrecognizable as being the same message. Caught between the demand of the people to hear something and the savage results of saying something "incorrect," 10:45 on Sunday morning finds its messenger frustrated and its congregation lost! Where are the likes of Jonathan Edwards who refused to preach unless he had a "message from God?" Where are the John Huss's who challenged the paucity of the Roman Catholic religious system and found martyrdom, to be but an eclipse in time? No one wishes to "dig in these wells."

The message from the angel who has delivered us from so much is still commanding that His people: "Go, stand in the Temple and speak to the people all the words of Life." Had the disciples not understood the difference between the "spirit of the Temple" and the Spirit of God, they would not have obeyed. The same is true today. "Go stand in your local church," is clearly a call to tell the message the Spirit will give you when one is "found standing and teaching." How long did they stand and teach?

The "sent ones" did not cease standing and teaching in the Temple until they received new orders. The problem with charismatica is that its halls are filled with "those who did not continue daily." Shouting "Hallelujah!" is no substitute for "thus saith My God!" Acts 5:42 said they kept hammering the message until the Spirit moved them elsewhere. Judgment demands that these warning be given. The prophet Ezekiel had a similar choice: deliver the word and have clean hands, or bear the guilt with bloody hands. The same choice is given in the Last Days.

STEPHEN, EXAMPLE OF *EN PUNTO*

Stephen (the namesake of my only son) glowed as he gave one of the greatest testimonies in all recorded history. His message incorporated the entire Law and Prophets with historical accuracy, crafted with beautiful finesse as he wove a scarlet thread to Golgotha. So powerful was this message given by the Holy Spirit through his yielded flesh that nothing mattered but the flow of that message from his lips. For this, the officials of the established religion stoned him. Acts 7:55 says:

> But he, being full of the Holy Spirit gazed into heaven...
>
> (NKJV)

His only orders from that moment forward were heaven-breathed, issued from a standing Jesus (who welcomed him home for a job well done). Who else but Jesus must be pleased? The religious crowd pounced on Stephen. (The hardest of rocks are thrown by the religious crowds; the cruelest of dictums fall from Prelate's lips.) No apology could be heard for Stephen's death but the apology of Paul who, in repentance, emulated Stephen's resolve. (Great God, the meager excuses of Pope John Paul, for the many Inquisitions throughout History will never be received in heaven. Only when the Pope falls in repentance and emulates Paul by crying out, "I will preach the Protestor's message under the Spirit with great resolve. I will unbind the clergy and free them to follow the Spirit, dismiss the convents, give them this message: 'Man is free from all mediation to enter the presence of God only through the atoning blood of Jesus.' I will resign a papacy that should never have existed and release the horded treasures of ill-gotten gain garnered from the mis-informed and mis-directed. I will resign in order to pour the true words of God before a dying and lost church. I will dissolve embassies; ambassadors will be recalled, and I will declare 'NO MORE!' to any hope of a 'Holy Roman Empire.' I will establish no more bishoprics, archbishoprics, priesthoods, or convocations of laity. I renounce all that the church has dictated, except Holy Scripture, as the compromise of man. I will denounce the Orders established by man. I will stand naked [without the robes of office] before God, pleading for His Mercy and Grace." This alone will suffice as repentance sufficient under heaven! Such a move would be a challenge for the entirety of Christendom to abandon its Catholicity and return to the living Holy Spirit.)

Following Stephen's martyrdom at the hand of structured religion, Philip was called to abandon his home base in Jerusalem and follow the Spirit to Samaria and the Eunuch.

PAUL'S, BOLD WITNESS IN THE SPIRIT

Soon after the death of the church's first martyr, Paul was confronted by the very Jesus who welcomed Stephen home. After a mute question, the blinded Paul was balled up in a trembling heap of: "What do you want me to do (Acts9:6)?" He was told to: "Arise and go to the city." This was Paul's first command. Following years of studying God, listening to endless debates, and traversing an academia second to none in the ancient world, he finally heard from God. (See Addendum One and the testimony of a nun who experienced a similar wilderness wandering; until one day, she heard from God.)

Those who were with Paul directed him to the city of Damascus, Syria. He was not directed to the Temple, not some re-energized synagogue, but to a man who was obedient to the leadership of the Spirit. He was not taken to some famous cleric, but to Damascus, considered by many of his day as the camp of the enemy. There, through Divine Appointment, he was healed at the hand of a servant of the Lord. Ananias, like Philip, had to obey the word of the Lord. In a vision, the Lord told Ananias to: "Arise and go to the street called Straight and inquire at the house of Judas for one called Saul of Tarsus, for behold, he is praying. And in a vision he has seen a man named Ananias coming in and putting his hand on him, so that he might receive his sight (Acts 9-11)."

Don't be amazed at the accuracy by which the Lord reveals to Ananias, names, streets, and other men's visions and dreams. All these things came to Ananias "right out of the blue." Don't assume that this kind of revelation is over and that only during the apostles' days would this kind of thing occur. (There is not enough paper to write the addendum testimonies of believers who, in this day and age, move by the Spirit in similar manner. The writings of C.G. Bevington (1.) in the past century is sufficient proof of such visitation and leading. God is reasserting His sovereignty in these Last Days in juxtaposing his men in mysterious ways.) Unfortunately, Ananias did not follow the command of the Lord without questioning. Having heard the awesome accounts of men like Stephen, he related to God what he knew about Saul of Tarsus. One might think Ananias was telling God something He did not know, or factoring a variable He had not considered. Interestingly enough, God's answer was emphatic, yet sympathetic. "Go," is followed by a revelation of what will be Paul's ministry to the Gentiles. It parallels what the Lord had revealed in the vision to Saul about waiting until he met His messenger, and then he would be told what he must do. (A later chapter will be dedicated to the "spheres" of authority that were afforded the ministry of Paul.) Paul was about to experience a double portion of anointing.

Receiving sight and being filled with the Holy Spirit is a double portion. Paul received his healing and received the infilling of the Spirit prior to baptism (which is against some theologies). He arose and was baptized following his healing. His was a baptism of repentance, and surely the same must be for all those who receive the Holy Spirit. Think of this chain of events. A man (Paul) waited for an unknown guest, while a stranger (Ananias) received direction from God to go to a specified place and speak a specific message from God— to a murderous zealot. This is the way of the believer. Not only will this be an increasing dimension among believers in the Last Days, but it will be the method most used by the Lord. As darkness envelopes the world and systems of government and religion solidify against those who walk in the Spirit, life and limb will depend on such hearing from God. Miraculous meetings will be concertized by the Spirit, and wonderful ministries will come from those "chosen from the foundation of the world."

What is truly amazing is that Saul began to preach Stephen's message! Verse 20 says, "immediately he preached the Christ in the synagogues, that He is the Son of God." The word *immediately* is a qualifying word for those in the early church. Once having heard the voice of God, the immediacy of the response is an absolute in the character of the believer. One common characteristic runs through the camp of the redeemed, and it is that they do not delay carrying out the command of God in exactness. (In the next chapter, exactness will be examined as a vital component to receiving the command of the Lord.)

CORNELIUS AND PETER: EXAMPLES OF *EN PUNTO*

Another "Divine Appointment" followed on the heels of Paul and Ananias, that of Cornelius and Peter. An Italian named Cornelius, a centurion for the Romans, received a vision at three o'clock in the afternoon. An Angel of the Lord addressed him by name and told him that the Lord was pleased with his prayers and alms (how unlike the things the world system finds worthy of praise). The Angel says specifically, "Now <u>send</u> <u>men</u> to Joppa and <u>send for</u> Simon whose surname is Peter. He is lodging with Simon, a tanner whose house is by the sea. He will tell you what you must do (Acts 10:5-6)."

Notice that Cornelius was immediate in his response to the Angel's message. He sent three men. Two were household servants, and one was a soldier under his command. (Three is a significant number and worthy of note. Consult a biblical numerology book for this number.) The three were dispatched immediately after they were informed of the reason for their mission. At the same time, Peter was having a vision about Gentiles receiving the gospel. While Peter was in a quandary about the trance, the Spirit (Acts 10:19-20) said to him, "Behold, three men are seeking you. ARISE therefore, and go down and go with them, doubting nothing; for I have sent them."

Verse 22 explained to Peter that Cornelius was "divinely instructed to summon you to his house, and to hear words from you." Such divine instruction must of necessity be followed, so Simon went with the men. (How many are there in churches, who deem themselves leaders, who are ready to drop everything and do the will of God?) Cornelius was expecting him, for in verse 33 he states: "So I sent to you immediately, and you have done well to come."

SAO PAULO: ANGELO AND *EN PUNTO*

I shall never forget in Sao Paulo, Brazil, a car mechanic named Angelo. After a week of my preaching and saying, "The Lord spoke to my heart and I did thus and so," he could tolerate no more of it. Little could I imagine that this was his mindset, for the services were drawing between 700-900 in attendance, and it was impossible to become acquainted with every attendee. I did not meet Angelo until the second Sunday of services, shortly before church members were dispersed to witness about Jesus in the streets. The second Sunday was harvest time when church members took tracts and went wherever the Spirit lead them. Angelo took a number of tracts but later confessed that he did not believe that God spoke to anyone, let alone gave directions as to His will. So, at 2:30 that afternoon, he departed like all the other church members who attended—but with one variance— he had determined that he simply would wander down a few streets and return home if the Lord did not speak to him and lead him. He did exactly as he determined with one exception, he had to walk further than he expected so that it would not to be obvious to the other members what he was doing. This took him down streets normally not traveled. As he exited from the main street, he walked about a half block when he noticed a man standing by an open garage door. He approached the gentleman who greeted him in this manner: "Are you the angel?" Angelo looked startled. He replied, "My name is Angelo, but I am not an angel." The man explained that he and his family had been praying that morning for the Lord to send someone to tell them more about Jesus. They had been given some gospel tracts earlier in the week by some foreigners, and they did not fully understand the way to salvation. The man further explained that the Lord had given them a vision with this instruction: "Go at 3 p.m., stand by your garage which is next to the street, and I will send an angel to instruct you." Angelo entered his home, and in less than hour, he emerged reeling in the joy of having brought an entire family into God's kingdom. This was not the end of it, for as he was winding his way home, he got lost and had to walk several streets out of the way to get where he intended. He mulled over the events which had just taken place as he traversed the side street. He was startled from his thoughts as he almost stumbled over a lady who was seated very close to the street. The steps leading to her modest home jutted up behind her. She said, "Are you the angel?" Haltingly, he repeated for her the same words he had given the former inquirers; he thought: "Here I go again." She said that she and her daughter had received gospel tracts from some foreigners as they came from the bus terminal a few blocks away. They experienced such conviction from the message in the tracts, that they had cried out to God for salvation. Having no Bible and no instruction, they felt hopeless until a voice told them, "I will send my angel to you this afternoon, wait by the steps." She had been waiting a long time. Within minutes, two more precious souls were born again.

Angelo literally ran from her house, leaping with joy and full of repentance for doubting that God could speak to him and direct his life. He burst into the pastor's study and fell at my feet, speaking Portuguese faster than my ears could comprehend. The pastor motioned me to remain silent, so he could hear all that was being said. With Angelo's tears literally bathing my shoes, he was asking forgiveness for all his thoughts and doubts. He declared he wanted to testify of these events at the evening service, which he did. It brought a mighty conviction upon the body and caused much repentance among those who heard. He told them he would close his auto repair shop and do this kind of work everyday if the Lord would lead him like this. He did, and he did.

The same Lord that led Philip, Cornelius, and the others was leading Angelo. Following the Spirit in the last days is an absolute; it is not an option, for every believer must commit to this principle if he or she is to prosper. (The ensuing chapters will be a study in the embracing of this most important aspect of the believer's walk.)

In the next chapter, Paul predicates his whole ministry on the premise of "doing nothing outside the Spirit." In reviewing Paul's ministry, the reader will examine just how far-reaching this formula is in its scope.

CHAPTER THREE

Paul, a True Son of Benjamin

Symbolic Analysis of Benjamin and Judah/ Paul and Jesus

Literally thousands of books have been written about Paul and his ministry. The focus of this chapter will differ from the majority of those works. The view in this chapter is not so much about what Paul preached, as it is how he ordered his ministry. He paid strict attention to the leadership of the Spirit and made the Spirit the director and corrector of life's every move. He embraced the wonderful principle of "doing nothing aside from the Spirit." Paul was well integrated alongside the other apostles in this matter. Each of the Disciples followed this same rule. As John wrote Revelation, he prefaced it by declaring he was "in the Spirit." Paul also walked transparently in following the Spirit, thereby giving an example to end-time believers who must emulate him.

By taking Paul's own written accounts and the accounts of others who wrote of his work, there emerge some principles which heretofore have not been emphasized. For instance, if the Spirit did not allow Paul to travel using his own schedule, Paul would abandon his course without hesitation and follow the Spirit (ie: entrance to Asia). This is the first principle which must be applied to the life of the believer. The last days require renewed thinking along these lines; these days require divergent patterns gendered by the Spirit, patterns which are contrary to the patterns of major religious thinking. To allow one's life to follow the standard courses set out by present church leadership is to blindly walk into spiritual death. Just as the Jewish regulatory bodies were no longer the source of Paul's direction, so the current regulatory bodies cannot be the source for today's believers.

There is a dearth in Christendom today of Paul's principles for governing life and ministry by being attentive only to the Spirit. Currently, Christendom is offered pre-agreed paths and methods for "doing ministry" in as many denominations (and their offspring) as there are people. The adherents to these several standards attempt to support their views by writing simplistic books using their similar models of ministry and theology. They copy each other's themes and purport to have new revelation when in reality, they rehash each other's belief forms. Intentionally these books give credence to each other by mimicking one other. Their multiplicity in number and volume overwhelms the Christian book market. Christendom can almost be catalogued along lines of their reading taste. Soon these multitudes find themselves the followers of man by ingesting man's work on a regular basis. Any review of current literature will uncover this truth.

Adding insult, the several and often connected churches of these writers limit their pulpits to those who give service to their point of view. By limiting their pulpits to those who reflect their views, they further distance their congregations from true Spirit direction.

Network volumes fill Christian bookstores and are front-runners among Christian booksellers. Bookstores are packed with "look alike" volumes. A survey of content in the Christian marketplace will reveal the paucity of ideology. A prominent Baptist minister of another year, Dr. R.G. Lee, once surveyed the bookshelves of his day and commented, "Mountains of paper, rivers of ink, all for a teaspoon of knowledge." Today, the mountains have grown higher, the rivers deeper, but the quotient of knowledge has shrunk to a drop. Booksellers have developed an art in predicting their public, serving only those selections which bring favorable sales. The Booksellers know who will purchase what. They define their market simply by selecting the publisher—forget the author. Publishers are classified by their stable of "best selling" authors. One bookseller in Washington State said, "I have my devotional readers, my religious fiction readers, my word and faith readers, but then I have a small group who emphasize holiness and righteousness without variable, and I have little to offer them." This statement alone should send a chill through the halls of Christendom.

There should be a caution sign above the religious section of every secular bookstore: "Caution: consuming some materials from these shelves will cause spiritual blindness." The same sign could be over the door of most religious bookstores.

It is time to consult the Spirit. He alone must determine the printed material which enters the heart of the believer. Without His express permission, direction, and approval confusion will reign in the heart of the reader. (No video, no tape [secular or religious] should be allowed an airing to the believer's eyes or ears without the permission of the Spirit.

No website, no incoming email should be opened or read without the scrutiny of the Spirit.) Without the Spirit's requested intervention, the believer has no other source for scrutiny and is left to his own wiles of reason.

Christians have proven the Sorokin (2) concept that history moves on a compendium of time like a swinging pendulum moving from the moral right to the immoral left. If Sorokin's compendium moves to the left (towards liberalism and acceptance of life styles outside the realm of the Spirit) through history, then it can be concluded that the "right" of today is the "left" of yesterday! Notice then the disparity over such a compendium as many centuries have been eclipsed since Paul. Let it be understood that the moral "right" of today is in reality the moral "left" of truth! (the immoral and unacceptable of yesterday). Multiply this premise over the years since the upper room, and one must surmise that the "disciples would have to severely backslide to be in fellowship with the modern church."(3)

If history repeats itself, then this age is ripe for a judgment on its systemized Christianity. What Jesus said of the Scribes and Pharisees must be said today. It could be paraphrased as, "Unless your righteousness exceeds theirs, then in no way will you enter the kingdom of heaven." The error that dawns with the twenty-first century is tantamount to the error of the dark ages. Rising out of that bleak morass, there stood men who marked history by their refusal to conform any longer to religious standards devoid of the Spirit. Battling error cost the Reformers their lives. They battled the religious "in" group of their day — now such battle may require the blood of true believers again.

The most tertiary study of the "times" tells one that spiritual similarity has created a religious "in group" today, and in order to be accepted by that group, one must enter their form of spiritual death. The visualization of this truth stirs the modern seer and causes new day Jeremiah's to prophesy against it.

Paul came to grips with this truth at the very beginning of his ministry. His religious heritage, his orthodox upbringing, his legal genealogy, both human and spiritual, lay in ashes before him. He sacrificed his former religious training in the same way a true priest must in approaching the altar of God. He chose to be in God's "in-group" and be hounded by God's enemies. He, however, never lost sight of his spiritual heritage, which had great influence upon him. (There is a difference between religious training and spiritual heritage.) Spiritual heritage emanates from God. Paul never forgot that he was of the tribe of Benjamin. The tribe of Benjamin had a unique spiritual heritage to offer.

Recently, upon the prompting of the Spirit, I made a study of the blood lineage of Paul and the lessons in history attributed to the tribe of Benjamin.

I discovered some cogent realities from this review. (This study was initiated as a witness to a Jew of the tribe of Benjamin who adheres to the Rabbinical teaching of today, which is, "once converted to Christianity, a Jew ceases to be a Jew."(4) This teaching is difficult to defend, but is most widely accepted in Jewish circles.) Paul and the early apostles, along with the many Jews who followed them in the teachings of Jesus, were still Jews. (Being a Jew meant more than establishing a bloodline; it involved the total person, even to having ready rapport with other Jews [which remains true in both the ancient and modern world]. Their brotherhood and acceptance of each other afforded a powerful deterrent to conversion to the service of Christ [A similar case can be made for any systematic religion and must of necessity include charismatic fellowships.]).

Paul relinquished dependence on his religious society based on one thing: He was convinced the Spirit would introduce him to and connect him with any person or group ordained by God. If individuals or groups were to be a part of God's plan for his life, the Spirit would introduce them. He could not rely upon his Jewish connectivity as a substitute for the Spirit. In these last days, religious connectivity must be abandoned for the Spirit in the believer's life as well.

God's plan for the last day is that the Spirit, just like in the Disciples' day, be the final determination in who or what is part of one's life. The Spirit becomes the sole source for the soul. (Spiritual heritage, however, which plays a large part in the identity of the Jew [ie: Paul from the tribe of Benjamin, Romans 11:1] is not to be abandoned. The Bible does not indicate that it should be. The Lord Himself identified with the tribe of Judah, and space is given in the New Testament concerning His lineage. Jesus did not lose his identity with that tribe because He sacrificed Himself for the sins of the world [that world included the people of Judah]. As a matter of fact, Jesus became more identified with this tribe as attested by writings found in the book of Hebrews. The book of Hebrews emphasized Jesus' spiritual lineage with David in the same way the Gospels had connected His natural lineage.) Jesus was of Judah just as Paul was of Benjamin.

PAUL'S SPIRITUAL HERITAGE: BENJAMIN

Because Paul was of Benjamin, he may have learned strict attention to spiritual matters due to his spiritual background. At first, he was a legalist who believed in exactness in regard to carrying out the letter of the Law. Later, he became a strict adherer to the exact will of God through the Spirit. This obedience allowed him no place for personal tolerance. The loyalty he displayed in both communities (Jewish and Christian) found its root in the heritage of Benjamin.

Paul considered himself a "Jew-Christian" of Benjamin. It is important to know the history of the tribe of Benjamin then, if one is to study of Paul. Such will help in understanding the deep link between his tribe and the tribe of Judah (the tribe of Jesus). As a matter of importance, Jesus' question on the road to Damascus in Paul's vision may have had some connection to the Judah-Benjamin relationship. (Hopefully you, the reader, will consider this study applicable to the overall message of "doing nothing outside the Spirit." The study of Benjamin is a spiritual study. Such study reflects how they [as a tribe] touched on this principal of faith and how it found its consummation in Paul.) Any study of Benjamin must go back to his nativity and each event that unfolds after his birth. To review the life sequences of the tribe will be the foundation for much of the spiritual heritage reflected in its most illustrious son, Paul!

Benjamin's Birth

Benjamin was Jacob's youngest son. His name means "son of my right hand." Paul may actually have fulfilled the deepest spiritual meaning of this name. Born in Rachael's death, *Benoni*, "son of my sorrow" may also have found its fulfillment in Paul as well. Many instances in the life of Benjamin are reflected in the life of Paul.

Benjamin and Joseph: (A matter of Deliverance)

Benjamin played an important role in delivering Israel through one of its most famous sons, Joseph. Look at the Bible instance in detail. Jacob, remembering Joseph, sought to preserve Benjamin by detaining him when he sent his sons to Egypt. Joseph, not seeing Benjamin among his brethren, insisted the boy be brought to Egypt, and to insure it, he retained Simeon as pledge. In other words, Benjamin became a point of testing for his brethren. Unless Benjamin came to the "non-Jewish" world (Egypt) as a testimony, there would be no provision for the other sons. Paul may have fulfilled the identical role among his people when he came to the "non-Jewish" world (Gentiles—*Goyim*, "the nations") for a testimony. As Benjamin was integral to Jacob's provision, so Paul was integral to Jesus' provision for Israel and the Gentiles. Paul could pray for the provision of all who were left behind, both Jew and Gentile, since he bridged the gap. Paul verbalized that he would be willing to become "*anathema*" (outside Jesus) in order for Israel to come to Jesus.

Benjamin and the Blessing of Jacob

Benjamin received a strange blessing from Jacob on Jacob's deathbed, a blessing with multiple symbolism. To Benjamin was said,

> *Benjamin is a ravenous wolf: in the morning he*
> *shall devour the prey,*
> *And at night he shall divide the spoil.*
>
> Genesis 49:27 (NKJV)

Now, counterpose the blessing of Moses over the twelve tribes and look what Moses said of Benjamin as he changed the order of blessing from that of Jacob:

> *The beloved of the Lord shall dwell in safety by Him,*
> *Who shelters him all the day long;*
> *And he shall dwell between His shoulders.*
>
> Deuteronomy 33:12 (NKJV)

Both of these words came true in Paul, for first he was a ravenous wolf against the believers and then he became the "beloved of the Lord." Most of the believers he persecuted were brethren of his who were following "The True Lion of the tribe of Judah." To them, Paul was a ravenous wolf. After Paul's conversion, he became the "beloved of the Lord."

Just as Jesus was the fulfillment of all that was in Judah, so Paul fulfilled all that was in Benjamin. (Neither of them lost their place in Jacob, neither failed to fulfill his destiny, neither of them depended on natural lineage as their hope.) Notice the following unique arrangement postulated by Moses in Deuteronomy.

Benjamin and Moses

When Moses called for the reading of the "Blessings and the Curses" of the Law, Benjamin was on the side of the "Blessings." Surrounding him was Simeon, Levi, Judah, Isachar, and Joseph. This grouping has significance.

In the dividing of the tribal lands, Jebus (or Jerusalem) was given to Benjamin (Joshua 18:20ff). Again, this is an interesting event, for Judah and Benjamin dwelled together and in accord in Jerusalem under David and Solomon and their heirs. The book of Chronicles is filled with references to the two tribes, their contiguity and the events which affected them. Early in their lives, this closeness is not observed, but various circumstances drew them together.

Benjamin's Lessons:
Lesson One: God-determinism

This lesson was learned when Benjamin did not following exactly the will of God. Like all the children of Israel, they were told to cleanse the land assigned them of all inhabitants. They did not carry out this order. Because they exercised their will instead of following God's plan, certain events flowed from their disobedience. Herein lies the importance of being in total agreement with the Spirit, because disagreement leads to disaster.

A series of tragic events began to occur in the lives of the Benjamites. Early in Israel's conquering and possessing of the Promised Land, Benjamin was given a sad commentary:

> *But the children of Benjamin did not drive out the Jebusites,*
> *who inhabited Jerusalem; so the Jebusites dwell with the*
> *children of Benjamin in Jerusalem to this day.*
>
> Judges 1:22 (NKJV)

This failure to follow the exact instruction of the Lord proved to be a "thorn in the flesh" for Benjamin. But this would not be the only "thorn," for when a people are self-determinate and not God-determinate (human reason and popular vote determines what is best for self and others), other moral and spiritual infractions occur. Becoming self-determinate led Benjamin to choices that found them defending error.

Lesson 2: Align with the Lord, not family.

Benjamin discovers the importance of aligning with the Lord, not their relatives. The beginning of this lesson is found in the book of Judges.

Judges 20-21 tells the account of a Levite, his concubine, and the sodomites of Gibeah. This account is notorious because of the gang rape of the wife and the daughter of two Ephraimites. The Levites' concubine suffered death, and the host of the Levite suffered the moral loss of his daughter at the hands of descendants of Benjamin. Because the tribal family did not adhere to the moral code of the other eleven brethren, they suffered the loss of most of their tribe. Because the male citizens of Gibeon wanted to have homosexual relations with the "stranger in their gates," a chain reaction occurred. Seeking to appease these citizens of Gibeah, the elderly host offered two young women to satiate their lust—and the men took them.

It is necessary to understand the depravity that is found in the homosexual-bisexual community in order to comprehend Gibeah's fate. Those calloused men abused these women sexually (perhaps sodomizing them all night). The concubine died from the cruelty of her abuse. Her husband-owner grievingly returned home and cut her body into twelve pieces and sent a piece to each of the twelve tribes. NOTE please that the tribe of Benjamin was not excluded. Two groups did not answer his call to arms.

The tribe of Benjamin defended their homosexual brethren (preferring their relatives above the Lord's Law). The camp of Jabesh Gilead opted not to take sides on this issue and did not show up either (Judges 21:8).

The other children of Israel gathered before the Lord to ask who must go to battle first against their own brother. Notice that the Lord said, "Judah." Why did God choose Judah, especially when Israel would lose 22,000 in one day of fighting and Judah would suffer first? Though the scripture is silent on this point, evidence will point to a time when instead of being on opposite sides, Benjamin and Judah would fight for the same causes. What **is** recorded is that Benjamin intended to preserve their brethren and that the Gibeonites were fierce defenders of their homosexual way of life. The same is true today in the realm of militancy and obstinacy! (Read II Peter 2 for greater understanding.)

Israel regrouped and approached God weeping for their losses. God sent them out again to face further losses. When the Lord is sovereign, those who follow Him are willing to pay whatever may be the cost. God-determination in a person or a nation costs!

Israel again inquired of the Lord, and He said, "Go up against him (Judges 20:23)." Eighteen thousand more Israelites lost their lives doing God's will. (Why do modern Christians believe they will not have to shed blood to carry out the Lord's exact commands? Revelation 12 says what few sermons emphasize: "and they loved not their own lives unto the death.")

Israel again inquired of the Lord and Phinehas received a word from God, "Go up, for tomorrow I will deliver them into your hand."

Twenty-five thousand Benjamites fell before the sword of Israel in one day. (Remember the first avengers and casualties were from the tribe of Judah.) All of the Gibeonites lost their lives. All the non-homosexuals died alongside their neighbors who practiced this abomination. (Instead of the church debating the value of their homosexual constituents, the church needs to learn to read and obey God's word.) The lesson is clear: defend what God abhors and risk losing everything, even life. The Benjamites held higher regard for their blood relatives than the will of God and sacrificed the lives of themselves and their loved ones, their friends, relatives, belongings, cities, and most of all— their standing among the children of Israel. They lost because of defending what the Lord declared evil. (A great price is exacted for not carrying out the exact command of God, but a greater one is exacted for defending that which is against Him. Think of the people who lived at Gibeah who abhorred the reputation of their city and but said nothing. Where were the righteous dissenters? (It was the prayers of Abraham and God's mercy which removed Lot from Sodom.) Six hundred Benjamites escaped the battle and hid four months in caves until they felt they could emerge. They alone survived because Israel did not know of their escape.

Israel wept over the plight of their brethren, but Benjamin learned a lesson that caused the next generation to order their lives closer to Judah. Yes, the six hundred survivors took wives at Shiloh. NOTICE PLEASE, they were not homosexual. Yes, even when the other tribes would eventually separate and live in a divided state, Benjamin stayed close to the king, close to Jerusalem, and close to God.

The Lord did something in Gibeah that He did not do in Sodom. The Lord cleansed Gibeah, so He could once again work in that city. It was in Gibeah that Solomon received the vision from God asking what he wished for the Lord to give him. Here, he received the wisdom that propelled his life. "The Lord is good and His mercy endures forever!"

Lesson Three: Do not support the Un-anointed (Ishbosheth, the Wrong King)

This is the other instance found in the word of God where Benjamin defends the wrong side. This was their final lesson. One can imagine the mindset of those who survived the Gibeah battle, for they raised their children to be morally pure and spiritually straight. This heritage lesson taught to those of the tribe of Benjamin was undoubtedly available to Paul. He knew, for instance, the circumstances of King Saul, a Benjamite. (King Saul, who represented the "spirit of rebellion," came from Benjamin). The term "spirit of rebellion" is chosen, for the people cried to God for a King and told God they did not wish to be governed by His choices (His Judges) anymore. They wanted their way above God's way.

Saul was a perfect example of their rebellion. In a state of rebellion himself, He was replaced by David, who represented a kingdom under the Hand of God. Isn't it wonderful that in the New Testament, that rebellious Saul, the Benjamite-zealot, brings his heritage to the feet of Jesus. (It is worth observing that in Revelation 7 the 144,000 are enumerated beginning with Judah and ending with Benjamin.) Oh, that the church of today would hurry and abandon its lineage and heritage of rebellion and bring them to feet of Jesus.

Gibeah once again comes into focus, for it is King Saul's hometown. Once again, Benjamin allows their heritage to outweigh their commitment to God. When Saul falls, Benjamin aligns behind Ishbosheth and Abner.

> *But Abner the son of Ner, commander of Saul's army, took Ishobosheth the son of Saul and brought him over to Mahanaim; And he made him king over Gilead, over the*

> *Ashurites, over Jezreel, over Ephraim, over Benjamin, and over all Israel.*
>
> 2 Samuel 2:8 (NKJV)

Later it says, "Only the house of Judah followed David." Battle lines were drawn, but David knew the kingdom belonged to him.

> *...there was a long war between the house of Saul and the house of David.*
>
> 2 Samuel 3:1 (NKJV)

Not long after, however, a dispute arose between Benjamin and Judah. Ishbosheth accused Abner wrongfully and the "sheet was torn." Abner declared he would unify the kingdom under David and defected. Proving "blood is thicker than water," Benjamin continued to follow Ishbosheth. Erosion of loyalty to Ishbosheth began to surface, and slowly, Benjamin realized their mistake. They defected in small groups until Ishbosheth was finished. From this time forward, the house of Benjamin aligned itself with the Kings of Judah. Benjamites were in the guard of David and were among the chiefs of Solomon. Not until the son of Solomon ascended the throne did their loyalty reach a climatic point, for when Israel rejected Rehoboam, Benjamin remained. While Israel spoke of rebellion, Benjamin knew that rebellions' path is dangerous.

> *'What portion have we in David?*
> *We have no inheritance in the son of Jesse,*
> *To your tents, O Israel!*
> *Now see to your own house, O David!'*
> *So Israel departed to their tents.*
>
> I Kings 12:16

Benjamin remained!

Notice the passage in I Kings 12:19:

> *So Israel has been in rebellion against the house of David to this day.*
>
> (NKJV)

This is more of a key prophecy than it looks on the surface. (When Paul realized that Benjamin stood with Judah, he separated from Israel. It is necessary to see that Paul aligned with the Lion of the tribe of Judah, real Judah.)

Benjamin did not throw in with the other ten. The Benjamites stayed with Judah. This is a significant point. Israel suffered the same judgment that Benjamin suffered previously. Israel became the devil's advocate and entered into a period of sin marked by spiritual adultery and idolatry. Benjamin remained faithful.

Benjamin realized that whoever linked with Israel in its fallen state would meet the same judgment they met. Alignment is important in the realm of the Spirit. (This is why it is important for the believer to be associated only with obedient saints.) Each occasion in which Judah aligned with Israel, Judah ended up in defeat and loss. Being outside the will of God is a difficult road to take. Not aligning with the EXACT will of God is the same as aligning oneself against God. It is truly a matter of position, a case of not being "en punto" or in the *place* where God is blessing (Each of these *places* may be different for each person. Just because one hurries to a place where "God is blessing" does not mean that this is the *place* where every person will receive God's blessing.). Ministers placate this dilemma by using phrases such as "being in God's perfect will versus being in His permissive will." Their preaching is error! Their tolerances are not God's.

The theology of the "permissive will of God," is a myth. Anyone who believes the deception that "one can leave God anywhere down the line and get right back in the will of God" by simply speaking a few words that sound like repentance should review Saul's life. Return to the example of Benjamin.

While the scriptures say, "there was none who followed the house of David, but the tribe of Judah only (I Kings 12:20)," it quickly qualifies itself by citing a sequential event which modifies the statement. Verse 21 says, " ...when Rehoboam came to Jerusalem, he assembled all the house of Judah **with** the tribe of Benjamin..." Never again would Benjamin be on the opposite side to Judah. They valiantly fought alongside Judah to restore the kingdom, but they did not enter willingly into the sins of the kings of Judah by covenanting with Israel.

Lesson Four: Remain faithful to God (and align with Judah)

From this time forward, mention of Judah is followed by mention of Benjamin. Shemaiah, the man of God, addresses them like one entity. The man of God cautioned them both with a directive not to fight with their brethren. This too is an important facet because scripture speaks in deliberate terms:

> *Therefore they obeyed the word of the Lord, and turned back, according to the word of the Lord.*
>
> I Kings 12:24 (NKJV)

Listen, by doing the exact will of God, they were demonstrating their determination to follow God above the design of their human reasoning. Following man's reasoning gets man's results: death. A great example of this is in Nehemiah. Had he followed man's reasoning and what seemed like a workable plan, he would have been murdered and the work of his ministry destroyed. Shemiah advised him to hide out in the Temple because the enemy would target him. Nehemiah's integrity would not allow him to seek protection while all his fellows were exposed to danger. Notice in Nehemiah 6:12:

> *"then I perceived that <u>God had not sent him</u> at all"*

Treachery whispers in the ear of the church today. Instead of following the exact command of God, their ears are attuned to those around them. Nehemiah 6:14 speaks of the erroneous prophesies of a prophetess, Noadiah, and other prophets who "would have made me afraid." Nehemiah did not listen to them. What seems like a grand plan from God may really be the road to death. Time is too short for the Virgin daughters to awaken and discover that seduction has taken place.

Israel, under Jeroboam, followed their own will. They ordained priests from whoever wished to enter the clergy. Get this! The qualifications were spelled our in I Kings 12:31, and they did not heed them. Jeroboam installed priests loyal to Israel, not God. They lifted up unacceptable offerings and called them "blessed." (Is this not the church's practice today?) Jeroboam did whatever "he devised in his own heart (I Kings 12:33)." He despised the word of the man of God and polluted the prophets to the point they misdirected one another. His awful estate is summed:

> *After this event Jeroboam did not turn from his evil way, but again he made priests from every class of people for The high places; whoever wished, he consecrated him, and he became one of the priests of the high places. And <u>this thing was the sin of the house</u> of Jeroboam, so as to exterminate, and destroy it from the face of the earth.*

> I Kings 13:33-34 (NKJV)

Heaken to this message! THIS THING was a matter of professional clergy. THIS THING of making one's self a religious leader without the anointing of God is akin to rebellion, which is next door to witchcraft. THIS THING was a slap to the face of God. (THIS THING is the sin of the modern church and the same result is taking place.) God scattered them "beyond the river." (Notice the mercy of God in Ezra; God gave authority to Ezra " beyond the river," thus reversing the matter.) The most serious matter on earth in the Last Days is not "the great outpouring, or the theories of rapture," but of judgment upon those who do "their own thing" in pulpit and pew! THIS THING universally prevails under the guise of "following God."

> *And He will give Israel up because of the sins of Jeroboam,*
> *who sinned and who made Israel sin.*
>
> I Kings 14:16 (NKJV)

Notice Nehemiah. Nehemiah disqualified some priests because they did not meet biblical qualifications. They were considered "defiled" and were not allowed around the holy things. They would not be reinstated until God gave the command (Nehemiah 7:65). Thousands of churches would be without ministers if this applied today.

What was going on with Judah and Benjamin during this time? Victory, prosperity, and honor was coming their way. Asa became king and built cities in Benjamin.

> *King Asa built GEBA of Benjamin, and Mizpah.*
>
> I Kings 15:22 (NKJV)

We see Geba again in I Chronicles 6:60, when Benjamin gave this city to the sons of Aaron for the priests to LIVE IN. (Talk about wanting to bless those who were chosen!) When Asa began to bless Benjamin, he did so by rebuilding the priestly city. It pays off in Nehemiah 11:36: "Some of the Judean divisions of Levites were in Benjamin." It pays off in Zechariah 14:10 when the Lord establishes His power:

> *All the land shall be turned into a plain from Geba to*
> *Rimmon south of Jerusalem.*
>
> (NKJV)

(Rimmon is where Benjamin's fathers hid and repented, and Geba is where Benjamin established the Priests.) This reference is to a repented people who bless God's ministry. The link between Benjamin and Judah continued through their relationship with David.

David's relationship with Benjamin is interesting. When David wrongfully ordered a census of Israel, Joab, his nephew, did not count Levi or Benjamin. Levi was not counted for obvious reasons; Joab did not want their number to be known. Why did he not count Benjamin? Is it that Benjamin, being the smallest of tribes, due to the judgment upon Gibeah, did not need to know just how small were their numbers? Could it be that Benjamin was skipped because the son of Abner (the man Joab killed) was ruler? Could it be because Jerusalem was in Benjamin? Joab offers no explanation. By not being numbered, they did not enter into the sin of

David just as the Levites were exempted from it. This is another instance of God's plan for Benjamin.

Benjamin remains linked through scripture with Judah. So significant is this union that it will become symbolic spiritually. Notice in Ezra as the decree to rebuild the temple went from King Cyrus, that Ezra 1:5 states:

> *The heads of the father' houses of JUDAH and BEN-*
> *JAMIN, and the priests...with all those whose spirits God*
> *had moved arose to go up and build.*

> (NKJV)

When God spoke, they moved. When the stirring of their spirits by the Holy Spirit came forth, they arose. Better to go at the first stirring than to be churned in turmoil, fearing the stirring is over!

With a clear mandate from heaven burning in their hearts, both Judah and Benjamin withstood their adversaries as one. (This is the only basis for fellowship.) To share the move and call of God upon your life allows a "knowing" in one another that cannot be replicated even with the high covenant of David and Jonathan.

So strong is the link between Benjamin and Judah, represented in the covenant with David, that David's songs bless the two as though they were one.

> *Bless God in the congregations, The Lord, from the foun-*
> *tain of Israel. There is little Benjamin, their leader The*
> *princes of Judah and their company...*

> Psalms 68:26-27 (NKJV)

So favored is Benjamin that in Psalms 80, David groups Benjamin with the two sons of Joseph, Manasseh and Ephraim. David calls for the Lord to stir up His strength in saving all three. Believe it or not, that prayer IS answered in Paul, the apostle. "Let Your hand be upon the man of Your right hand," refers to Jesus and is a reference to the words of Jacob about Benjamin, "Son of my right hand."

In another place, Benjamin takes a symbolic position; the place is in the prophesies of Jeremiah. Anathoth in Benjamin was the city where the Lord first began to talk to the prophet. It was in this city that Jeremiah purchased a piece of real estate from his uncle, during the siege of the city. His uncle thought it to be worthless and took the money, but Jeremiah knew that the Lord would give that land to his heirs. When he went to Anathoth to check out the boundaries on another occasion, he was captured and put in prison for his prophecies. It is significant that Jeremiah had faith that one day his real estate investment would pay off, but it has deeper meaning. Anothoth means "answers," and Jeremiah bought into God's answers, not man's workings.

Soon the link between Paul and his ancestral heritage would be complete. When the final understanding comes forth, shouting will take place. There are still some links to be investigated before the picture can be completed. A step deeper into the Old Testament will reveal some strong spiritual battles that have raged between Benjamin and his neighbors throughout history. Those battles continue to this day.

Lesson Five: God's Timetable is not set to Man's Timetable

This lesson is mammoth in scope. It incorporates studies in Esther, Numbers, Nehemiah and back to Paul in the book of Acts. In the next chapter, these areas are explored in detail.

CHAPTER FOUR

God's Timetable, not Man's

A New Perspective: From Esther to Acts

Author's Note: As a continuation of chapter three (the spiritual heritage of Benjamin), the focus of this chapter is war between God and the forces which align with spiritual Amalek (who symbolically stand as representing every force which seeks to hinder, deter, and distract the people of God in their quest for the Promised Land. In order to gain an overview of the timetable God uses in His dealing with spiritual Amalek, it is necessary to first review the book of Esther in light of the continuing battle between Benjamin and Amalek. Aside from all other teaching in Esther, and there are many, the primary concern of this book is the war between Benjamin and Amalek, hopefully the reader will ascertain this truth.)

A STUDY IN ESTHER

*T*he Lord's people may meet defeat in a battle, but God remembers their defeat over a long period of time called history. Ultimately the Lord will defend his people and defeat their conquering enemy. One case in point is found in the book of Esther, which has far reaching implications in regard to God's timetable. Hundreds of years may pass, but God will bring judgment upon his children's enemies. He did in the case of Benjamin and Benjamin's conflicts with Amalek.

Caught up in one of those long remembered battles is a great man of history who was the deliverer of both Jews and Gentiles. His name was not Paul; his name was Mordecai. Esther's account of this man ends with a great tribute, "For Mordecai the Jew was second to King Ahasuerus, and was great among the Jews and well received by the multitude of his brethren, seeking the good of his people and speaking peace to all his kindred." (Esther 10:3, NKJV).

Mordecai found himself in warfare with personalities who had links to former skirmishes with his ancestors; those events made the Amalekites hate the tribe of Benjamin. Mordecai and Haman became symbolic figures of this battle in the book of Esther. Mordecai was a Benjamite; his archenemy was Haman, an Agagite. On the surface, the battle seemed to be confined to the account of Esther, but beneath the surface was a strong spiritual current. Haman was from Amalek. Haman's heritage made him an enemy to Benjamin and basically to all Israel.

THE REAL BATTLE IN ESTHER: BENJAMIN AND THE AMALEKITES

(A brief study of the Amalekites is important to this text because of the far-reaching prophecies about them. Judgment was hanging over them, and their judgment hinged upon their strife with Benjamin. Remember: Mordecai represents spiritual Benjamin, while Haman represents spiritual Amalek and ultimately the rogue, Agag.)

The sons of Amalek (who were the grandsons of Esau) had maintained deep resentment for the sons of Jacob throughout time. When Moses returned from Egypt, the Amalekites were living in the area just south and east of the land, which would belong to Benjamin. They came against Moses and were defeated by Joshua.

Again, when Moses sent spies to the land to determine whether the children of God could take the land, the people sided with the majority report, which was against immediate confrontation with the inhabitants of the Promised Land (most of the time the reasoning of man is against God's will). Eventually, the people understood the consequences of their action and made a decision to go ahead and attack. Again they followed man's reasoning and reacted outside the leadership of God.

When Moses told them that the Lord was displeased with their decision not to follow the minority report, it was then they decided to retract their vote and to go up immediately against the Amalekites (remembering their defeat under Joshua); however, this time Israel was defeated. (Just because God defeats an enemy one time using a certain method, He does not give license to use the same method again outside His permission.)

A pattern was about to emerge. The Amalekites, who dwelled among those of Moab, were the people Satan used to keep the children of God separated from their promised reward. The Amalekites/Ammonites/ Moabites urged Balak to hire Balaam to use sorcery to curse Israel and prevent the occupation of their lands. Moab had heard of Israel's victories over the Ammonites and how Joshua prevailed. Since Israel was a spiritual nation, their enemies turned to a spiritual leader to offer a spiritual solution. (The world has its spiritual leaders, and they have spiritual answers, just not the answers of the Holy Spirit.) The triumvirate reasoned that a spiritual curse was their answer.

Balaam could offer no curse, but in Numbers 24 turned from sorcery, and with the Spirit of God on him, blessed Israel and gave prophetic words about Amalek. Bible geography reveals that Balak escorted Balaam to three different mountain locations. Each of these locations drew them closer to Jericho and to Benjamin's territory. Finally, standing on Mt. Peor directly across the valley from Jericho, God intervened with His own message. (How important it is to realize that God's message points to a near day defeat of Agag, and a distant defeat [in the last days] of Amalek.) In other words, Benjamin symbolizes the people of the Lord to those who are God's enemies. It was toward Benjamin's land that the prophecies of Balaam were directed. Benjamin will be an integral part in the destruction of Amalek prophesied in the last days (see Numbers 24:14).

Numbers 24 records these events. In verse 7, Balaam speaks of Agag in terms of defeat. "His king (God's) shall be higher than Agag, and his kingdom shall be exalted." Because the Amalekites sought to curse Israel, they must fall under the judgment of verse 9:

> *Blessed is he, who blesses you, and Cursed is he who curses you.*
>
> (NKJV)

Balak was furious. He sent Balaam home, but not before the Lord used Balaam to deliver an end-time message. It is a message to "your people." (Here is a very important message for the last days, and very few end-time ministers even know its content.) Balaam prophesied about Jesus, calling Him the Star of Jacob, <u>Scepter</u> of Israel, and batterer of the brow of Moab and the sons of tumult (those who are against God and do battle with His people). Because Moab and Amalek were joined in their plot to defeat the plan of God, Balaam turned his prophetic word toward them.

In verse 20:

> *Amalek was first among the nations, (goyim) But shall be last until he perishes.*
>
> (NKJV)

Balaam is the first to use the term *goyim* for "the nations." Normally, this word is used by Hebrews to refer to the "Gentiles." Bible scholarship divides the classes of people the Word of God addresses as:

1. Israel

2. The Nations (*goyim*)

3. The Church of the living God.

Amalek is representative of all who stand to oppose the plan of God for His people. Even in the prophecy of Balaam toward the Kenites, which spoke of affliction against the tribe of Asher—Amalek stood as a representative of all who afflict God's people. Amalek represented the *goyim*, or the nations, which God will judge in the last days. Balak was not satisfied until he took his conversation with Balaam and turned it into reality. He desperately wanted to defeat Benjamin and Israel. Inadvertently, Balaam revealed through sorcery the "Achilles heel" of Israel, which was harlotry (both spiritual and physical). The harlotry of Israel was symbolized in their taking Moabitish women, which was the beginning of their prophesied affliction. (Nehemiah 13:25 deals with the severity of this sin.)

Affliction is often subtle and in the case of Israel, it was found in their joining themselves in liaisons with Moabitish women (Moab, the Kennites, Amalek, the Hittites and the Canaanites were so closely linked that they were united under the curse of Balaam. They stood as one in judgment).

When Israel accepted Moab's women, they incepted Moab's pagan gods. (Here is a tremendous parallel to the church and its people today.) God was angered that they spiritually cohabited with Baal of Peor by developing relationships with the women of Moab.

Why is Baal of Peor so important? One reason might be found in that this was the last place viewed by Balaam and the place where his final prophesy was given. Another answer might be found in Benjamin, for he was the only child of Jacob born in Canaan. Being a Canaanite was his special citizenship that made him the spiritual target to defeat in Israel. Like Paul, his citizenry gave him rights that others did not possess. Benjamin had a right to be in Canaan, both as one of the inheritors and as a citizen through birthright. Although a Simeonite was the provocateur of the hour (who was thrust through), the scene happened in the front door of Benjamin.

MORDECAI AND ESTHER

Now look anew at the matter of Esther and Mordecai. Old battle lines were drawn, and the persecution of the Jews which took place in the book of Esther was the outcropping of the battle between Benjamin and Amalek. Because of God's timetable of judgment, God defeated Haman in a wonderful deliverance of His people, including Queen Esther. The Lord did not settle the entire score but used this incident to encourage the people of God—while showing HE HAD NOT FORGOTTEN though centuries had passed. The battle was still alive between Benjamin, the vanquisher of Canaan, and their neighborhood of villains.

After the Balaam prophecy, the villains regularly appeared to carry out what they did best—seeking to thwart God's people from doing the exact will of God and seeking to keep them from their blessing. They acted to prevent His people from receiving God's best. (Look at the string of incidents that took place; soon it will be apparent why God chose a Benjamite named Paul to go to the *Goyim*.)

Review the history of Amalek and his cohorts. They attacked Jericho (in the land of Benjamin, Judges 3:13). They did battle with Ephraim (Judges 5:14). Gideon defeated them in Judges 6:3. They oppressed Israel (Judges 10:12). They were the reason for the dethronement of Saul (I Samuel 15, note the next chapter). They did battle with David (I Samuel 27). They captured David's wives (I Samuel 30). Hezekiah did battle with them and Simeon avenged himself upon them (I Chronicles 4).

Historically, all that was necessary to elicit a response from Israel was to mention them. Nehemiah, for instance, reflects in Nehemiah 13:1 on a passage in Deuteronomy 23:3:

> *An Ammonite or Moabite shall not enter the congregation of the Lord; even to the <u>tenth</u> generation none of his descendants shall enter the congregation of the Lord <u>forever</u>, because they did not meet you with bread and water on the road when you came out of Egypt, and <u>because they hired against you Balaam</u>, the son of Beor from Pethor of Mesopotamia, to curse you. Nevertheless, the Lord your God would not listen to Balaam, but the Lord your God turned the curse into a blessing for you, because the Lord your God loves you. <u>YOU shall not seek their peace nor their prosperity all your days forever.</u>*

(NKJV)

This incident stands out in written history on the same level as Sodom and Gomorrah in the minds of Israel. Those *goyim* who seek to hinder the work of the Lord, those who stand to discourage, fail to assist, or persecute God's people, face the same condemnation as is recorded in Numbers 24! ("They who curse Israel [even spiritual Israel] shall be cursed.")

Nehemiah believed that the sin of Balaam's day was taking place in his day. Intermarriage of Jews with the pagan women of Ashdod, Ammon, and Moab was again taking its toll upon them. He warned them by reading the Word in Chapter 13. The response of the true in heart to that Word was to separate themselves from the mixed multitudes. Mixture in that day was the attempt to combine the pure word of God with the godless practices of paganism. The pure in heart sought to correct themselves by living separate and holy lives. Those who were locked into relationships they did not wish to break stood without shame. (This is the sin of the modern church; it has sought to mix the pure word of God with the godless lifestyles of its congregation. The compromised church forgives where the Word does not forgive; their ministers are like lawyers who seek to mediate between God and the godless. This mixture of the profane with the holy will not work; it did not in Nehemiah's day and it will not work now. Without shame, congregations seek the face of God with people who are teaming with sin.) Nehemiah was tired of looking constantly upon a people laden with sin and its relationships, so he finally resorted to what may be the only tactic that will work today.

> *So I contended with them and cursed them, struck some of them and pulled out their hair, and made them swear by God, saying, 'You shall not give your daughters as wives to their sons, nor take their daughters for your sons or yourselves.*
>
> Nehemiah 13: 25(NKJV)

Nehemiah took a tough position and carried out his reforms in the face of people who really did not consider their relationships to be the source of their problems. Nehemiah looked backward in history to another day and reminded them of the subtleness of sin. Nehemiah was pragmatic about Solomon's down fall and attributed it to Solomon's marrying pagan women.

> *nevertheless pagan women caused even him to sin.*
>
> Nehemiah 13: 26(NKJV)

His prayer (to be remembered) is concluded by a blanket statement that is true today,

> *Remember them, O my God, because they have defiled the priesthood and the covenant of the priesthood and the Levites.*
>
> Nehemiah 13:29 (NKJV)

What was his final act? He cleansed them of everything that was pagan, including their relationships. That IS the most important work in life of the believer today!

ESTHER AND THE FORCE OF GOD IN OVERCOMING A DIFFICULT RELATIONSHIP

In many respects, Esther had to be willing to end her relationship with the King in order to provide for her people. She spiritually divorced her allegiance to her adopted nation and clothed herself with the mantel of Mordecai. She, in essence, assumed the position of Benjamin. Note the scriptures in Esther 2:20:

> For Esther obeyed the command of Mordecai as when she
> was brought up by him.

> (NKJV)

Mordecai learned of a plot to overthrow the king and informed Esther. Benjamin is always loyal to the king. Esther informed the king about a plot against him but did it in Mordecai's name. Satan is against the king because the king has taken one of Benjamin's daughters into his bosom. The thickening plot of the devil continues through the ascension of Haman. Esther 3:10 says:

> So the king took his signet ring from his hand and gave it it
> to Haman, the son of Hammedatha the Agagite, the enemy
> of Israel.

> (NKJV)

Haman was given power to destroy, kill, and to annihilate all Jews and to plunder their possessions. When the King sat down with Haman politically and socially, he became identified with Amalek.

Great prayer, weeping, mourning, and wailing went up from the Jews. God's *En Punto* is yet to be revealed!

Mordecai, who has never led her wrong, makes one of the strongest appeals in history. Esther 4:13-14 (NKJV):

> Do not think in your heart that you will escape in the king's
> palace any more than all the other Jews. For if you remain
> completely silent at this time, relief and deliverance WILL
> ARISE FOR THE JEWS FROM ANOTHER PLACE,
> but you and your father's house will perish. Yet who knows
> whether you have come to the kingdom for such a time as
> this?

In essence, he offers the possibility that her ascendancy to the king's bosom is God's *En Punto*. Just as in days past, the term, "now it happened," signals the intervention of the Lord. (In the treacherous hours between her decision and God's provision, the forces of hell were moving against her. Faith force overcame relational ties.) Esther waits in the court for the power of God to deliver her message. Note that she is favored and immediately goes to touch the scepter. This is direct fulfillment of the promise of God that His scepter shall be greater than Amalek's. A battle will ensue in which the Lord will be victorious for His people and recompense upon the head of Amalek his just reward. Haman is furious with Mordecai's faith (Esther 5:9) and takes it for insult. In the meantime, a restless king commands to have the chronicles of his achievements read to him. Mordecai's name is recorded with no reward for his patriotic loyalty. Haman is chosen to carry out the king's reward program. Symbolically, he has already succumbed to the curse of Benjamin, but not before his own wife prophesies:

> *If Mordecai, before whom you have begun to fall is of Jewish descent, you will not prevail against him but will surely fall before him.*
>
> Esther 6:13 (NKJV)

Haman is instantly hastened to the banquet of Esther just after these words. In Chapter 7, Esther declares to the king at this banquet that she is a Jewess. She pleads for her people and God is in that plea! She further pleads, "How can I endure to see the evil that will come to MY PEOPLE? Or how can I endure to see the destruction of my kindred?" (If Esther could plead today, her supplication would be before the rulers of churches, but her plea would be the same.) The Son of Benjamin and the Daughter of Benjamin were empowered to write the decree which freed the Sons of Israel from death, annihilation, destruction, and plundering. God's *En Punto* IS in history. Oh, that the result of their decree were to find fruition today, for when it went forth, the Jews had light, gladness, joy, and honor, and many in the land became Jews for fear of them. If believers would trust our God for their deliverance, He would give them the same. It has never taken great revival plans to bring conversion; it has always taken faith seeking the Hand of God! Seventy-five thousand of the enemies of the Jews fell under the hand of the Lord. They who align with Amalek will suffer greater numbers! (Note: the Jews did not take one possession from those they slew. Why? The sons of Benjamin did not wish to bring into their bosom the items handled by pagan hands. Thus, the hand of God prevailed for Benjamin as it will in the last days.)

Purim is celebrated throughout Israel as a remembrance of this occasion, but God favors this celebration as a symbolic anniversary to his Kept Promise. This is a day when life was "...turned from sorrow to joy for them and from mourning to a holiday." Currently on this day, Jews send presents to one another and gifts to the poor. This day of remembrance was not the beginning but the foreshadowing of a different day when God will defeat the enemies of the gospel and turn mourning into joy.

PAUL, THE PARTIAL FULFILLMENT OF ESTHER'S PLEA

As a son of Benjamin, Paul was like Haman to the Christians, but became like Esther in the end. With pockets stuffed with Jewish decrees to kill, destroy, annihilate, and plunder every man, woman, and child of "this way," he breathed wrath upon those who embraced the Lion of the Tribe of Judah. He was as much Amalek as Haman in spiritual terms. BUT, he repented.

It took no threat of gallows for Paul to change, but it did take a shocking visit from heaven to shake him into reality. That shaking was enough to change him forever. (What kind of shaking must take place in the modern congregation to bring them to such awareness? No shaking will take place! God dealt with a man, not a congregation. God dealt with Paul, who would repent, not a Sanhedrin, which refused to hear. God did not send Jesus to reform religion in the Temple; He sent Him to die for the sin of the world. Now the world must repent and come to Him one person at a time. Now the church must repent of its horrific relationships, its compromised liaisons, and its chambered promises whispered into seductive ears. No shaking will take place until, one at a time, repentant individuals decide— NO MORE!—nothing will stand between my God and me!)

Paul had to become like Benjamin when they divorced their shameful marriages to the Moabitish women: he had to divorce himself from his relationship in order to deliver his people. Identity with paganism makes the pagan.

Paul realized his grave departure from truth, cleansed himself of all that was pagan, despicable, and worthless. His three wilderness years purged him of all that was against the truth; he emerged a different man in the Lord. As a flaming evangel for the living Christ, he stood in the shoes of the biblical "man of God." Those who call themselves "men of God" today can do NO LESS!

As a Benjamite, who had been so zealous for his nation Israel, allowing nothing to stand in the way of carrying out his legalism, he now allows nothing to stand in his way in carrying forth the truth. Until the Damascus road happened, he had not departed from the traditions of his people and had remained loyal to the Temple. When he saw he was waging war against the Lord's people, he changed. Would to God that the leadership of religion would follow Paul's example.

In the twisting of time, Israel had become Amalek. Israel had become Ammon, Moab, and Canaan. It was not Egypt they followed; it was the path of Balak and Balaam. They sought to spiritually curse God's chosen people, the believers in Jesus. On the Damascus Road, the chief of the Tribe of Judah confronted a son of Benjamin and asked him a question that has puzzled scholarship. "Why do you persecute <u>me</u>?" and "is it hard to kick against the pricks?" were both loaded questions. The first was symbolic and so was the second. Look at the context and it will become apparent.

Throughout history, Benjamin had been aligned with Judah, so the question in context is: "Why are you persecuting Judah when until now Benjamin has been harnessed with Judah?" Is this too difficult to see? "Saul, why are you kicking and trying to break out of harness." This is why Paul was so adamant about history being used as proof that Israel must have a relationship to Jesus. The Lord used him (Benjamin) to preach peace to the *Goyim*, so that righteous judgment would be able to come from the Prince of Judah. Benjamin and Judah are now standing against the other brothers.

Oh! the church of today has become like Amalek. They fall under the curse of Amalek. They have aligned with Moab and Ammon in seeking to prevent the blessing from flowing to the people. Sound an alarm in Zion! Post signs upon the highways for the people of God! Place signs before churches which will read: "Caution: traveling the road set before you will lead to judgment!" Paul, the Benjamite, hated the likes of Balaam. Paul, the Benjamite, sought to correct Israel but soon realized the depth of their sin. They had not just married so many pagan women; they had embraced the pagan gods loved by those women.

Having cleansed himself, Paul was UNLIKE them. Having been cleansed, he was suspect in their ranks and unwelcome in their fellowship. Alas, this is true among those who cleanse themselves today. Alas, they are <u>unlike</u> their peers and find themselves unwelcome in their fellowships. Balaam may have been unsuccessful in Israel's day but has succeeded in this present one! The Achilles heel of the modern church has been discovered: they love the world and the things of it. The people stand cursed! They have embraced the pagan customs of their marriages. Jude and Peter both warned that this would happen in the latter days—they were right!

What has this to do with Paul, the Benjamite? It has to do with his place in the plan of God. His heritage and his time in history is as exact as the birth time of Jesus. Our Lord's plan is vast and exact. He arrived on the scene of history and changed it! In these last days, it is more important to focus upon what (and whom) God is sending than to decry what is disintegrating in the economic, social, and political world. In Paul's day, the decrees of Caesar meant less than the decrees of Paul. The road to Damascus broke the social and religious ties established through Phariseeism. It did not break the spiritual ties to his family and tribe of Benjamin; yeah, it established true Benjamin.

Realizing his roots in Benjamin, Paul was qualified to link with Judah more than Israel. He was able to write to his fellows with the irresistible appeal of Stephen. He recognized his times. He knew that he was the exact man for that exact moment in spiritual history. He was God's choice as a Benjamite to deal with the *Goyim*. He uniquely could take advantage of Israel's blind refusals and admit the Gentiles into the kingdom. Who would be better qualified than a Benjamite? Prophecy supported him.

He also recognized the limited time frame of this spiritual gap, which at the end of history would be closed. Benjamin would draw the net of inclusion for all who would choose Christ as Lord, both Jew and *Goyim*. This would explain Revelation 7's account of the 144,000 and why it begins with Judah (son of Leah) and ends with Benjamin (son of Rachael).

Paul touched the spiritual keys in both societies. He surgically entered the Jews domain of pride and exclusivity and engrafted a new Israel of God's choosing. He challenged the new Israel, not based upon blood lineage but spiritual lineage, to come forth and be seen. He aligned with the Abraham of faith, whose roots were in Melchizedek not the Chaldees. Standing next to Judah (Jesus), Paul was as separate from Israel as Rehoboam was separate from Jeroboam. He and Jesus became the two-pronged fork that could rightfully draw from the pot! They were sanctified and made of solid gold, fit for a heavenly sacrifice. Their similarities outweighed any differences and they became ONE. Mention the name Paul and immediately a flood of cognition takes one past flogging, shipwreck, and prison to his place in Christ. Oh! that the mention of modern leaders would cause the same reflection.

History is fast moving to its most important era, the era of the last days. What is needed is a Damascus road followed by a Pauline commitment to be exactly in the perfect, visible, accurate will of God, twenty-four seven. Damascus road experiences slaughter the machinations of man, while the Ananias annointing establishes a relationship where man hears only from God, receives only from God, leans solely upon God, moving only when directed by the Lord.

EN PUNTO IN THE LIFE OF PAUL

Look briefly into the life of Paul and see Ananias prophesy sink into his very being. The words of the Lord to Ananias ring clear:

> *Go, for he is a **chosen** vessel of Mine to bear My name before **Gentiles (goyim), kings, and the children of Is-rael.** For **I will show him** how many things he must suffer for My name's sake.*
>
> Acts 9:15-16 (NKJV)

Do not forget the three pronged assignments in these verses. Paul started his task by confronting the Jews at Damascus. The Jews in that area had heard of him and already spiritually catalogued him. They were not ready for a changed Paul who refused their classification. Where once his papers were signed by a High Priest, now they were disavowed. His papers were now signed by a different authority, Jesus of the tribe of Judah, and not the high priest of Jerusalem's Temple. That change alone was sufficient for the death sentence among the religious leaders. It is the same today!

Narrowly escaping a Jewish plot, he exercises his newfound task in the camp of the Hellenists. Whether these were Jews with Greek mixture or just *goyim* of the vicinity, we are not told. We are told they wanted to kill him.

Look at his situation. He has been newly sent out and already two opposing forces seek his life. Never in the history of Christendom is there a situation riper for a repeat of this than today. No one dares cross the establishment and stand for truth. Ranks are closing on all sides and the same verdict comes from both camps: death! (Fearing the worst, the disciples sent Paul home to Tarsus.)

Then it happened, the occasion which drew him out. God draws upon his cadre of believers for their assigned tasks. It did not just happen that the disciples, who had only worked among the Jews heretofore, filtered down to Antioch. There, men from Cyrene and Cyprus preached to the Hellenists (These were Greeks who were wrapped in their culture.). The Hellenists were receptive and were born again. Barnabas was sent to them and increased their number. (Note the qualities of Barnagbas: "good man, full of the Holy Spirit and faith [Acts 11:24].") Seeing the magnitude of the work, Barnabas went to Tarsus in order to take Paul back to Antioch.

At Antioch, a prophet named Agabus initiated the first official journey of Paul. He prophesied a worldwide famine. He and Barnabas were sent back to Jerusalem with relief money because of a WORD from God.

Again, a "word from the Lord" united Barnabas and Paul. Acts 13 says, that prophets and teachers were **ministering to the Lord** (something we see little of today), and the Holy Spirit told them to separate these two for their chosen work. A supernatural word was given them because both of them were exactly in the right place (*En Punto*) for that blessing.

Being sent by the Holy Spirit is different than "deciding to do something for Jesus." They went to Salamis via a route charted by the Spirit. They encountered men who needed their ministry when they followed that route. Moving only through the Spirit, one after another person or group was encountered by them. Such God ordained witness is worlds apart from the haphazard approaches advocated by evangelical zealots. Sergius Paulos sought them out (Acts 13:7)!

Taking their lead only from the Spirit, Paul and Barnabas entered Antioch in Pisidia. Preaching to Jews and Gentiles (proselytes), using the double streams flowing in his life, Paul had unusual results. Most of the Jews left, but the Gentiles remained and begged for more. (Lately, how many occasions have congregations reassembled and begged to hear more? Is this not the difference between Paul's ministry and the ministries which proliferate today?) Take this event as a God-ordained response to a God-ordained ministry.

From these Holy Spirit directed events came preachments which drew the whole city. Juxtapose the "citywide" campaigns of current evangelism to what the Bible said of Paul: "the whole city came together to hear the word of God." No one remained at home in that city when Paul preached; imagine that! No person decided his or her agenda was greater than hearing about God's agenda. What is the difference in the twenty-first century? The difference is simple: the people were led and convinced by the Spirit that these men were men of God who had the message of God!

A cutting difference between Paphos and modern evangelism is found in the response of the audience. The religious leadership heard the same message as the Gentiles that day, they opposed it—the Gentiles were glad and glorified the word of the Lord. Look for the same responses to the true "Gospel of the Kingdom" in these final hours. (It is at this point that a distinction should be made between the "gospel of the Kingdom" and that which is posed as the gospel message. Paul, in Romans 2, spelled it more specifically in verse 16,... "in the day when God will judge the secrets of men by Jesus Christ, according to MY GOSPEL." His gospel spelled out total commitment to the will and leadership of Jesus. It was His kingdom, His Gospel that the world would hear and the one promised to be preached before the end of the ages. Do not confuse the many "gospels" prevailing today with the "gospel of His Kingdom." His kingdom does not reign in every sanctuary and is not preached from every pulpit. The sign on the door may read "church," while those who adhere to its tenets have no concept of the KINGDOM! Objection will be raised from the lips of religious leadership just as in Paul's day, while the sinners of this world who seek to escape the fate of judgment, will cry, "More!" A new maxim will be coined: "If the clergy shouts 'Amen,' run! If the sinners cry, 'Let us hear more!' stay!"

Full of the Holy Spirit, Paul went to Iconium where those who were to believe heard the word and those who were filled with the devil rejected it. It was organized religion that organized against the man of God. So it is today!

Fleeing under the hand of a protective Lord, they came to Lystra where their paths crossed the crippled man's need and he was healed. Here they were almost deified yet in finality were stoned. The roads between these two extremes are very close. Paul knew the Spirit was teaching him what they must suffer for Jesus. He knew he was in the Spirit's path.

Because their ministry covered the broad spectrum of Gentiles, kings, and Jews, when Paul arrived at Jerusalem, a "circumcision debate" was on. Often religious beliefs must be discarded in the face of the Spirit. The Holy Spirit settled the issue, not by a democratic voice vote. They returned to Antioch, under the letter of the Spirit, and a spiritual ministry took place with prophets and preaching.

Paul gathered steam in his work to liberate the Gentiles from spiritual death. New men in new circumstances were needed, and by allowing the Spirit to lead him, he moved toward Phrygia and Galatia. Notice what took place.

> *they were <u>forbidden by the Holy Spirit</u> to preach the word in Asia.*
>
> Acts 16:6 (NKJV)

Had this taken place today, two responses would have occurred: first, most churches would not have consulted in that much detail what the Spirit wanted. The second is simple, for had the Spirit forbade, some well-meaning churchman would have risen to say, "We started to go there, and I believe, bless God, we ought to continue; after, all someone must be mistaken; the Word is to be preached at all times and everywhere." Therefore, thousands of works done in the name of our Lord were never given permission in the Spirit, and the world is reaping a harvest of spiritual miscarriage. There is no such thing in the Spirit as uncoordinated effort, no such thing as duplication of effort in the same field.

Paul stopped when the Spirit stopped. "Shall we go to Asia?" No! "Shall we go to Mysia?" Yes! "Shall we go to Bithynia?" No! "Shall we go to Troas?" Yes! Is this too difficult for the body of Christ today? Is this much dependence on the Spirit provocative to the religious circles of the twenty-first century? Yes! Computer analysis and neighborhood surveys have not taken the place of the Spirit. A community profile in which "pockets of reachable social strata" are identified (or some feasibility study) does not placate the Spirit!

"Come over to Macedonia," exceeds leadership's opinion of "we see a need." Notice Paul's reaction, "Now after he had seen the vision, immediately we sought to go to Macedonia, concluding that the Lord had called us...(Acts 16:10)." Following the "Spirit Map," they came to Philippi in

Macedonia. A series of events began to take place. From the prayer meeting at the riverside to ministering at the Jailor's side, the Spirit arranged a series of God-ordained "happenings." (When one experiences a God-ordained "happening" no other kind will do. Stop here and read appendix One: "It happened at Rotatona, Sri Lanka".)

Acts 17 found Paul and Silas walking along the Spirit-trail to Thessalonica where they encountered both Jews and Greeks. It was here they were accused of the one thing for which they gladly heard, "These who have turned the world upside down have come here too (v.6)." Although their accusers sought to have them arrested for treason, instead, they were propelled by "their circumstances" to the next appointment.

From Berea to Mar's Hill to Corinth is a trail of blessing which leads to Aquila and Priscilla. Without the hand of God, how dismal is the "earth trek," but with His hand, how wonderful it is to meet His people at the chosen place and at the right time. In their company he preached; the Scripture says, "Paul was constrained (pressed) by the Spirit (Acts 18:5)." Ah, the word "constrained" speaks volumes to the Spirit-trained ear. Spirit encouragement is different than the shouts of an exuberant audience. With Spirit constraining, there will be Spirit results. Oh! to speak under that kind of anointing causes the "constrained" to know that "something wonderful is about to take place." When one feels the "constraint" of the Spirit, one's spiritual antennae raises because this signal must be transmitted. Something different is in the air; it is the fresh anointing that breaks the yoke.

Barriers are going to fall, and sin captured souls are going to be liberated when the Spirit constrains. When the Spirit constrains, His powerful leadership takes charge, and no matter what event follows, it is a Spirit-event. Crispus, the ruler of the synagogue, followed Jesus, which was a Spirit-event. Corinthian *goyim* were saved, that was a Spirit-event. Paul heard from God in a vision, that was a Spirit-event. The Lord says, "don't be afraid and don't stop preaching," that is Spirit encouragement. Later on, Paul saw the accusing ruler Sosthenes (Acts 18) get his just deserts in front of a civil court, that was a Spirit-event.

Under the Spirit, Paul sailed to Ephesus. Here, the Spirit baptized the saints in fire, following their baptism in the name of Jesus. At Ephesus, God worked unusual miracles by the hand of Paul. Special handkerchiefs were put on the sick, and they recovered as evil spirits left; this was a Spirit-event. When the Spirit ordains the trip, expect miracles.

Paul saw other miracles; converts who were formerly into witchcraft burned their books and paraphernalia in fires set by their own hands. From this point forward, Paul was a different man. Moving in the Spirit became Paul's way of life. He did nothing apart from the Spirit. Acts 19:20 says: "Paul purposed in the Spirit," to go to Jerusalem and to Rome. Purposing something in the Spirit is different than "making up your mind." When you clear your decisions with the Spirit, He will bring into your life whatever circumstance or provision is necessary to get you to your desired destination. From Ephesus to Macedonia to Greece to Troas, through riots, Jewish plots, and falling saints (Eutychus), he wended his way to his destination.

> *I go bound in the spirit to Jerusalem, not knowing the things that will happen to me there,   EXCEPT THE HOLY SPIRIT testifies in every city saying that chains and tribulations await me.*

> Acts 20:23 (NKJV)

Over and over, the Holy Spirit testified to Paul that he would undergo harsh treatment and suffering at Jerusalem. Talk about revelation! How much more revelation would Paul need to order his steps? Yet, in the modern church, the Holy Spirit often says nothing, testifies nothing, and the aimless wandering that takes place under the guise of Christ is a shame to those in the New Testament who lived and walked ONLY in the Spirit.

From this point on in Acts, there is a continuous trail of Divine Appointments. Paul testifies before Jews, Kings, and Gentiles just as was prophesied. His contacts were with the highest ranking officials in religion and government. The effect of his contacts resulted in two very different conclusions: they either revealed the hypocrisy of the hearer or they ended in salvation. His oration before Felix is a masterpiece, showing his personal understanding of his life and work.

> *...this I confess to you, that according to the Way which they call a sect, so I worship the God of my fathers, believing all things which are written in the Law and the Prophets. (His confession reveals his continuing identity with his Benjamite heritage.) I have hope in God.... I myself always strive to have a conscience without offense toward God and men....*

> Acts 24:14.15.16 (NKJV)

Acts concludes with Paul preaching to the Jews a message of repentance found in Isaiah 6:9; he follows it with a rebuke:

> *Therefore let it be known to you that the salvation of God has been sent to the Gentiles, <u>and</u> <u>they</u> <u>will</u> <u>hear</u> <u>it</u>.*

> Acts 28:28 (NKJV)

Today, one thing haunts the ministry-at-large and especially those who know the truth and perhaps preach some of it, "I preached, but did they hear it?" With the Spirit, Paul did not have that quandary. He knew that those to whom he brought the "gospel of the kingdom" were foreordained to respond to his message. Why? Because he was led ONLY by the Spirit. "KNOWN TO GOD FROM ETERNITY ARE ALL HIS WORKS (ACTS 15:18 NKJV)."

(**Author's Note:** Just as Philip and Paul are examples of those who walked in the exactness of the Spirit, the following chapter is devoted to one who stands symbolically for all those who do not.)

CHAPTER FIVE

The Burden of Spiritual Relativism

Study of Saul and the Church

KING SAUL, THE SPIRITUAL RELATIVIST

Saul, though anointed of God, was never careful to hear and carry out God's exact commands. Although a commander of a nation of blessed people, he was not submissive to the Supreme Commander of the Universe. He stood symbolically in Israel's history as the answer to a rebellious people's cry for a king, but he was just that, the symbol of rebellion and not obedience. Over and over his decisions turned to disaster because he depended on his "soulish" reason and his human intellect. Perhaps his having an imposing physique and quick elevation to kingship can be cited as the reason for Saul's conduct. Lying deep within him was the cancer which eats at many spiritual leaders. He symbolized all spiritual leaders who have kept stronger touch with the pulse of the people than in touch with the heart of God. Soulishness is a condition which causes men to depend on their senses rather than the Spirit of God. Saul stumbled through his kingship, eventually losing his kingdom to a man opposite to himself, a man who relished God's voice. Juxtaposed in history, they are opposites. One sought "the secret place of the Most High," while the other sought a place with the people. One listened with sensitive ear to what God's voice was saying; the other turned a deaf ear (God refused to speak to him). One received the rebuke of the Lord; the other sought to ameliorate the judgment of God through the mediation of Samuel. One learned to wait for a "rustling in the mulberries;" the other waited for no one. One asked, "Shall I go forth?" knowing the wisdom of hearing from the Lord; the other counted his troops and assumed the will of God. Men of leadership must hear from God or be destined to join the ranks of those who stand in judgment for their failure to do so.

SAUL, ROOTED IN RELATIVISM

Saul is chosen in this study to exemplify why it is important to hear and execute the exact will of God. His relegation of God's commandments to circumstances and his view of those commands as merely suggestions to be strained through man's reason stand as a Biblical example of spiritual relativism. It is from this format the following questions arise.

How important is it to carry out the <u>exact</u> command of the Lord? Just why is it necessary to carry out each detail of His desire, down to the letter? The answer is simple, because religious relativism is as deadly as moral relativism. Such inquiry into absolutism versus relativism is valid because the Twenty-First Century church has emerged from fifty years or more of being taught, through design and demonstration, spiritual relativism. (It may be argued that the ruination of the Pharisees and the Legalistic Jews was their insistence upon legalistic absolutism (adhering to every jot and tittle of minute Scripture while weighing the wisdom of Rabbis to be equal with God's Wisdom). Why then would God condemn this super-religious body, while demanding strict adherence to His Word from the Church? Hopefully from this study, the reader will understand how adherence to standards which have been modified by man is the essence of relativism.

Spiritual relativism is as damnable as moral and ethical relativism. The last decade of the Twentieth Century was characterized by all three. Regardless of the intentions of the U.S. President, Bill Clinton, he stood as a prime example of moral and ethical relativism. (In my Philosophy classes, there was always included a two day session entitled, "The Clinton Clinic On Relative Truth." During the course of study, the class was led to examine the moral, ethical, and spiritual ethos surrounding the Clinton Presidency. Such questions as, "Did he actually believe he was telling the truth to the American public?" Yes! Under the banner of moral relativism he, in fact, did. Under the influence of ethical relativism, his actions were excusable even up to his relationship to the Arkansas Bar. Under religious relativism, he also gave all the explanation necessary to appease his Baptist congregation. Rather than viewing many actions portrayed in the media as scandalous, he was used as a symbol by a society which embraced the tenets of his relativistic philosophy.)

Relativism considers circumstances; it asks the question, "What is best for people according to one's personal point of view?" In its more benevolent use, it considers how one might spare the feelings of another. These considerations have to be dealt with alongside truth, as judgment lies within the rationale of man. Relativism always weighs the impact of actions upon others. Relativism excuses exactness in favor of a more global view. Globalism demands one to say that "given all the truth that is out there, how can we know the truth, for there are many truths?" As truth becomes relative, real truth is required to share its throne with any statement, action, or belief which may have an element of truth in it. Nine-tenths error stands in credibility alongside one-tenth truth. (Hence, the "Clintonism" which said, " It's according to what you mean by...[supply the subject]." In other words, a portion of truth qualifies the total package of statements, actions, and beliefs as truth. Getting close to truth is just as important as hitting the mark, according to relativism. Close counts! It says, "We must consider every circumstance." [In a game of horseshoes, a "leaner" doesn't count the same as a "ringer," but it counts for something—because it is almost there. Being close counts! In a game of darts, if a dart is on the board, it counts for something.] Even in the field of Education, relativism has forged a hearing as can be seen in the trend which says, if a child does his best in school, the value of his self-esteem is as prized as his academic prowess. Relativists reward getting close to a standard, for they believe standards are mediated by circumstances and issues and are constantly in a state of flux.)

Now, consider the effect of a society saturated with relativistic arenas (government—the diplomatic and military corps; the judicial—having lost its impartiality; the legislative—passing laws and setting trends which are bathed in relativisitic tenets) and clearly understand that the religious arena is even more saturated than other institutions because of religion's dependence on volunteerism. A strict standard would diminish participation, and the last thing any church or religious organization wants is diminution! How then is religion, government, morals, ethics, business, and education affected through their interconnected interaction? (In present society, there is no clearly marked separation between these institutions.) Their network of decision making is primarily the same, based on circumstances and pushed by public opinion. To have a better concept of this interaction, consider the next position.

Consider a textbook explanation of ethical relativism. After all, the Philosopher or the Behavioral Scientist must have some basis for assessing the attitudes or actions of those occupying the camp of the relativist. Hear one Philosopher explain his view:

> The revolt of the relativists against absolutism is, I believe, part and parcel of the <u>general revolutionary tendency of our times</u>. In particular it is a result of the decay of belief in the dogmas of orthodox religion.

> Belief in absolutism was supported, as we have seen, by

belief in Christian monotheism. And now that, in an age of
<u>widespread religious skepticism</u>, that support is withdrawn,
absolutism tends to collapse....ethical relativism is, in its
essence, a purely negative creed. It is simply a denial of
ethical absolutism.(5)

(Because there may be a misunderstanding as to the definition of absolutism in this context, it is used as the <u>standard</u> of the Lord, the <u>sovereignty</u> of
His Word, and the choice of the <u>leadership</u> of the Holy Ghost, as opposed
to the rationale of man.)

Just as one cannot be the "healed" and the "sick" at the same time,
so it is impossible to embrace ethical, moral, and religious relativism
and be considered a purist. The two are incompatible, yet there are
several other aspects which must be considered beyond the obvious
ones first postulated.

There is another form of relativism which is really the opposite side of
the same coin. It is an elitist-relativism. Briefly mentioned in the first sentences of this chapter, it boils down to this equation: "We are a select group
by birth and/or social standing, and if an 'outsider' wishes to enter our
group, he or she must adhere to the rules we enjoin." Saul considered
himself such an elitist. He was the chosen of God, and he felt the choosing
was based on fiat rather than grace and mercy. He was Israel's first King.
He was handsome and he was determined to make himself regal. When he
entered a room, the room was to pay attention. His pride of office eventually overcame him. This is why he is symbolic of all spiritual leaders who
cease to govern by the Spirit. Their office becomes more of a political
office carrying with it the power granted by men, rather than a spiritual
office whose power flows from the Spirit.

So often, those who have departed from spiritual exactness begin to
demand an exactness of their own. They seek to exclude themselves from
the common or ordinary and make demands which are neither spiritual nor
Godly. Often, they surround themselves with others who have attained
their favor and who seek to maintain their exclusivity. Here, exactness is
demanded of the "outsider," but not always of the insider. Exactness is
designed to be used as a tool to obfuscate. It is the reverse of globalism,
which seeks to encompass everyone. Legalism is enshrined because it
reduces the universe to a set of rules. One's standing is based on who one
is and how closely one adheres to those within the same strata. Thus, we
have the sin of the Pharisees and the Legalists of Jesus' day. Everything in
their world was relative to their own framework. This is where the modern
church has brought itself. Denominational bodies, as well as those who
consider themselves "non-denominational," have devised neat rules which
are mutually accepted and exclusive, and allow the establishment of an "in"

and an "out" group. If a person chooses to operate <u>outside</u> that group's set of rules, then he or she is castigated, or maybe even sentenced to death (in the case of Jesus, this was physical death, but this must also include social castigation, character assassination, business and professional persecution). It's adherents practice a form of relativism, for once admitted to the group, they tend to excuse one another, all the while judging one another. This "in-group" forms its own universe and measures even the commands of God along their own guidelines. They determine what is to be emphasized and what is not; they determine what is relevant and what is not. Every one of them is under heavy obligation to tow the line of the "in-group" while making relative judgments about all other aspects of life. (This issue is raised, "How often is the Sunday morning message determined along the same lines? Who determines what will be included and what will be excluded? What is the criteria which determines all the action within the convention, the church hall, or the cathedral?" Are these decisions made by man or the Spirit?)

JESUS VERSUS THE RELATIVISTS

Enter Jesus, who delighted in emphasizing the Scriptures and the higher principles the religious hierarchy de-emphasized. He delighted in punching the buttons they left untouched. He applied principles in a way their "in-group" had long ago counted as trivia or excluded as being an impossible imperative. He pointed out that their God was themselves. He was given the death sentence by them, for He refused to be governed by their relativism. Hear this modern relativist speaking under the guise of an advocate of "moral freedom:"

> ...morality involves autonomy, that is, the ability to think
> for oneself and decide, for oneself, what is right and what
> is wrong, whom to obey and whom to ignore, what to do
> and what not to do. (6)

Scripture has already shown the fallacy of this type of relativism, which is based on individual self-determination and varies with as many individuals as may occupy the earth. This truly is the world's concept of morality which excuses some actions, while not excusing others, based on individual taste. The moment Israel sought to be like the world and have a King, they ushered in the format for such relativism. Instead of judgment by the King of Kings, their judgment would rest upon Saul or his successors. Within the confines of Israel's first kingship, relativism reared its head. (Each step away from the absolute sovereignty of the Living Lord is a step toward relativistic compromise. With the elevation of man within religious circles, there comes the same portent.) Enter King Saul.

KING SAUL, SYMBOL OF RELATIVISM'S FINALITY

Saul lived in Gibeah; he was a Benjamite. This is important! When Samuel did the bidding of the Lord and made Saul King, he did so with trepidation. In I Samuel 10:25, the prophet tells the people they have lost the freedom they enjoyed in the "<u>liberty</u> of the Lord." By identifying with the world and seeking a king, they would embrace the burden of royalty. "Then Samuel explained to the people the behavior of royalty, and wrote it in a book and laid it up before the Lord."

The first verse of chapter 12 showed Samuel telling the people, "Indeed I have heeded your voice in all that you said to me, and have made a king over you." Just a few verses down, he sorrowfully lamented for the days of yore, "when the Lord your God was your king...(v.13)." Shortly after, Samuel reminded the people about the conditions relative to their action.

> *If you <u>fear the Lord and serve Him and obey His voice</u>, and do not rebel against the commandment of the Lord, then both you and the king who reigns over you will continue following the Lord your God. However, if you do not <u>obey the voice of the Lord</u>, but rebel against the commandments of the Lord, then the hand of the Lord will be against you, as it was against your fathers.*

I Samuel 12:12-14 (NKJV)

Samuel then called rain and thunder to emphasize their great wickedness in seeking man instead of God to be their king. The people asked Samuel to pray for them, for they recognized the sin they had committed. Then, Samuel spoke to them on the topic of exactness.

> *Do not fear. You have <u>done all this wickedness</u>; yet do not turn aside from following the Lord, but serve the Lord with all your heart. And do not turn aside; for then you would go after <u>empty</u> things which cannot profit or deliver, for they are nothing. ONLY fear the Lord, and serve Him in truth with all your heart; for consider what great things He has done for you. But if you still do wickedly, you shall be <u>swept</u> away, both <u>you and your king</u>.*

I Samuel 12:20,21,24-25 (NKJV)

The first action of the king (after these words were spoken) was an action which was based on relativism. He offered a burnt offering to the Lord and usurped the role of Samuel. Why? His explanation began, "under the circumstances." Relativism always begins at this point.

> *When I saw that the people were scattered from me, and*
> *that you did not come within the days appointed, and that*
> *the Philistines gathered together at Michmash, then I said,*
> *'The Philistines will now come down on me at Gilgal, and*
> *I have not made supplication to the Lord.'* THEREFORE
> I FELT COMPELLED, *and offered a burnt offering.*
>
> I Samuel 13:1-12 (NKJV)

Samuel now told him where he made his error,

> *You have not kept the commandment of the Lord*
> *your God... .*
>
> I Samuel 13:13 (NKJV)

Samuel explained to Saul that God was looking for someone like Himself, one who lived within prescribed parameters. (The world classifies God as an Absolutist. God lives within a finely tuned universe. Remember, it is a strange sounding piano which is not tuned by an absolute tone. In days past, it was A-440.) Because of his lack of discipline regarding the word of the Great Absolute, Saul lost his throne. Samuel spoke of David, his successor:

> *The Lord has sought for Himself a man after His own heart,*
> *and the Lord has commanded him to be commander over*
> *His people, because you have not kept what the Lord com-*
> *manded you.*
>
> I Samuel 13:14 (NKJV)

Just as verse fourteen declared, Samuel went to Saul's hometown of Gibeah in Benjamin. The prophet returned to "home plate" to call the King, "Out!" The King thought he had done right in giving an offering. He thought he was honoring God, but he failed to understand the "exactness" of God. God did not anoint him a prophet. God did not anoint him a priest. He anointed him king. (This is very important, for in the chapter dealing with "spheres" the whole thrust will be, "operating within God-defined spheres of authority.")

Ministries are suffering today because they have eclipsed the boundaries God set for them. They have sought to do good things for which they were not anointed. Why would the Lord be angry about Saul's sacrifice if this is not true? Why didn't the circumstances warrant a change in the rules to accommodate Saul? Why are there so many shipwrecks in Christendom when seemingly good activities of the church bring down judgment instead of blessing? This one act cost Saul his kingdom, a similar one would cost him his life! (O Church, look at your many acts which stand before you in judgment!)

Saul's life became a pictograph of mistakes and misjudgments. He was a true relativist. I Samuel 13-15 is a chronicle of error. When the Philistines challenged him, Saul was seen sitting not far from home (perhaps because Samuel was in Gibeah, he was reluctant to stay in that city) discussing his plan of action with Ahijah, the nephew of Ichabod. Ahijah was Saul's priest. Slowly, God began to separate Himself and His chosen ones from Saul and from his relativistic decisions. (The significance with Ahijah is his connection with the tainted Eli System [See *Sons of Zadok*].)

While Saul was steadily working against the Lord, his son Jonathan was steadily being blessed, "for he has worked with God this day (I Samuel 14:45) ." The dichotomy between the two was evident. Jonathan depended solely upon the Lord's command, while his father just assumed the Lord's will. When Saul inquired of the Lord after building an altar and sacrificing again, the Lord refused to answer. Saul's oath to kill whoever took food or drink was an "uncalled-for-intrusion" on the work of God. (How many times is this the case today, among ministries? Men determine what will be the rule and agenda for doing God's work, all the while stumbling because of that agenda.)

When Samuel again appeared on the scene, it signaled that the Lord was willing to give Saul a second chance to get things right. Chapter 15 opens with exact instructions from the Lord. Samuel tells Saul, "Now therefore, heed the voice of the words of the Lord." Samuel then gave Saul the exact instructions of the Lord so clearly that it should have been impossible not to know them.

> *Now go and attack Amalek,[after all Saul is a Benjamite]*
> *and utterly destroy all that they have, and do not spare them.*
> *But kill both man and woman, infant and nursing child,*
> *ox and sheep, camel and donkey.*
>
> I Samuel 15:3 (NKJV)

The Scriptures point out that Saul had two hundred thousand foot soldiers and <u>ten thousand men of Judah</u>. Isn't it interesting that Judah is singled out in this accounting. (Remember the closeness of Benjamin and Judah.)

Saul's relativism again showed its ugly head. The account in I Samuel said he attacked the Amalekites, then **departed** from the commandment of the Lord.

> *He also took Agag king of the Amalekites alive.*
>
> I Samuel 15:8 (NKJV)

Then he carried out in exactness one part of the commandment,

> *...and utterly destroyed all the people with the edge of the sword.*
>
> I Samuel 15:8 (NKJV)

How interesting to observe Saul as he picked and chose which of the commands of the Lord that he would obey. His relativism was showing!

> *But Saul and the people [note] spared Agag and the best of the sheep, the oxen, the fatlings, the lambs, and all that was good, and were unwilling to utterly destroy them. But everything despised and worthless, they utterly destroyed.*
>
> I Samuel 15:9(NKJV)

This act of relativism cost Saul his life. It made the Lord regret that he set Saul as King of His people. It grieved the heart of the prophet Samuel (he cried to God all night). In the face of all this, Saul set up a monument to himself. It was a "look what I have accomplished" edifice. (We see them all across the world and in every major city in the United States, brick and mortar monuments built by religious relativists to remind the world of their greatness. Almost every relativist worries about his legacy [Notice how relativistic this statement is.]).

Verse 13 showed Samuel going to see Saul, whose first words to Samuel were sincere utterances from a profound relativist:

> *Blessed are you of the Lord: I HAVE PERFORMED THE COMMANDMENT OF THE LORD.*
>
> I Samuel 15:13 (NKJV)

Can one suppose the next action might have been attributed to the fact Samuel had gotten no sleep the night before? His attitude toward the King looked like utter exasperation. Samuel's attitude might also be construed as a true reflection of the heart of God toward relativists. Nonetheless, the first King of Israel was told basically to, "Shut up." Samuel was to be admired, for he did wait until the King started out on his string of "reasons" before he silenced him. It was mercy that silenced Saul, for his tongue was uttering more and more the relativist's heart. Saul had ceased hearing from God because God refuses to talk to those who refuse to do His will. The problem lay in the fact that Saul was aware of God's silence. God's silence did not deter him from action, however. (Silence from God has not caused men or man's institutions of religion to stop and take notice; on the contrary, they function regardless of the silence.)

Since Saul was not getting any word from the Lord, it was necessary for Samuel, the prophet, to hear from God and relate the message to him. (Thousands rely upon clergy to hear the message of God be-

cause they have not heard from God themselves. The primary difference between today's clergy and Samuel is that Samuel prayed all night
and interceded. He heard from God, THEN he went with God's message. Modern clergy, like Saul, continue when they have heard nothing. Please note what happens on Sunday when a crowd appears: a
sermon is given—anointed or not!)

The message from God was simple; it touched the root of the issue,
"when you were little in your own eyes." (We have a saying in Texas,
"before He got too big for his britches.") In other words, when he was not
so self-determined, he relied upon God and the Lord made him King. Thank
God for the bravery of a prophet standing before a King, who ultimately
could have ordered his death. Sadly, there are none standing today!

Samuel continued with an unusual statement for Old Testament times:

> *Now the Lord sent you on a* <u>*mission*</u>.
>
> I Samuel 15:18 (NKJV)

Note the endemic factors surrounding Samuel's use of the word "mission."
Being sent on a mission involves several aspects. First, it is a form of
command from God, for being "sent" is different than "deciding to go."
Second, a mission implies a set goal to be attained within "being sent."
Something must occur, as the result of the "going," which would not have
occurred on its own. Thirdly, there are usually understood parameters of
authority in being sent "on a mission," for something of importance has to
be generated due to that "embassage." Fourthly, timing is a factor in a
"mission," for the sender is convinced that the time is NOW! A King on a
mission is an awesome prospect!

Within the framework of "Saul's Mission" was a chance for Saul to
prove himself reliable. He failed. When challenged by Samuel, his answer
was again unacceptable:

> *And Saul said to Samuel, 'But I HAVE obeyed the voice
> of the Lord, and gone on the mission on which the Lord
> sent me, and brought back Agag king of Amalek, I have
> utterly destroyed the Amalekites. But the PEOPLE took
> of the plunder, sheep and oxen, the best of the things which
> should have been utterly destroyed, to sacrifice to the Lord
> YOUR God in Gilgal.*
>
> I Samuel 15:20-21 (NKJV)

(Before Samuel's reply is reviewed, it is necessary to point out a few items
in Saul's answer.) Saul actually thought he had totally complied with the
commandment of God. He was not feigning compliance, for he had prac-

ticed relativism so long that he could now no longer perceive the absolute. (Literally millions of churches, denominations, organizations, and individuals are in this condition. Committees have made decisions, boards have made determinations, and ecclesiastical councils have handed down arbitrations for so long, that those who adhere to them have lost their sense of the original plan of God. They think, along with the millions who abide by those decisions, that they are doing the will of God. Where are the Samuel's? Would someone who fit Samuel's prophetic qualifications be heard today? To God and the purist prophet, the words of "explanation" sounded sickening. It is always the relativist's need to explain, to give a rationale for a behavior which is neither true nor pure. Listen to the worldly explanations given by Christendom today; they are endless. Somewhere in the core of these diatribes is a putrefying compromise oozing its odorous answer. The spiritual health of the issuer is evident to the prophet's heart, even though his words sound reasonable to the society hearing them. Sound the alarm! Alas, ears to hear are given by the Spirit alone, for the world wide deception is deep and pervasive. The multitudinous "amen" echoing acceptance to the quasi-truths of a disobedient church rake against the prophet's ear and sound like a rejoicing crowd surrounding a golden calf.)

Saul's answer injected a powerful undercurrent to his verbal explanation. He separated the people of the Amalekites from the King. In Saul's mind, the king was something different than the people. Psychologically, this was the key to Saul's problem. He had identified "kingship" as a separate class. (How many congregations have separated "their leadership" from "the people." Their leaders become a special class, a different rank to be dealt with on a different basis.) Had Agag been excused by God, a whole remnant of Amalekites would have been fathered by Agag. Samuel slew him. (Where are the Samuel's who will take such a stand? Someone had to rise to carry out the EXACT command of the Lord and it was His prophet. Oh, this is the question for this hour—Is there no one who will rise to the occasion?)

Saul's answer pointed to the people. Saul sought for security in numbers. If there was security in numbers, then those who accompanied Saul gave him solace. "Everyone thought like I did," might have been an appropriate summation for Saul's speech. "We all were concerned about bringing God a sacrifice from the spoils." Religious spin had early roots! Religious spin, because it is not truth, continues to talk, searching for acceptance from those who are separated from its ranks. Saul eventually excluded himself from God!

Saul inadvertently disassociated himself from the God of Samuel. He referred to "the Lord your God," in a manner which appropriated the "absolutist God" to Samuel, while maintaining a "relativist concept" of God for himself.

Samuel exploded with a strong revelation from the Lord:

> *Has the Lord as great delight in burnt offerings and sacri-*
> *fices, As <u>in obeying</u> the voice of the Lord? Behold, to obey*
> *is better than sacrifice, and <u>to heed</u> than the fat of rams. For*
> *REBELLION is as the sin of witchcraft, and stubbornness*
> *is as iniquity and idolatry, Because you have <u>rejected</u> the*
> *word of the Lord, He also has rejected you from being king.*
>
> I Samuel 15:22-23 (NKJV)

Samuel "cut no slack" as he obeyed the exact word of the Lord, not even for a king. (Although sermons abound using this text, few delve deeply enough to see the implications related to the heart of the king.) Samuel does not say that the Lord has no delight in burnt offerings and sacrifices, for surely this was proven in later events. Sacrifice was just secondary to the condition of the heart. It was so with Saul; it was so with Cain. (Thousands crowd into halls and sanctuaries weekly to offer the sacrifice of praise, but what is the condition of their heart? Have they carried out to the letter the will of God for their lives in that week? Have they accomplished their "mission" with accuracy? Silence would mark the services if only the qualified praised.) On a scale of 1 to 10, how does the Lord rank carrying out His exact command as compared to sacrifice? Obedience received a 10! Samuel said the Lord considered obedience to surpass sacrifice, even if that sacrifice is millions in money at offering time, even if the most lustrous singers package a music program equal to Solomon's dedication of the Temple. Awake, O' Church, this is God's answer to the humanistic relativism which seeks to pollute the clear stream from God's Throne. To deny God His RIGHT to demand strict adherence to His will is the highest form of anarchy. It is what caused satan to be satan and Saul to be Saul. REBELLION is a textbook example of revolutionary teaching and its child is relativism and self-determination. Its companion is liberation theology and the myriads of shades of variance within its ranks. Its greatest joy is mediation, whether by priest or pulpiteer. Its ranks are swollen by volunteers who find solace in "doing something for Christ" and feeling the humanistic thrill attained by looking over their "accomplishments." These are those who meet "needs" and take advantage of "open doors of opportunity." It matters little to this multitude whether the Lord has assigned them, called them, anointed them, or empowered them—their answer is that the right kind of offering will solve their every dilemma. There is one dilemma which it will not solve: when God is not appeased—but is provoked. His provocation will bring judgment, and His words will be similar to those spoken to Saul:

> *Because you have rejected the word of the Lord, He has*
> *rejected you from being king.*
>
> I Samuel 15:23b (NKJV)

Stiff-necked stubbornness kept the king from continuing as king. It will do the same for anyone who practices it. It is the heart of humility which says, "Not my will but Thine be done." It is intentional sin that demands self-determination. There is no provision in Old Testament Judaism for the intentional sin. There is no pacifism for the relativist either!

Saul's attempt to answer, like thousands after him, caused Samuel to utter an ultimatum. Saul did not want to hear ultimatums; he wanted approval. The heart of Saul sought to escape the punishment of his transgression as he cried out, "I have sinned, for I have transgressed the command of the Lord and your words." (The great sin of present society is that the relativist has found approval from all ranks of Christendom, but that approval has not come from the Lord.)

Saul's response caused a greater alarm than his first words (I Samuel 15:20). He sought to separate the word of the Lord from the words of the prophet. Alas, tyranny knows no limit. God and the prophet's words were one, for the prophet spoke only the word of the Lord. (Is the same not true in both organized and unorganized religion today? Has there not been an attempt to cause a separation between words? Is it not easy to choose which words religious bodies will hear? Yeah, there is one salient difference: God has spoken in His Word, and there are few Samuels who offer challenges.)

Saul requested Samuel to do what Samuel could not do—pardon his sin. Man has no authority to pardon. Saul also asked him to return with him, so he could worship the Lord. Pardon me, but did Saul miss the point of the words of Samuel? What worship could Saul offer? What was important to Saul was that he be seen standing beside the man of God when he returned. His design to dignify his sin failed! (In modern times, if a president, king, or leader gave this invitation, no hesitation would have been proffered. Not only would the clergy have responded affirmatively, they would have requested to bring a guest, fellow worker, and television crew! But, then again, there are few Samuels.)

Let the record be straight; Samuel did finally acquiesce and accompany Saul to worship before the elders. I do not believe he really wanted to do this. I Samuel 15:26 declares his first response to be, "I will not return with you, for you have rejected the word of the Lord, and the Lord has rejected you from being king over Israel (Past tense)." "Saul tore Samuel's robe." Samuel responded in kind, "The Lord has torn the kingdom of Israel from you today, and has given it to a neighbor of yours, who is better than you."

Nothing could have stung Saul more than to hear someone "who is better than you." This was followed with a strong word that even if the prophet accompanied Saul, God was not going to change His mind like mortal men change theirs. The judgment remained. God cannot be threatened.

Samuel accompanied Saul, but I strongly believe he did not view him as the "king." His kingship was wrested from him the moment Samuel spoke the word of the Lord to him. In that private session when he declared, "The Lord has torn the kingdom of Israel from you **today**," the word "today" constituted the end of the spiritual and natural kingship of Saul. Samuel accompanied a pitiful "has been," who had lost all authority and power, to a public sacrifice—what a sorry worship scene that must have been. (Yet, week upon week, similar sorry worship takes place.)

Samuel now carried out the exact order of the Lord and hacked Agag to pieces, after which the Prophet left the presence of Saul and NEVER returned. The scripture relates that he mourned for Saul until the Lord lifted him up and sent him on a divine assignment to anoint David. In doing this, the Lord gave Samuel a powerful principle of Heaven,"For the Lord does not see as man sees; for man looks at the outward appearance, but the Lord looks at the heart (I Samuel 16:14)." (Thank you Lord, for that wonderful truth.)

I Samuel 16:14 goes into a deeper level of judgment on Saul than Samuel was able to foretell, "But the Spirit of the Lord departed from Saul, and a **distressing spirit** from the Lord troubled him." Yes, he still occupied the throne. He still walked the halls of the palace. He still was waited on by his court. He still held the rank of "commander in chief" because his military was loyal. Abner was indeed a general of remarkable prowess and loyalty. His government still conscripted armies and fielded battles. Nevertheless, the "distressing spirit" haunted him, and the only time the "distressing spirit" would depart was in the presence of the anointing (David). When the anointing overrode his compromised heart, then peace and even the Spirit of prophesy would come upon him. (I Samuel19:22-24 reveals these truths.)

It was the heart of David (the opposite of Saul) who entreated the Lord to enter every aspect of his life, from decisions about going into battle, to the stabilizing of the kingdom. (I Samuel 23 revealed one occasion when David did not entreat the Lord, and it cost him the ability to build the House of the Lord—it costs to be outside the *en punto* of God and not be in the exact place of blessing. What is it costing the church today? What is the price for "doing one's own thing?" What is the cost to the hosts who align themselves with the hosts of Saul rather than the Kingdom of David?)

Saul ended his career in disguise at the house of a fortune teller. God revealed nothing to him (I Samuel 28:6). The prophet Samuel was dead.

Saul longed to hear even judgmental words from the true man of God. He begged Samuel to speak again. Whether the voice of Samuel or "the medium" was heard is immaterial. The words were the same words he had heard when Agag was alive. Nothing had changed! (I Samuel 28:17-20) The Word of the Lord remains in the atmosphere of the earth long after the deliverer is gone! The Word of the Lord had to be spoken in order for it to be established on earth as it is in heaven. Whether the Word of the Lord is spoken by donkeys or rocks, it <u>must</u> be spoken in the earth. That which was used to create a universe is used to create judgment or blessing. It is HIS word. (Readings from Whitfield, Finney, Spurgeon, Moody, Bevington, Wigglesworth, and Lake still thrill the soul and lift the spirit of the reader. Long silenced by the grave, their preachments did not melt away with time. Though their frames are dust, their words declare the timelessness of their message; it was a message from God!)

Saul fell prostrate on the ground when the word of the Lord added a final judgment to the one pronounced by Samuel. The Lord said Saul was going to die and his <u>sons</u> with him. (It is one thing to hear a personal judgment, but when it extends to one's posterity, the punishment is almost unbearable.) Words of judgment have a strange effect, for many people fall before God's pronounced judgment. When they should have fallen down before Him was at His first word and at that moment committed their lives to Him. Great tragedies of history could have been avoided had such action been taken. Since all history is spiritual history, there are no historical facts that are not connected to the spirit realm. The great prophets of old made clear that all history is known of God before it is revealed to man. No war is ever fought on earth that is not spiritual in nature. Sad is the passage, "And the Philistines killed Jonathan, Abinadab, and Malchishua, Saul's sons (I Samuel 31:2)." Saul, being deeply wounded, committed suicide by falling on his own sword. (Saul, like Judas, met the criteria for suicide: inwardly turned anger, hopelessness, anomy.) The Philistines severed his head and hung his body on the wall of Beth Shan. Unlike the boys at Mizpah, no one was there to fend against the birds of prey. His frame hung in ignominy, the sad reminder that relativism always falls before the Absolute!

(In the next chapter, Ezekiel is viewed as a man of God who did exactly as the Lord commanded him. He stands as an opposite to Saul.)

CHAPTER SIX

Ezekiel, Prophet of Exactness
(En Punto)

Ezekiel is a prophet studied in such variance that the wealth of his teachings often overshadow the underlying obedience he manifested throughout his life. Ezekiel is most commonly studied by theologians for his eschatological messages, just as historians establish his unique place in time. His writings utilized many literary forms such as flashback, flash-forward, and instant replay as techniques to catalyst his message. Although a deft writer, a marvelous illustrator, a fearless prophet, and an uncompromising loyalist to God, Ezekiel stands greatest as a man who carried out the exact will and word of God. When biblical scholars delve into his work, they are able to reconstruct spiritual history as it parallels political and economic history. The ancient world is, in many aspects, similar to the present one: Nothing is done aside from its spiritual dimension. Ezekiel, more than any other prophet, constructs a vision of the past, present, and future that involves every generation. Thousands of sermons are taken from his texts and as many conjectures are made about the true meaning of his prophesies. One thing remains immutable: He did exactly what the Lord told him to do, where He told him to do it, and remained in that mode until God released him.

Chapter six is devoted to one pursuit—to reveal how carefully the man, Ezekiel, carried out the commands of the Lord. This treatise will not emphasize his teachings. As a matter of fact, if the reader would take the time to examine Ezekiel apart from any prophecy, revelation, or message, he or she will be startled by the research. Revealed is a man dedicated to carrying out, to the smallest detail, the word given to him by the Lord. No assignment he was given was too onerous, no detail too exacting, no occupation too trying. If one can imagine a vast river (like Chebar) separating God from man, then imagine Ezekiel receiving his message on God's side of the river and returning to carry out every detail on the human (man's) side of the river, then a great perspective will be achieved. In visualizing such a divide, a picture of the prophet's manner of life will become real. Ezekiel knew the importance of missing nothing in his special assignments. The slightest detail was observed and carried out. He set a new standard for all who would come after him—a standard of excellence in exactness.

Ezekiel remains as an eternal standard against which to view the sloppy methods of the modern techno-church. His method of doing and being was like that of His maker. No detail missed his scrutiny, and the absolute disdain of his heart would have been to miss carrying out God's exact command (and as a result, having blood on his hands). His motivation was not fear, however, but love. Though the Lord explained to him the importance of his task and the consequences of missing the mark, Ezekiel's greatest motivation was that he cared about those things God cared about. He cared about one opinion: God's.

When the Lord equipped him for service, God carried Ezekiel through a a series of events. These began at the river Chebar. There, a panoramic educational process illumined the mind and heart of this meek prophet. Ezekiel was a man willing to be taught. Although he was a priest, the Lord chose to use him as a prophet. This is an important factor. Priests had a human requisite imposed on their office: Their charges often defined their roles. As a priest, Ezekiel's obligation would have been to the people. As a prophet, his responses were only to God. He was not just acquainted with God, he knew the Lord God!

Nearly three chapters at the beginning of the book of Ezekiel are dedicated to getting a true perspective of the Lord. The most important facet in the development of the man of God is to have a true understanding of who God is and how to relate to Him. Perhaps this is why there are so few men of God on the scene today.) Ezekiel saw "visions of God." These were visions of God generated by God. "Visions" is plural in these verses and when one views the multiple facets of His Holy Highness, there is but one position appropriate—flat on one's face. Cherubim, who feast continually on His prismatic Holiness, always cry out, "Holy, Holy, Holy!" To the human eye, His Prismatic Holiness resembles a rainbow. In order to function as a true "man of God," it is necessary to have the understanding that comes from such an encounter. For proof of this, review Ezekiel's circumstances.

Ezekiel was a prisoner in a foreign country. With him, there was none of the self absorbed sophist approach to God one sees today. Most of the time, Ezekiel was being picked up from having fallen on his face before the majesty of the living God. <u>All</u> of the time, he was being led by the Spirit from one scene to another. Most of the time, the pureness of Ezekiel's heart was glowingly evident. Perhaps this is why there are so few Ezekiels.

God provided His prophet a cycloramic presentation of His glory. Ezekiel saw living creatures, living wheels, and the living God. He heard whirlwinds, the noise of wings, the voice of God. He saw raging fire engulfing itself, lightening, and colors so vivid that jewelers and artists have never approximated their splendor. He heard the noise of wings, the noise of many waters, and the tumult of an army. He heard his new name spoken by his Creator, "Son of Man." He fell on his face. His thoughts were not upon rushing back to a studio and attempting to facsimilate his experience by creating a money-making drama of epic proportion.

"Stand on your feet," the voice said. He stood. He was then instructed to be a witness to the people of God. In order to be a witness, the Lord had to give him an overview of how He saw the people and their spiritual condition—as rebellious and transgressing, impudent and hardhearted, stubborn and refusing, critical and abusive, briars and thorns. These were the descriptors He used. (God is saying the same thing today as He looks over those who simply "do things in the name of Christ.")

Ezekiel was told to pay no attention to those prating sycophants. Instead, he was to arm himself spiritually to fend off their disparaging, distracting words and looks. He was told not to be rebellious like they were. He was to emulate the Lord, not them. (Spiritually, today's churchmen emulate each other, not God. Should the reader doubt this, then check the social and psychological "conditioning" that takes place throughout seminaries, Bible schools, and the unstructured "learning of the ropes" in training classes. This activity continues in even the most "free" churches, denominations, and fellowships!)

Ezekiel was handed the book, the Word of God, to masticate and digest. (Until God's Word belongs to you, becomes an integral part of you, and cannot be separated from you, that Word is not synonymous with you. To read the Word is one thing, but to own it— is another. Ezekiel owned it!) The Bible says, "He opened his mouth [no argument, no preparation, no hesitation]." Ezekiel opened; God caused. These are the verbs of victory.

Ezekiel internalized the Word so much, that the only regurgitation spilling forth from him was the pure flow from his source of nourishment.

He was given one <u>mandate</u>, "Go," "Speak!" One <u>qualifier</u> was proffered, "Speak My words." One <u>equipage</u> was offered, (paraphrased) "You will be a match for them, for I will see to it." One <u>modifier</u>, "receive it in your heart (Ezekiel 3:10)." The equipping power of the Word (the glory of God dwelling in His Word) and the equipping by being Spirit-possessed allowed him to stand before the true Glory. It will do the same for you.

Ezekiel recorded meticulously the times God said, "I have made." "I have made your face strong, your forehead strong," and "I have made you a watchman." (The *Song of Solomon* says that in the last days, we are to keep an eye on the watchmen, for they will betray the bride. These were false watchmen. Ezekiel was a true watchman. The Lord does not equip betrayers.)

Each of these events is predicated by the "Spirit's" involvement. Nothing is done or revealed without the Spirit. When one sees what Ezekiel saw, everything else fades to insignificance. When one hears what Ezekiel heard, no other voice will do. When one receives what Ezekiel received, no earthly concern matters. (Only when these credentials are one's own will there be place for God's direction.) Thousands seek to speak for God, having never heard from Him. Thousands stand weekly to divide the Word who have never owned His Word. Thousands of parishioners go away from services where they have received nothing, believing they have heard something because their clergy has received nothing while believing they have said something.

It is not until Ezekiel 3:22-23, that the real test takes place:

> *Then the hand of the Lord was upon me THERE (See chapter eleven of this text), and He said to me, 'Arise, go out into the plain, and **there** I will talk with you.'*
> *So I arose and went out into the plain, and behold, the glory of the Lord stood **there**, like the glory which I saw by the river Chebar, and I fell on my face.*
>
> (NKJV)

There is a THERE for every individual who resides in the Lord Jesus. My THERE may not be where your THERE is, but it is our individual THERE where we receive from Him. (Chapter 11 will go into greater detail on this subject.) Ezekiel had to obey and go to the plain to find his THERE. (For the Ethiopian, Abana and Pharpar were nice places, but they were not his THERE. The Jordan was his THERE!) In order to receive from the Lord, it is important that one is not just "somewhere" but "THERE." The Lord has a way, not just a "someway," just as He has a "THERE," not just a somewhere.

When Ezekiel heard from the Lord at one "there," then he had to travel to another "there" to receive a further word. When the hand of the Lord came upon him, he felt the guiding assurance of the Lord and listened to His exact instructions. "Arise," does not mean "remain here and meditate, until you hear an affirming word." Being "here" becomes disobedience, for God has shown another "there."

"Go out into the plain," is really not a road map; it is a matter of putting one foot ahead of the other. It means turning where the Spirit says to turn; "turn right, turn left, look and go that way." Upon arriving at the next "there," he witnessed the glory of God. The glory of God was standing waiting for him to arrive at his "there." When the same glory that was at the river Chebar manifested itself, the same response came from Ezekiel, he fell on his face. (It puzzles me to see how much teaching today incorporates instruction about the glory of both man and God. It seems such instruction manifests a "glory" unlike the "glory" Ezekiel witnessed. I say this for so many are able to stand in "this" glory who never could stand in "that" glory. Perhaps the "glory-concern" in Jude, which related to the last days, is coming true; perhaps the real crucible for the church will center around a false "glory.")

The glory at the river Chebar was accompanied with living creatures who had fire running between them and lightning emanating from that fire.(7) The glory at the river Chebar had voices and a tumult like a mighty army. The glory at the river Chebar had a sapphire-like throne (sapphires are in every color of the rainbow and some have many colors in one piece). It had the semblance of a man-figure above the throne with amber from the waist up and enfolding fire (He does not have to be seated with his weight on the throne; He is surrounded with glory and appears above it). From the waist down, He had brightness like the clean brightness which welcomes the rainbow after the refreshing rain (the brightness of the glory illumines the multi-colored specter of the throne). "This," exclaims Ezekiel, "is the LIKENESS of the glory." (The paltry counterfeit of manmade glory is not acceptable to the person who has seen the real.) Ezekiel would never have been deceived by the deception of the modern substitute-glory (any more than John would have been deceived concerning the "glory" he saw in Revelation). Once one sees the real glory, no substitute will do! Counterfeit glory and counterfeit teaching on the glory are an affront to God who dwells in the real glory. Those who have seen nothing, usually wind up describing it; those who have seen the glory can only describe a likeness.

> *Then the Spirit entered me and set me on my feet, and spoke WITH me and said to me: 'Go, shut yourself inside your house.' And you, O son of Man, surely they will put ropes on you and bind you with them, so that you cannot go out among them.*
> *I will make your tongue cling to the roof of your mouth, so*

> *that you shall be mute and not be a reprover to them, for*
> *they are a rebellious house.*
> *BUT, WHEN I SPEAK with you, I will open your mouth,*
> *and you shall say to them, 'Thus says the Lord God.' He*
> *who hears, let him hear, and he who refuses, let him refuse;*
> *for they are a rebellious house.*

Ezekiel 3:24-27 (NKJV)

Ezekiel was given specific instructions about his future, and it was revealed to him which events would come to pass. When they came to pass, he was not to utter one word of rebuke. To insure his silence (It is important that the man of God speak ONLY what God has given him to speak—Nothing MORE, Nothing LESS!), his tongue clung to the roof of his mouth. (This is uncomfortable. Clinging tongues make it hard to swallow, difficult to utter intelligible words, and because of the drying effect upon the whole mouth, such clinging encourages one to remain "closed mouth." Try it.)

In our world of endless speaking, relentless teaching, and prolific pronouncing (each person more anxious than the other to divulge some new word, prophetic revelation, or "can you top this" word of knowledge), it would be wonderful to only hear the man of God *after* the Lord has opened His mouth and imparted His abilities to him. There are so few Ezekiels!

Ezekiel was instructed along three lines. He was to enter his own house (a new "There"). Why did He have to go "there" to hear "go home?" While in his house, he would be bound with ropes (How many in number are those who remain virtually unknown and silent bound by some cultural, social, and religious rope? Do they stay home because they are unwelcome in the halls of structured courts? Their silenced, clinging tongues, which offer no reproof, may have occurred as the result of hateful slaps administered by those who never hear the pure living voice and do not wish to. Ezekiel stayed at home as a symbol of the multitudes bound by many cords. Modern Ezekiel's may never darken a cathedral's door!)

The second command was, "not to be a reprover to them." (For the man of God to sit quietly and let the uninformed speak their deception is a most difficult task.) Again, Ezekiel is a symbol. Discernment lays silent in most churches today. Justice is already silent in the streets as equity has received her bribe. Why is it strange then for a rebuke not to be heard? Psalms 11 says it ever so succinctly,"If the foundations are destroyed, What can the righteous do (verse 3, NKJV)?"

His third command was one of great relief, for clinging tongues must have a moment of release. "Thus saith the Lord," sounds so wonderful when those words fall from released tongues. "Thus saith the Lord," is like salve to the wounded heart of those longing to hear, but those same words are like a red flag in a bull arena to those who have no spiritual ear. "Speak that word again, please," sounds so different than, "Let the games begin." "Thus saith the Lord," when spoken from a heart yielded to doing the exact will of God (a heart which "owns" those words), sounds different than the clamor of ceaseless diatribe.

I know a man of God who stood before the highest legislative body in Colombia in South America and declared that one-third of their population would perish if they did not break a 150 year old contract with Papal Rome. He finished his comments with this phrase, "Tomorrow, before my plane touches down at my home airport, to prove that my words are HIS WORDS, an earthquake will shake this country from top to bottom and side to side." It did! The largest registered earthquake in Colombia's history shook the nation the following day, but not before he was airborne and just before the wheels of his plane touched down. There is a different ring to words spoken by the man of God! The senators who heard him speak did not comprehend the truth he spoke, just as religious authorities, untrained to hear the difference, suffer a similar judgment. The man who spoke those words had never appeared before an ordaining council, never attended a theological school nor carried "credentials" from the world's "authorities." He did like Ezekiel; he obeyed the voice of the Lord, and his released tongue spoke, "thus saith the Lord." It is very important to follow the exact command of the Lord, for only those words will accomplish the exact result from God!

Author's Note: From this point forward in this chapter, there will be a rapid fire investigation regarding the commands of the Lord and how a willing Ezekiel followed them. This study is rooted in one principle—Hear, then Do.

TILE PAINTING 101

Ezekiel was commanded to take a clay tablet and set it before him. On that tablet, he was to paint the city of Jerusalem. Jerusalem was symbolic of all of Israel, of all those who worship there. It was like touching "home base." Ezekiel was to do several things with that tile: he was to lay siege to it (whether this was to be a theatrical siege which would require acting on his part or a model siege where inanimate figures would approximate reality, we are not told.). He was to heap a mound, set camps, and place battering rams against it. (Whether this was a chess-like game inside his home or a front yard display, we are not told, but the results would be the Lord's as would be the building of it.) Ezekiel had to follow the Spirit in its construction and execution. Ezekiel did question God from time to time, but he did what the Lord laid out for him, for when he was finished, he knew he would be "**there**."

The Lord emphatically tied the siege of this city to Ezekiel's action. He was to set his face against it. Aligning the will of man with the will of God often requires assuming the posture prescribed by the Lord. Ezekiel is told when he assumed this posture, the Lord would affirm the word: "It shall be besieged." Man's coordinated efforts with the Lord will produce the results of the Lord. In the Spirit-realm, that city was already besieged. All that remained was the acting out of what had been done in the heavenly. God's man garnered his authority from the realm of the Spirit. Ezekiel took no self-determined action; he moved only as the Lord instructed. He was now ready to besiege the city with the instruments of war placed against it, but first he must take an iron pan and place it between the city and himself. Consider the tedious accuracy of Ezekiel in carrying out this task. Why?

Long after the prophet's voice no longer rings in the streets, tanks and artillery, soldiers and airpower carry out what has been spoken in the realm of the Spirit. It is here that great schools of prophets miss their trajectory. Seeing fuzzy innuendos is not in line with the clear picture projected to Ezekiel.

COUNTING DAYS AND CALLING NAMES

Ezekiel was told to lie on his left side for 390 days. This was a sign of the number of years of the great iniquity of Israel. He was to bear the iniquity of Israel in his mortal body. God said that he would "constrain you so that you cannot turn from one side to another till you have ended the days of your siege (Ezekiel 4:8, NKJV)."

When he finished the first portion, he was to turn and lay on his right side for 40 days. The Lord knew the difficulty of this task. He enabled Ezekiel to do it exactly. Think, though, of the discipline required to lay according to the number of days required. At best, Ezekiel had to strike each day on the calendar, and this meant an interminable ordeal of examining future days remaining. Think of what coursed through his mind in such a state. Imagine the effort of neighbors and friends, who casually dropped by and could not understand why he would not move or make exceptions for their visit. Consider the potential pain of remaining in a static state, the awful increase of the burden in doing so, knowing that it is symbolic of that which will take place in the holy city.

An unquestioning Ezekiel did as he was instructed because it was God who required him, and it was God's mind that determined the number. He knew that one miscalculation of the determined days, or some breach of the appointed sides, or some compromise of position, would mean that in the Spirit-realm Satan would not be defeated and victory would not come to the people of God. God's judgment would not have had an earthly keeper and history would be forever changed. (En Punto is a serious matter with serious consequences!)

With uncovered arm, he prophesied. (The word *chasaph*, "uncover," can mean "to draw out." This scene is the classic prophetic stance, where the prophet draws out his arm with pointed finger and declares the prophetic words given to him.) He prophesied against a painted replica surrounded by instruments of war. He spoke daily, hourly, moment by moment to something that had no ears, no voice with which to reply, no eyes to see or brain to comprehend. He prophesied as the Spirit moved upon him. He prophesied with as much intensity on day 389 as on day one. He prophesied until the earth was affected. He prophesied until God's day was declared. He prophesied until the spirit realm was sieged. He did not cease until day 390 and the clock struck midnight and seconds past. Then, he changed to his right side for forty more days. From this new perspective, he cried out toward Judah. Exactness is demanded from the presence of a Perfect God!

MEASURING SPOONS AND SMELLY FUEL

Eight ounces of bread and 21.3 ounces of water per day constituted Ezekiel's diet. He cried the cry of Proverbs 30:8, "Feed me with the food You prescribe for me (NKJV)." Ezekiel was to eat a cake of wheat, barley, beans, lentils, millet, and smelt. The bread was nourishing enough, except 8 oz. per day is meager fare. Couple this with a very limited intake of water and it makes for a very lean Ezekiel. These elements are to be eaten "from time to time (God determines the time. It may differ daily.)." Exactness is terribly important to the Lord.

There was a specific manner these baked goods were to be prepared. They were to be baked over patties of human dung. (In India, I have witnessed many times, women gathering cow dung from the streets where many cows were wandering. Patting the dung, which contain remains of straw vender, they set them to dry on sidewalks and curbs. These patties will fuel the fires that bake the bread for their families [ca. 1986]). Ezekiel shrank from this prospect. He cried out to God to amend the command. God changed the ordinance to cow dung for fuel.

Is it not enough to do part of what God requests? Can one change the rules and substitute his own formula for God's formula? Ezekiel did not take the levity to change one portion of God's commandment without coming before the Lord, giving his reason, and offering his request. Why do churches, congregations, fellowships, individuals, who seek the will of God, feel so often they can substitute this ingredient or that substance in God's formula. (Is Proverbs only for the palatable?)

Is it admissible to delete those disagreeable aspects of God's choices, those that we find nauseous? Why is it necessary to follow to the letter the Lord's prescription? Is it not because of God's ultimate proscription that such a demand is precluded? His reasons reach beyond the fathom of human reason; they align with what He has proclaimed from eternity. Leave out one ingredient, and the glory of God cannot accompany the person. It is the glory of the Lord that demands strict adherence to God's formulae. His glory will not fail in one detail to bring about the universe He projects. To be at one with Him in detail is to be at one with His glory! There is satisfaction to be gained in strict obedience. Thousands seek His glory without understanding the connection to strict obedience. (In Chapter 9, focus will turn to Jesus and this very aspect of His ministry.)

CLOSE SHAVING

Although many people would have fallen away upon receiving the first two commandments, Ezekiel continued undaunted. Again, the Voice instructed him. Again, the commandment of the Lord would be judged by the outside world as an act of a demented obsession. Clearly, no one in his or her right mind would believe that the Lord would tell someone to do these kinds of things in public and expect a good result. Even among those who claim to hear from God, there would be few who would consider these overt acts demanded of Ezekiel as valid. There are so few whose only questions are clothed in silence, as were His. Throughout these passages, where God gave specific directions, Ezekiel offered no response after the Lord's first accommodation.

He was told to take a sharp sword, use it as a straight razor, and start to shave his head and beard. This was the beginning sign of complete submission in ancient times and was the sign used by Paul in the taking of a vow before the Lord. He was to weigh and divide the hair into three sections. His long hair and beard had been grown during the days he was laying siege against the city. He was to go to that city (replica) and burn one-third of the hair in the city. He was to take another one-third and strike the hair with the razor sharp sword, chopping it up. He was then to take the remaining one-third and cast it to the wind. Among these thirds, he was to leave a little remnant of hair from each section and bind some in the edge of his garment. The rest was to be burned in the fire kindled for the first group. This added fuel to the existing fire.

Repeated acts involving hair from his person were symbolic of many things. First, it would cost him something. Second, it would set him apart in any crowd. Third, it would signify a vow was in the making between Ezekiel and His God. Fourth, the repetition would tend to amplify the significance of the hair dispersal, which represented the personal sacrifice of that which was living to be rendered in judgment.

God continued to call Ezekiel to strict obedience by saying he must prophesy to a mountain—imagine—a huge inanimate pile of rock and dirt that rises as a silent landmark. This landmark will hear the judgment of God, it will be present when the judgment takes place, and will remain after it is over to preside as testimony to God's righteousness.

MOUNTAIN MOVING

Strange as it seemed for Ezekiel to prophesy to a mountain, Jesus said if we want them moved, we must speak to them as well. He was to set his face toward the mountains, an act which carries with it great intensity. The sequence of events is interesting in its order. First, he laid siege and prophesied to the city of Jerusalem. Next, he prophesied against the people within the city. Now, he spoke to the surrounding mountains, which were the protectors and had been the providers for much of the blessing of Israel. Specifically, the mountains of question were the "mountains of Israel." Nothing was forgotten in this prophesy: the hills, the ravines, the valleys. Each was treated equally. Because the earth shares its place with man, Paul pointed out that the "earth groans." David, in many places, used graphics which included facets of God's creation which bore witness for and against man. (I think these words of prophesy are still "out there," and at the time of the end will give reason for earthquakes and falling rocks. Strangely enough, a recent trade magazine reported "a coming world wide earthquake [an economic one] is on the horizon.")(8)

A specific speech was to be made to the mountains of Israel, beginning with, "O mountains of Israel, hear the word of the Lord God!" Imagine the opinions of Ezekiel's fellows when it came to observing the prophet speaking to mountains. Regardless of their opinion, He prophesied in a loud voice, publicly, and within their hearing. Words given by God, when spoken by man, have the power of God in those words. Words directed to places He directs, have a profundity unlike other words spoken by man. The "I Am" has become the "I Will," and the mountains melt before Him. The Creator was speaking through Ezekiel, and His mountains took heed and listened. He who is above every name, named them as co-conspirators who had sheltered altars, idols, and "hidden" works. Out of a "crushed heart," He who had planned a wedding, now plans a funeral! Instead of harboring the incense altars of Baal, the mountains will cradle the fallen (Ezekiel 6:7). Instead of being the citadels of Holiness, they will become the repository of the horrors of famine, pestilence, and sword.

Ezekiel was to pound his fist and stamp his feet and while doing so, say: "Alas for all the evil abominations of the house of Israel! For they shall fall by the sword, by famine, and by pestilence." (Pounding fists and stamping feet are not acceptable behaviors in religious circles today, neither are true prophet's words. If, in the pulpits of America, the "Alas's" would begin, a falling away would quickly occur. "Alas for all the abominations," would call for the mountains of bureaucracy to fall. It would call for the ceasing of building new altars of deception. It would call for religion to be seen as God sees it—His people bent upon a spiritual harlotry unequaled in history. Ecumenical bonding, which is the mode of the day, speaks to the issue of building greater altars in order to accommodate greater sacrifices to harlotry. These are altars which will send forth more foul smelling odors to pollute an already saturated air—odors which already demand, "Thus saith the Lord God!" No wonder mountains will be moved into the sea and cosmic disaster pose an unthinkable universe in the last days. On to this scene there is coming a voice, not the voice of the prophet, but the voice of the Announcing Angel.) When Ezekiel completed his mountain pronouncements, he was shown even greater revelation. In order for the modern church to have greater revelation, first ,let them pronounce that which He has spoken!

LANDMARK MESSAGE

Turning from the mountains, the prophet was told to direct a prophecy to the land of Israel. The link between people and land and surrounding mountains had always been in the mind of Israel. They were not separate entities. When Orthodox Jews are buried, they place some soil from Israel alongside the body to show their link to the land. When Jews visit Israel and do not remain, they take some soil from Mt. Zion with them. Like those of old who brought two mule loads of dirt home with them so they could kneel on the soil of Israel and direct their prayers to the God of Israel, they showed the link between the soil and God. God and the soil of Israel have been linked like a chain to the mind of the Jew. Now, instead of the curse of Balaam, the land was under the judgment of the Almighty.

Ezekiel's strange assignments were not over. There was a progression involved in them, for each one built upon the other. O' Church, grasp this theme! Nothing is done in a corner!

WALL DIGGING AND DOOR PEEKING

Ezekiel was tried and found true. He had carried out the exact command of the Lord, even when, in the eyes of the beholders, he may have been judged "strange." In Ezekiel 8, he received a fresh call, a fresh vision of the glory, and with it—new orders. He saw the glory like he did in the plain. Notice, He did not stay by the river. This was to be an ever unfolding revelation of the glory. The Glory of God revealed to the servant of God was incentive enough for credulity. A fresh charge burned within him because of the fresh vision of the glory. Going forth under the glory is different than going forth under man's mandate. Being lifted by a lock of hair and transported to a city a thousand miles away will also do something for the recipient! But alas, there are few Ezekiel's. God chose Ezekiel; it is that simple.

It is amazing when one reviews how God chooses a man in the midst of a hierarchy of men to be His prophet. This vision came to Ezekiel WHILE he was sitting talking with the ELDERS of Judah. The same kind of verse is found in the gospels when the Lord had Luke write:

> *Now in the fifteenth year of the reign of Tiberius Caesar, Pontius Pilate being governor of Judea, Herod being tetrarch of Galilee, his brother Philip tetrarch of Iturea and the region of Trachonitis, and Lysanias Tetrarch of Abilene, Annas and Caiaphas being high priests, the word of the Lord came to John the son of Zacharias in the wilderness.*
>
> Luke 3:1-2 (NKJV)

Past kings and priests, the word of the Lord came to the back side of nowhere to a man anointed of God and not men. Luke meticulously named all those with political, economic, and spiritual power, then glibly remarked, "the word of God came to John." So it is with Ezekiel. Past the elders of Judah, right to the "willing One," the vision chose its mark.

"Lift your eyes now toward the north. So I lifted my eyes toward the north, and there... (Ezekiel 8:5,NKJV)." Yes, it is easy to say, "Well anyone would have followed directions given these circumstances in their life." However, what if the visions had not been present, just an inner voice saying, "Look there!" Would the prophet have responded as unhesitatingly? YES! No hesitation was in the heart of Ezekiel. Just as the words began to fall on his ears, he turned to look. "So I lifted my eyes toward the north," is not characteristic of a hardened, stiff-necked, disobedient heart. Though alarmed at what the Lord revealed to him, he plunged readily into each new realm.

Now, he viewed abominations at the entrance to the house of God. A command followed: "'dig into the wall;' and when I dug into the wall, there was a door(8:8)." "Go In." "So I went in and saw, and there—." Is it not easy to see that "**there**" is the place for receiving revelation? Without a place called "**there**," all that remains is conjecture and assumption. There is nothing like being "**there**." "**There**" is the place where God shows (with "word of knowledge and wisdom") the hidden things.

"Turn again," was the next command given him, "and you will see greater abominations that they are doing(8:13)." Such vision could not be released to the pitiable crowd that gathers under the banner of "prophet" today. First, the consuming flames of the glory would decimate them; second, such revelation would be trounced as a column of gossip in their monthly publication. (If, however, the reader is one to whom the Lord speaks, then be advised that he or she must be as exact and careful as Ezekiel to speak <u>only</u> what He says, when He says, to whom He directs. One's ear must also constantly listen for His further command.) What Ezekiel was privileged to see was "how God sees." Holy eyes, peering through private doors, are a specter to behold.

Ezekiel saw the women of the church worshipping Tammuz. (How does this differ from ladies' groups today? Don't take offence; simply review the topics chosen in order to insure a crowd. You will see Tammuz again! Though under the guise of religion, their adoration is more to Adonis than to Adonai.)

"Turn again, you will see greater abominations than these(8:15)." Next, he beheld men of God falling before idols amid zodiac trappings. God's glory was about to depart from all worship activity and from the midst of the worshippers, yet none of the religious leadership was even aware of the tragedy. The prophet was aware, but alas, there are so few Ezekiels.

The Lord ordered death to begin at the entrance to the house of God and proceed through the city, sparing no one. This revelation was overwhelming to the heart of the prophet. The first words spoken to God since the "dung" experience were words found in Ezekiel 9:8. He inquired of the Lord as to the depth of His judgment. Ezekiel did not question the righteousness of God's judgment because he had been shown the scope of saturation connected to these abominations. He wanted to know only the extent of God's judgment. He was answered by a fresh vision of God's glory.

A SPECTER OF GLORY

If it had not been for the continuous vision of the glory of God, Ezekiel would have been overwhelmed. It was manifested glory that drew him, unafraid, to greater heights. How can there be higher levels of faith, new levels of understanding, greater revelation without touching the glory? Within the glory, there is a call upon one's life that adds an ingredient which cannot be garnered in any other place. It is the "**there**" for which no substitute can be applied. It enveloped Enoch, transported Elijah, illuminated Moses, and magnified the Son (on the Mt. of Transfiguration).

Chapter 10 took Ezekiel back to the glory. The problem was that the glory was departing from worship in His day and no one but he and God knew it. When Jesus beheld the Temple, He and God were the only ones who knew that the glory had departed. During the lifetime of the disciples, there had been no manifested glory present at the Temple; they could not ascertain the loss. Having known no glory, thereby they could not appraise the state of affairs that surrounded them. This is the tragedy of the modern church regardless of the name above the door. The glory is not present and no one knows the difference, but now a new day of demarcation has arrived. In these last days, the Lord is manifesting His glory to those who seek Him. That manifestation is so consuming that the absence of it in worship propels the "knower" to fall on his or her face and weep!

The Lord pointed out to Ezekiel twenty-five men who were the ring leaders of a wicked council. To the public, these men were upstanding and appeared righteous. The prophet was to prophesy <u>against</u> them. In his prophecy, God directed him to reveal,

> *I know the things that come into your mind.*
> Ezekiel 11:5 (NKJV)

Pelatiah, one of those men, died while Ezekiel was prophesying. Remember, these were the most highly esteemed religious men in the city. No one would have dreamed of their tyranny. (One of the great tragedies in the memory of Rev. Carlos Gruber, a <u>native of Latvia who fled to Brazil</u> with his father and mother at an early age, was when his pastor suddenly disappeared and <u>returned as a Communist Officer</u> who afterward informed on every church member.) Lord, it is time for Holy Spirit discernment in the church.

At the death of Pelatiah, consternation fell upon Ezekiel. He had delivered exactly the message God gave to him and this was the result. He fell on his face and cried with a loud voice. Does the message of the man of God today cause the messenger consternation? Yes! (Even in the writing of this book, there are times when tears flow freely, and I fall from my chair on my face and groan in my spirit.) Look at what happened when consternation overwhelmed Ezekiel.

In Ezekiel 11:14, he recorded this:

> *And the word of the Lord came to me...*
>
> (NKJV)

There is a tenderness in this verse which communicates an aspect of the Lord which is unknown to the majority of the religious world. Dawning upon the heart of the prophet was the true extent of the depth of his society's sin. The Lord told him:

> *Son of man, thy brethren, even thy brethren, the men of thy kindred, and all the house of Israel together, are they unto whom the inhabitants of Jerusalem have said, 'Get you far*

from the LORD: unto us is this land given in possession.'
Ezekiel 11:15 (Jubilee Bible)

The saturation of this kind of reasoning exposed by the Lord about Ezekiel's day is tragically present in modern Christendom. (One prosperity evangelist said, "Demand your money from the Lord; it is your right under the covenant." Just how far is that from the sin of Israel? The amount of deception today is almost unfathomable. It permeates the society called religion. It reaches outward to the whole of modern society. Should the Lord open the eyes of readers to the true depth of arrogance and pretense which pervades the religious universe, the political scheming which seeks to territorialize the revelation of God, the amount of unbridled ego that callously dares to come before God [Isaiah 1:10-17], they too will weep, fall from their chair, and groan in their spirit.)

This is why Ezekiel carried a pure message, untainted by his hand, but directed by the Most High. It had to be an exact message in order to cut through the yoke of sin. Its anointing was fresh from the glory. Because of the taint on man, that which is often called the "anointing" is really little more than man's compromised enthusiasm. The real anointing comes from above, in flaming tongues, upon a waiting and obedient people, who explode rather than implode! To this overwhelming message, the Lord continues to lay further revelation before Ezekiel.

PACK YOUR BAGS

After faithfully delivering God's message, the word of the Lord came to Ezekiel with specific instructions. Regardless of the intrusion time, the prophet responded immediately. He was told to get out the suitcases and pack his luggage and other belongings just as if he were going to journey into captivity that very day. He was to do this in full sun in front of all the people. (Can you imagine the stir when suitcases and boxes and sacks and clothes boxes began to appear on the front porch?) "You moving out, Mr. Prophet?" "Somebody must'a called the movin' van, Is it 'cause your preachin's got too rough?" "What are you doing brother? Have you gone nuts? Why are you going to move out of this nice house?" "Where are you going?"— "CAPTIVITY!" "Did I hear you say you were going into captivity?...Man, you've lost it! We are free men, no oppressor is here!" He replied, "NOT YET!"

He was told to dig a hole in the city wall, wait until twilight, carry the stuff through the hole with his face covered so as not to see the ground.

So I did as I was commanded.
Ezekiel 12:7 (NKJV)

When the prophet did exactly as he was instructed, THEN he had a word from the Lord. Somehow, this is how it works today, just in that sequence!

EARTHQUAKE CAKE

The prophet was told to eat his bread with quaking and drink his water with trembling and anxiety. (Such would be the unfolding nature of each revelation given to his populous.) Perhaps the multitudes could only receive limited amounts of truth, which caused the pauses between preachments. They rationalized that his words were for a time in the future and did not directly affect them. God responded with Ezekiel 12:25,28:

> For I am the Lord. I speak, and the word which I speak
> will come to pass; it will no more be postponed; for in your
> days, O rebellious house, I will say the word and perform
> it, says the Lord God.

> Therefore say to them, 'Thus says the Lord God: None of
> my words will be postponed any more, but the word which
> I speak will be done,' says the Lord God.

The time between pronouncement and delivery was now shortened. (Many end-time ministers have pronounced there is an acceleration of time in these last days, their point being a short time between sowing and reaping.) In Revelation there is evidence of accelerated judgment. There is a short time between the pronouncement and the carrying out. There is an immediacy which approximates the confession of the Lord God in these verses. The current generation has made the same mistake of Ezekiel's day, it has banked on the extended mercy of God, while believing judgment is distant.

The wait and see attitude of the prophets was challenged. Ezekiel disassociated himself from those "others" who considered themselves "men of honor, men of the cloth, men in the know." The man of God was told to <u>prophesy against the prophets,</u> <u>against the daughters</u> of the people (who were prophesying), and <u>against those who practiced witchcraft</u>. Prophets who prophesy without a word from God, and daughters who add their blessing to those prophecies are no different than those who practice witchcraft and claim to see things in the future which are of their own making.

God turned Ezekiel toward the elders who were assembled before him. (Ezekiel does not have to seek an audience, announce a meeting, or call for media coverage. God gathers the hearers.) He was to prophesy to the whole of Jerusalem, and those prophecies had both unkind and hard words mixed into them. The shock effect of being called "stupid harlots, good for nothing vines, adulterous women, and kinfolk to Sodom," found its mark. It was God's view of their inflated self-esteem. (The reader must ascertain if such a prophetic word could be uttered in the assemblages of today due to the control factor against negative words and the filtering of all pronouncements through man's system.)

From every angle, the Lord directed arrows of truth toward the elders of Israel. Ezekiel was to pose a riddle for them (Ezekiel 19). If they wished to play games with the Lord, then games it would be. (Samson toyed with the Philistines in this manner.) Ezekiel was told to set up a lamentation (like a funeral dirge). Perhaps this is what prompted Jesus to say, "We have played the flute for you, and you did not dance; We mourned to you, and you did not lament (Matthew 11:17, NKJV)."

Moving in the Spirit, Ezekiel spoke not only to men, but to all the economic support systems by which they prospered. (Isaiah wrote: "strangers devour your land before your presence [1:7].")

The Lord had him speak to the <u>forest land</u> to the South. The message was that the commercial use of timber would cease, for it would be burned. The Lord made it easy for those who could not distinguish the forest from the trees— NO MORE TREES. Economic, political, social, and religious infrastructures were the major realms of attack by the Lord. He who knew, left nothing uncovered.

> *Set your face toward Jerusalem, preach against the holy*
> *places, and prophesy against the land of Israel*
> (Ezekiel 21:2, NKJV).

These words of Ezekiel may have become common place, but they were poignant and unavoidable to those about to feel judgment. God was warning, and heed it or not, His righteous judgment would be carried out.

SIGHING WITH A BREAKING HEART

When the sighing time began, the crowds must have thought, "Oh, no, what is he up to now?" With bitter weeping and sorrow-filled eyes, he would pass them and just weep the more. He would stop and look at little children playing games and cry aloud because he knew their sounds would soon be heard no more. He would observe a wedding party and begin to throw dirt in the air and weep loudly, sighing with a breaking heart. He would meet an old friend and just stand and look at him and break down weeping. When one sees as God sees, this reaction is not foreign (Ezekiel 21:6,NKJV).

The vision of the Lord increased and he cried, "A sword, not a scepter."

SIGN MAKER

Ezekiel was told to make two road signs (22:19). These signs were to show the path of the sword, coming from two directions but from the same land. Rabbah, of the Ammonites, and Jerusalem are to be the destinations. Ezekiel was not short on details. His obedience as a sign maker graphically accented the messages he had been preaching. It would be like posting large billboards directed to a nation with messages from God!

His message from the Lord was about a conspiracy between politicians and the religious leaders of the land. It was mutual abuse of power which darkened the understanding of the general public. For this crime, there was severe punishment.

> *Therefore I have poured out MY indignation on them; I have consumed them with the fire of MY wrath; and I have recompensed their deeds on their own heads*
>
> (Ezekiel 22:31, NKJV).

So exact was the Lord in his word to Ezekiel that he had him write down the day, the person of the conquering king, and the hour the city of Jerusalem was under siege. Nothing was held back from the obedient "man of God" (24:2).

FUNERAL TIME: EZEKIEL'S WIFE WAS STRUCK DEAD BY GOD

The most difficult task of all was assigned Ezekiel. He was told by the Lord that his wife would die quickly and that he was to have no appearance of mourning. The Lord called her "the delight of thine eye." There was to be no mourning, no weeping, no tears running down his cheeks; he was to sigh in silence. He was to put on his street clothes and carry out the ordinary duties of an average day as if nothing had happened. (Carrying out this exact command must have been the most difficult of the "God assignments," but he carried it out!)

Having been given the knowledge of his wife's impending death, he entered the streets and greeted the people. He spoke to the masses as if nothing was going to occur. At evening, his wife died. Next morning, he was going about his regular duties. (One either does the exact will of God or one doesn't.)

> *And the next morning, I did as I was commanded.*
>
> Ezekiel 24:18 (NKJV)

Consider the inner comfort that comes from hearing and doing the exact will of God. Who could know the inner peace of the soul solace resting upon Ezekiel? Should anyone question the difficulty of this task, let that person question the difficulty of not ever hearing from God, not ever knowing His exact will, not ever having a task. Embracing the comfort that comes from the Great Comforter is an experience that puts to silence grief (unlike those of modern psychology who, through educational advances, seek to categorize stages and map sequences of grief—while relishing the therapeutic aspects of grief management).

Because this study is about doing the exact will of God and speaking the exact word of God, it is not necessary to interpret the many passages that single out various nations and cities which received a prophecy. There is one aspect which must be addressed. Each of the nations and individual cities which are mentioned in these passages represent a type of nation or city found in the last days. History may or may not repeat itself, but the ways of man are open to the Lord. When Ammon and Tyre are coupled together and brought to judgment because they said,"Aha," it might do well to seek the heart-reason for such an ejaculation. Moab, Mt. Seir, Edom (land of Esau), and Egypt are personalities made up of a common attitude. (What is the attitude of nations today? Never in the history of the world has such polarity been evidenced, all the while speaking of globalization and mutual participation.)

As soon as Ezekiel finished his task of prophecy to the nations, he began a new set of prophetic utterances concerning the <u>attitudes</u> of various groups <u>within</u> Israel. (Notice, he was faithful to prophesy to the mountains and the forests. Then the scope is narrowed to the people who occupy those various terrains. Now, a further narrowing takes place. Prophesy is directed against individual groups who have affected Ezekiel's nation. An interlude separated these two sets.)

In the interlude, the Lord re-commissioned the Prophet. Recalling Ezekiel 3:17, the Lord reiterates Ezekiel's watchman status, in 33:7:

> *So you, son of man: I have made you a watchman for the house of Israel; therefore you shall hear a word from My mouth and warn them for Me.*

> (NKJV)

The most cursory study of the "watchman/watchmen" in scripture will reveal their place of responsibility. For Ezekiel to be the kind of "watchman" God envisioned, he must fully understand the office with which he is charged. He alone stands in this station according to the Lord. He IS the Lord's mouthpiece. (Review the "watchmen" of the Song of Solomon and discover their sin. Instead of protecting the "precious," they succumbed to the vile!)

In year twelve and month ten and day five, the hand of the Lord was upon the "Watchman," and the Spirit of the Lord prepared him to receive a runner from the city of Jerusalem. The Lord lifted Ezekiel's commissioned silence.

> *After this, I was never dumb again.*
>
> (Ezekiel 33:22, Jubilee Bible)

The runner bore evil tidings. Jerusalem had been smitten down. Ezekiel was not moved. He spoke the word of the Lord to the runner, and God has him reaffirm his prophetic office, "then they will know that a prophet has been among them."

He cast a word to the evil shepherds of God's flock and told them the Great Shepherd is coming. He returned to prophesying about Edom and singled out Mt. Seir, which is now Petra, the city of the rose-red rock. (Obadiah spends much time with Mt. Seir and rightly so.) Standing as a citadel on the trade route from East to West, they hindered Israel and assisted her invaders. They occupied the only mountain pass and stood as gatekeepers for sin. Their sin was the transgression of Esau and Cain. The nations that used their hospitality were tallied and found they had mingled their destinies with Mt. Seir (with whom you associate is with whom you are judged). Mt. Seir depicts all who hinder the hand of the Lord. (The great societies of the world are not exempt, for the overall judgment of the nations in the end time will be based on this same principle. Trade, alliances, contracts, and treaties, will link the judgment nations.)

The sins of Israel were summarized in the venue of a menstruous woman, biblically unapproachable. As unapproachable in strict law as that woman, so was Israel. After her purification, her cleansing, then she could be embraced again by the lover of her soul. Isaiah's "righteousness as filthy rags," is a similar portrayal. Their unapproachable status was the result of occupying their land and defiling it with their "ways and deeds (36:17)."

Consider the next events in Ezekiel's prophetic ministry. He had prophesied of the death to those who considered themselves alive; now he will prophesy life to those who are considered dead.

SPEAKING TO THE DEAD

Twice in this passage Ezekiel said: "So I prophesied as I was commanded (Ezekiel 37:7,10)." First, he prophesied to the dry bones, which the Spirit caused him to survey. Here, he proclaimed that AS he was speaking, the bones came together. He saw muscle and flesh come upon these bodies WHILE he was prophesying. It is one thing to believe that God can raise the dead, it is another thing to believe that upon your command—limb will join to limb. Thus, in speaking His word, the bone-yard became a pleasant field. (Thousands of ministers have commented that we need prophets to raise the dead of the churches and to speak words of life to the disjointed masses. Their comments are well taken, but the case in point is greater than this. When will they believe that under their voices the living dead will come to life?)

Ezekiel took the Higher Law of God and spoke it over a lesser law, the law of sin and death. "Thus says the Lord," prefaced each prophecy. The Creator told him the words that He used. There was no doubt, no hint of unbelief, to be found in his words.

Isaiah declared:

> *He will teach us His ways, and we shall walk in His paths.*
> (Isaiah 2:3 NKJV)

As Ezekiel used those words, his expectations were the same as the Lord's. He beheld a miracle as he spoke verses 5 and 6. We are not told if he repeated these phrases, but there is one thing certain, the bodies came together. Oh!, that men of God, under the control of God, would speak again like God speaks. "God-speak" sounds different than "man-speak!" When man speaks like God speaks, no force on earth can prevent "a happening." Stephen spoke like that and he was irresistible. Only the living can speak to the dead. (Perhaps this is the difference between the clergy and Ezekiel.) Grasp the expectancy and urgency in the voice of Ezekiel. Visualize Ezekiel as he saw flesh begin to reveal the personal variations found in man. Empty bones became visionless faces and motionless torsos. His words did not reverse order; he simply established Divine Order. The created must answer the Creator, God speaks—flesh responds.

Second, he prophesied to the breath. He told the bodies to breathe and they did. He called for "the breath" to come from four directions, and it did. Life flooded those mortals, and the warmth of personality asserted its place. They stood as an army of the Redeemed, for they were.

Now, Ezekiel could prophesy to a crowd which would not disdain his words. Those who stood before him knew their undone condition and God called them, "My people." (So, it is today!)

This was a sovereign move of God proclaimed by God's man. Ezekiel stood in faith and did exactly what the Lord commanded. (We are not told if he yearned for the body of his wife to be among them. What we are told is that he did as he was commanded.) If ever in history there is a time for someone to call for a sovereign move of God, it is now! Throughout

Christendom, all that has been observed is the contemptuous move of man. Alas, who would proclaim it, for there are so few Ezekiels!

TWO STICKS

Having witnessed a multitude of people assembled from a valley of bones and knowing that as he spoke, they lived, it seemed ludicrous for God to command so mighty a man of faith to gather two sticks and write on them. It was not ludicrous to Ezekiel.

Which is the greater work, speaking to dry bones, or doing the exact will of God, at the exact moment in time, in the exact manner described? If the Lord of glory could trust Ezekiel's lips to speak life, can't He trust his hands to obediently gather sticks? Is this principle foreign to the religious world, who caters to the slightest whim of a benevolent benefactor and daily fails the Lord of Glory? Two sticks, just two sticks, with an inscription dictated by God was as great as two stone tablets with the engraving of God upon them; God wrote them both!

> *For Judah and for the children of Israel, his companions...*
> *For Joseph, the stick of Ephraim, and for all the house of*
> *Israel, his companions.*
>
> Ezekiel 37:16 (NKJV)

Ezekiel stood like Moses, fresh from God's presence, with an anointed message from Him. "They shall no longer be two nations, nor shall they ever be divided into two kingdoms again (v.22)." Who dares enter the throne room of God and return with a prophetic message for the people of God today? Many claim to do this on a regular basis, but what of their words? They ring hollow against the dictum of the Most High.(10)

Ezekiel's obedience strengthened his resolve, for having one's words never fail is the highest accolade of a prophet. When the Lord told him to set his face toward Gog and the prince of Rosh, Mesheck, and Tubal, the face of the prophet turned like a canon finding its range. Each volley found its mark and the report is a phrase, "**then** the nations shall know that I am the Lord, the Holy One in Israel. (39:7 NKJV)."

Ezekiel was told to speak to every <u>bird</u> and to every <u>beast</u> of the field (39:17). He called for the assembly of those creatures to a great sacrificial feast. Imagine, a solitary prophet standing and talking to birds and beasts. Is this different than Elijah speaking to the clouds? Is this different than Jesus speaking to a storm? Could it be that the pride of modern man dismisses such to the realm of the ridiculous and misses the realm of the miraculous? (I remember praying and laying hands and anointing my dog with oil when he had been hit by a speeding vehicle. His leg was badly hurt and internal injuries seemed apparent. What a joy to see him recover in a few weeks and never have a limp!)

Ezekiel continues his prophesy toward Israel ending with, "then they shall know that I am the Lord their God....(39:28)."

THE TEMPLE AND THE VANISHING GLORY

Spirit journey was nothing new to Ezekiel; he had made an earlier trip by the hair of his head. Spirit travel brought the man of God to the city of God and the temple of His Glory. Ezekiel was instructed by the man who met him at the end of the journey thusly:

> *Son of man, look with your eyes and hear with your ears, and fix (set your heart) your mind on everything I show you; for you were brought here so that I might show them to you. Declare to the house of Israel everything you see.*
>
> Ezekiel 40:4 (NKJV)

Those instructions were specific and clear. Ezekiel was human, and it is a human trait to allow the mind to wander. Focus was necessary for very detailed items were pointed out to him. He was given a vision of the real temple, not an earthly one. The Glory of God had departed from the earthly temple, but the Temple of heaven still held the Glory (43:1-3). Here, Ezekiel returned to a familiar position, flat on his face before the living God. Once having seen the Temple with the Glory of God, no temple will suffice where the Glory is not. (Could this be the reason for so much unrest among those who have fallen on their face before the living God? How is it possible for them to continue in the house where no Glory resides?)

The Lord spoke to Ezekiel FROM the temple (43:6). In verse 10, He instructed Ezekiel to:

> *Describe the temple to the house of Israel, that they may be ashamed of their iniquities; and let them measure the pattern.*
> *And if they are ashamed of all that they have done, make known to them the design of the temple and its arrangement, its exits and its entrances, its entire design and all its ordinances, all its forms and all its laws. Write it down in their sight, so that they may keep its whole design and all its ordinances, and perform them.*
> *This is the LAW OF THE TEMPLE: the whole area surrounding the mountaintop shall be most holy. Behold, this is the law of the temple.*
>
> Ezekiel 43:10-12 (NKJV)

Several aspects surround those commands. Ezekiel was to describe, to the house of Israel, the temple WITH the Glory on it and in it. He was to relate the splendor and the power of a place where the Lord dwells. This was to make the listeners ashamed that, for many years, they had worshipped in a temple where God was NOT. (How many churches should be ashamed today? Relentlessly, services continue where God is NOT.)

Ezekiel was to be the judge of those who had repented and were worthy to have further instructions about the temple. Notice two things: the prophet as judge and the reward of repentance. In Isaiah, the Lord groups the judge with the prophet (Isaiah 3:2). Long before there were kings, the judges were sent by God to judge the people. After the kings were established, due to the will of the people, He sent his word by the prophets. Understand that the people were to be kings and priests as well as judge and prophet. The realization of these offices is predicated on repentance. Repentance is a rare commodity in today's churches.

Ezekiel was to teach this special group (the repentance group), the intricacies of a temple where the Lord is enthroned and not man. He was to teach them the Law of the Temple, which is Holiness. Unless repentance leads to holiness, the mysteries of the Lord cannot be revealed. It was the principle of Ezekiel (the Law of the Temple), and it has never been rescinded.

Continuing with his guide, Ezekiel encountered the "Sons of Zadok." Their holiness became the hallmark used for all further instruction:

> *Son of Man, <u>mark well</u>, see with your eyes and hear with your ears, all that I say to you concerning all the ordinances of the house of the Lord and all its laws. <u>Mark well</u> who may enter the house and all who go out from the sanctuary.*
>
> Ezekiel 44:5 (NKJV)

Holy people with holiness in them are those he marks. His journey continued until he was brought to the river of God in Chapter 47. Here, he was made to pass through the waters with increasing depth, beginning with ankle deep. Finally, he was unable to touch the bottom and was completely surrounded and buoyed by life giving waters. He was unable to touch any of the foundations heretofore relied upon. He was unable to stand on his own. He was unable to control the flow or himself in it. He was unable to master his direction or determine his stay. He learned seeking to siphon this life-flow ends in death. He learned all it touches multiples. He learned trees that touch it bear fruit. He learned its source is the Sanctuary of the Most High. He learned those who depend on it lack nothing. (Prerequisite to serving in the Temple of Heaven, one must enter the River. This is not just any river, it is the river of God which flows just like Jesus promised in

Mark, "out of your belly will flow rivers of living water." To come to grips with the river is part of the rites of passage to the Zadok priesthood. To glean from its banks is common fare, to become a part of the flow forms a dynamic imprint in the person of the chosen. Each aspect discovered by Ezekiel must be the personal experience of every person who wishes to establish himself or herself in the Lord.)

When the Lord charged Ezekiel to divide the land and form the spiritual boundaries of Israel, a portion was set aside for the Sons of Zadok. The Temple was to be cordoned off with a "holy" area. Here, the faithful priests would find their residence and welfare. The Temple was to be in their midst. This was to be designated as "most holy."

One other lesson was given Ezekiel before the close of his vision and the end of his prophecy. He learned the name of the great city: "THE LORD IS **THERE**." There really is a place called **There**! It is where the Lord dwells.

Author's Note: In the following chapters great emphasis will be placed on the place called **"There."** In order to get **"There,"** the judging tools of Ezekiel must be applied to the believer's heart. "And if they shall be ashamed of all that they have done—make known to them the design of the Temple," which is in the center of God's **"There."** "Ashamed" comes before "make known." This is Divine Order.

CHAPTER SEVEN

A Tale of Two Situations:

Studies in modern exactness *(En Punto)*

*E*veryone rejoices when reading of the great patriarch's and their spiritual journeys which led them to the place called, "There." In the previous chapter, Ezekiel was lauded for his execution of exactness, thereby standing as a giant symbol of a man's decision to dwell in God's "There." Looming next to Ezekiel's lauding is a giant question, what about today? Who stands in that exactness in the last days?

In this chapter, two personal situations will be reviewed. The first, involves a direct order from the Lord to go to Romania and pronounce His words in designated cities. The second was a mysterious event that required Dr. Ed Tapscott, (now deceased) who was then Academic Dean of Houston Baptist University, to obey an exact command from the Spirit. Just by answering a phone call, he changed this author's life forever.

Each incident reviewed in this chapter required people to put aside their personal agenda and go to a specific place and perform certain acts governed by the Spirit. In order for the Lord to accomplish His work in their lives, sensitivity to the Spirit was required. In the Spirit-realm, there are no chance meetings, but there are many Divine appointments. This chapter deals with those Divine appointments that would never have occurred apart from obedience to the Holy Spirit.

Near the beginning of chapter five, a question was posed, "How important is it to do the exact command of the Lord?" After reviewing the life of several biblical giants, hopefully, the answer is, "very important." Spiritual commands, however, must be from the Lord and no other. Because of the complex nature of religious activity in society, most religious deeds are generated by the prompting of a religious leader or an organized effort.

Many of these assigned tasks are initiated in order to enhance a specific ministry or to follow through on a designated program or activity. Many of these tasks are great missionary efforts or powerfully run ministry advances. Most assuredly, there is nothing wrong in going to a mission field and doing benevolent works and deeds of kindness and mercy. This chapter is not about those kinds of things.

When ministries decide a need must be met, often they recruit the faithful to that cause and do the things necessary to fill that need. Paul, the apostle, said that these acts were to be commended. This chapter is not about those kinds of acts.

There is always work to be done, schedules to be kept, meetings to be organized, and a whole spectrum of activities that are deemed "good" and "righteous." This chapter is not about those organized, routine, classical "church related" kinds of deeds. Scripturally, their progenitors base their reasoning around: "show me your works and I will show you my faith." This chapter is not about random acts of kindness.

This chapter will emphasize those kinds of Spirit-directed activities that do not show up on man's calendars and, in actuality, supercede man's schedules and memos. This chapter wishes to direct attention to the manifest, overwhelming, over-riding, agenda erasing events that God directs and shares with His children.

In the following personal illustrations, there is a single thread running through both. Simply stated, that thread is the direct intervention of the Holy Spirit upon the lives of those involved. These are not to be construed as great exempla but as detailed events that occurred in the author's life. Both have one theme, and that is: It's important to hear from the Lord every moment of the day and night, and it's important to be willing to drop whatever pursuit one has, to carry out the exact will of God. This chapter is not about "what man decides to do for God;" it is about what "God wants to do through man." These illustrations involve special assignments and have absolutely nothing to do with the ordinary. (See Addendum Four)

In most religious circles, the "doing" that goes on in the name of Christ is most often commanded by man or his written instruction. "Doing" the command of man is not the same as hearing from the Lord. This is a significant difference. Pastors, writers, leaders in various specialty areas all have advice, good teaching, and perhaps even worthy paths, but nothing must placate "hearing from the Lord." Sermons are filled with directives. Seminars abound on every subject imaginable. Bookstore shelves are lined with wonderful patterns for living the Christian life or having a successful marriage or remedying some neurosis. Man's interests find many outlets!

In the Christian arena, there emerges a basic problem—it is easier to prescribe to others than it is to incorporate those prescriptions into the life of the prescriber. Then again, there are so many prescriptions that the believer often comes away with a single numbed observation—"that's nice." Whether the direction-giver is well known or not, whether his or her teaching is a Divine revelation or simply man's configuration, the numbed response is the same.

There is hope, however! To some, there arises a deepening sense that the Lord is the only prescriber for all their life situations. It is studious to know differing views regarding various subjects and be conversant about various religious matters, but it is better to know the secret place of the Most High. The secret place is referred to in this study as, "**there**." Facts garnered "there" are immutable.

If only one quality is to be gleaned from this book, let it be its emphasis on hearing directly from the Lord. To hear from some writer, minister, or prophet may be profitable, but to hear from God is Absolute. David, for instance, did not write Psalm 32:8-9 in order to affect just his day, or for that matter his own life; it was written to affect every age and especially this one. Its universality is profound:

> *I will instruct you (the Lord speaking) and teach you in the way you should go; I will guide you with My eye. DO NOT be like the horse or like the mule, which have no understanding, Which must be harnessed with bit and bridle, Else they will not come near you.*

> (NKJV)

God is not calling for "horse sense," which is endemic to man's reasoning; He is calling for "God-sense," which comes from listening to His instruction. David's Psalm contains a promise, "I will guide YOU with MY eye." Any person relying on that promise discovers the Lord willing to show them "a way."

Of all the manifestation and revelation which finds its way onto bookshelves and in video presentations, let none supercede this most basic premise—we all must be instructed by Him. Let Him TEACH you, let Him guide you with His eye. As simplistic as this may sound, it is TOTALLY foreign to most Christians. This is why the religious model must be changed to a spiritual one. Had Ezekiel waited for the local religious authorities to instruct him in the path he should go, no book would bear his name. If Job had adhered to the theology of His day, he would have died in ignominy and misery. This volume is dedicated to changing the model that for years has acted as a standard in pulpit and pew. Simply stated the past religious model is that of a clergy guided constituency, dependant upon that clergy for all their instruction and guidance. This must change! Observe how much of a "track" of thought has been handed down as "proper."

In most religious circles today, what is discussed is mostly a rehash from some message, book, recording, or mail-out. Scan any newspaper's religious advertisement and note the connected themes of them all. This is not to say these religious vehicles are not worthy sources, but they are secondary sources. (Isaiah, for instance, knew the Primary source.)

There is a searching today for a someone, or some book, or some leader, to point the way through all the deception and error which covers the earth. The Lord alone is that someone!

> And He will destroy on **this** mountain the surface of the
> covering cast over all people, and the veil that is spread over
> all the nations...
>
> Isaiah 25:7 (NKJV)

One great premise of Revelation is there actually is a prophet and a beast which operate by deception and seek to cause the very elect to stumble. Just how would such a prophet and beast deceive those who are trained and well established in the "faith?" The answer is obvious, by distancing man from God. The deception has already begun.

Regard the remarks of a Baptist pastor recently speaking at a New Orleans convention (Jack Graham of Texas):

> 'Most Christians in our churches are nominal, carnal, and
> living in disobedience to God.' Graham declared,
> 'Churches have become stumbling blocks into hell rather
> than stepping stones to heaven.' (10a)

Accepting Mr. Graham's comments as indictments to the masses who approve the status quo, truly there is a veil and covering over today's congregations.

The Lord said this was a covering and a veil that must be removed. What is that covering if it is not some universal tenet? Media has saturated the public, yeah even the religious public with ITS issues. There is a "leading" by the media, which is known in real estate circles as "steering." ("Steering" a person toward some particular house or away from some neighborhood is illegal.) Religious "steering," however, seems to be in vogue. Pastors "steer" their congregations in the paths they deem as appropriate for their needs. Media providers "steer" their audiences into topics which they feel are "the issues." The religious press determines which topics are suitable for discussion and which are not. Trigger-subjects emerge as "hot items" for those engaged in interviews and talk shows. (If the reader will pay attention, a definite narrow field of "in-subjects" will begin to surface both in print and electronic media.) It is time to hear the LORD! It is time to pray for Him to remove the covering and the veil. It is time to change the steering mechanisms, which are neatly in place, and let our Lord be at the helm! Let Him decide the real issues. Let Him draw back the curtain that has provided a covering for deception, and let Him point out, through the Spirit, what a believer's position should be.

It IS important who holds the "steering wheel" to one's life. The Lord directs the believer's paths through the Holy Spirit. Such direction should be as succinct as "turn here," "stop," "go straight." Such personal guidance is almost unheard of among congregants and their leaders. Today, little time is given to hearing the "still small voice."

This "still" voice was the reason of last resort for the prophet Elijah. Fire from heaven, blasting wind, and earthquakes could not convince him to return to his duties, but when the Lord introduced the reason of High resort, the "still small voice," that changed everything for him. The "still" small voice will change everything in the life of a believer who will seek that voice.

Christendom faces an "out of control" situation when left to its own devices. Just as drivers wreck and destroy themselves when "they lose control," vast enclaves of religious people are about to go "over the edge." If the wrong spiritual road is chosen, the wrong turn made, or the wrong person is found commanding, then spiritual disaster awaits. It is time for the "still small voice."

The Lord knows the right roads, the right times, the best situations, even the right persons with whom to be in fellowship. He, alone, is able to provide those elements which no mortal can provide. Corporate prayer ought to corporately confess, "Lord, we have a covering that keeps us from hearing your clear directions. Lord, remove the covering with the One who decimated the Temple veil."

As the world deteriorates, the necessity to hear from the Lord accelerates.

Not to be at the Mall is important when the bomb explodes. Not to be in the street when terrorists attack is important business. To be in a particular locale when others have a need and you have resources to meet that need is a thrilling adventure, especially when led there under Spirit direction.

The following illustrations are spectacular events, but what constitutes a spectacular event to one may not be spectacular to another. However, they do represent how the Lord worked these truths into the author's heart. These are classified as spectacular events in the thinking of the author.

WHEN GOD PLANS THE JOURNEY

It was early August in Texas and the heat was searing. Sitting in an air-conditioned office, with a dozen different tasks in front of me, a "still small voice" on the inside said, "Go to Romania." I remember leaning back in my chair and thinking, "that's not the Spirit, that's just some thought passing through my mind." (Earlier that year, I had attended a seminar on missions to Romania, and I attributed the voice to a latent brain quirk. Besides, a business office is far afield from a church study.) Though the voice did not speak again, the seed was planted in my heart. I did not respond to the voice. Days slipped by as easily as reality does to the aged.

It was now late August, I was seated in the same office staying as far away from the scorching sun as possible. The secretary informed me of a call waiting on line 3. At the other end was a man requesting some business information. Since he was just a short drive from the office, and he was on his cell phone to seek directions, I invited him to share my cool surroundings. I was glad he did not want me to venture out. Within minutes, he entered my domain.

I did not know this man or his business partner. When they arrived, I greeted them and invited them to my private work area. The usual pleasantries were exchanged and a discussion regarding a business transaction ensued—for all of ten minutes—then it happened. Harold (the only name I can recall) asked if he might secure the office door so his conversation would be totally private. Naturally, I thought he wanted to negotiate privately about some financial consideration. I was soon to find out differently.

Harold looked at his partner and said, "Shall I tell him or will you?" His close friend insisted that Harold do the talking. The words coming from the lips of Harold were not of his own making. It was as if he was delivering an oracle from some distant shore. "Sir, you were told by the Lord to go to an Eastern European country recently; I do not know which one, but you do. Because I listen to His voice and seek to obey His commands, I encourage you not to hesitate any longer. You have evaluated yourself and your life below the evaluation God has of you. You have not seen yourself as God sees you." (Many times the people of God are guilty of self-assessing themselves and their value in the kingdom. It is God who determines value.) He then continued by revealing certain events in my life that had taken place recently, to which he could not have been privy. He then pronounced a blessing. Tears began to spill from my eyes. (My astonishment must have been evident; my acknowledgement was profound.) Harold and his friend excused themselves and shut the door behind them saying,"We can see ourselves out."

How long I sat mulling this strange event, I do not remember. Were these men human or divine? If human, how on earth could they know this much about the voice? If divine, then angels really do visit men, but are angels conversant about business? I repented and turned my attention to Romania.

A few days went by before I began to make plans to go to Romania. I informed my business partners that it was expedient that I go to that nation. They were amiable.

The airlines cooperated as well by dropping the fare to Budapest by twenty-five percent. As the Lord directed every detail, a strange feeling emerged which kept me from making any decision about this trip without prayer and fasting. Within a few days, I had secured a small hotel in Budapest for the first and last day of the trip but was warned by the Spirit not to make plans for accommodations beyond this. When I set out to determine the times and length of travel, the Lord instructed that exactly 30 days must be the limit, not one day shy or one day beyond that limit. (To go beyond would be dangerous and anything shorter would be insufficient.) I did as I was commanded. He was preparing me for a venture into total dependency, where I would wait for His every direction.

The Lord wanted to speak through my (human) voice to various cities and to the entire nation. The message He laid upon my heart was simple, I was to stand in the central plazas of the designated cities and declare a "new day for Romania." Like an ancient prophet, whether there was a soul around me to hear or understand what was being spoken didn't matter. What was given must be said. I must be obedient to the "voice." (Ezekiel proved the necessity to hear and do the exact command of God, and I strangely felt akin to him.)

ARAD ROMANIA

Arriving in early October during a drizzling rain, the city of Arad (which was almost a day's train ride from Budapest and near the Hungarian border) was not an enticing place. I knew little about the city except it was more Hungarian than Romanian. I trudged toward the center of the city from the rail station (in jeans, a denim cap, and jacket), wondering about the sanity of this situation. Upon passing a shop, I stopped to inquire about lodging and was directed to a hotel by the river. It was chilly. Walking toward the hotel, I occasioned to pass in front of a monument for those who died during the overthrow of the communist regime. What looked like blood stains in the concrete were all around as were bullet holes in nearby buildings. Upon seeing this place where valiant souls gave their all, it seemed their blood cried out.

Unable to do otherwise, I lifted my hand and my voice and declared:

> Arad, the Lord has heard your cries. He has declared you a city of blessing. He has heard your cries from continually being conquered. I declare in His Name that your economy will flourish, your society will prosper, and a spiritual awakening shall come upon you and Romania. This blessing will sweep to all the surrounding nations— Bulgaria, (Yugoslavia, then), Hungary, Poland, and Russia. This revival will begin among the poorest of your people and will call forth an awakening like none that has ever swept these nations.

It just rolled out, these words, under such an anointing as I had not felt for a long time. I wept alone, as there was no one to weep with me. A joy then filled my soul, for I had released on this city and nation, the words of the Lord. (I admit that afterwards I felt that this task could have been accomplished without my traveling such a long distance and by some different voice than mine. I did not understand at that point in time how He gives certain spheres or domains of authority to His saints. Nonetheless, He who reads the human heart began to speak to me about His choices and about how He places authority for certain tasks into the hands of those he empowers for the task. He then added this comment, "I want to teach you to be so sensitive to my voice that you will not attempt even to walk ahead or speak without hearing my affirmation.")

Consider these Biblical words:

> *Your ears shall hear a word behind you saying, 'This is the way, walk in it,' Whenever you turn to the right hand or whenever you turn to the left.*
>
> Isaiah 30:21 (NKJV)

You see, Man reasons, but faith waits to hear a voice! Man wants to know the "how and why" behind every command of the Lord, while faith ceases such tyranny. David often referred to "the paths of the Lord," while modern churchmen rarely consider there is a path different from their traditions and their own choosing. (This is precisely why the place called "**THERE**," is not overcrowded, for one must follow a path not fathomed by reason, but known by the Spirit, in order to find it.)

When the clearance came to move ahead, I found the hotel. The front desk clerk welcomed me as if I had reservations. I pondered Isaiah's words as I rested.

Before I departed from Arad, the Spirit lead me to an intersection not far from the hotel. He had me stand and observe. Soon, an auto pulled in front of me and within it a person who could be classified as a "symbol of established religion." The driver was waiting a change in the traffic signal. As strange as it may sound, I spoke prophetic words toward this noble passenger and cursed the spiritual blindness he was engendering (Not all things of the Lord are blessings, sometimes radical judgments are pronounced.). Having accomplished this, I was free to go and rest. I was released to continue to Sibiu.

TO SIBIU

The October early morning air was freezing as a soft wind caused me to turn my back to its direction. Five-thirty a.m. found me enclosed in darkness, while waiting for the train. As I stood looking about at the gathering numbers (there were many people waiting), my eyes fell upon a man shivering, sitting on a bench not far from me. He was hungry but said nothing. I thought, "Dear God, why am I here? Did I miss your leadership? This is so crazy!" (It is amazing how quickly our flesh returns to its reasonings.) It was then I observed an old man and woman walking slowly, arm in arm, toward me. He was carrying a basket covered with a white cloth. I just stood there. As straight as an arrow, they headed toward me. His eyes met mine. Not knowing the Romanian language, I nodded my head and said, "Good morning." Now they were standing directly in front of me, whereupon he placed both his hands together which were as work-worn as Durer's famous "praying hands" sculpture. He wanted me to pray for him. He pointed to his wife's eyes, and I could see they were clouded. "Dear God, how on earth did they seek me out? I know I believe in divine healing, but on the platform of Arad Station?" Having no oil, I gently laid my hands upon her eyes and prayed. I really wanted her to see. I prayed. When the prayer was finished, He took my hands. His eyes thanked me as he then reached under the cloth and broke off a large cluster of grapes. He placed them in my hands. This was my "prayer pay." Instantly, I took one or two, showed delight, and asked by sign motions if I could give them to the man who was hungry on the bench. Yes! The starving man ate stems and all as the whirring train came to stop and engorge its passengers. The elderly couple scurried to first class; she went without assistance.

After I settled in my seat and the train began its journey, a man entered the compartment where I was reading my Bible and said, "The old man sent me." On the journey to Sibiu, this gentleman came to know the Lord. He requested that I come home with him and tell his wife and family about how to trust and believe in Jesus. (I knew there was the appointed task of speaking blessings to Sibiu, but here was a new adventure planned in heaven!) Far into the night I shared testimony with his wife, children, parents, uncles, aunts, and his neighbors.

(**Author's Note:** The reader has been brought through this travelogue in order to focus upon the manner and method the Lord uses to direct His children. As you enter the portion related to Braþov, many more spiritual facets will appear.)

ON TO BRASOV

Braþov represents one of the strangest occasions of my life. High in the mountains of Transylvania, Braþov symbolizes two historical crossroads. Not only was it a resort near the fabled Count Dracula, but it was known as the seat of the Romanian Roman Catholic Church.

At this juncture, it is important to lay emphasis on the importance of God's timing. Because my journey allowed me to arrive on a Saturday morning, it would seem reasonable that I would not experience stress in locating lodging, yet there was an urgency within me. I searched diligently for the right place, walking away from two prospects.

Upon entering a modest downtown hotel, I felt a peace about my choice. I checked in and was going up two flights of stairs when I encountered three men coming down. As I looked up toward their approach, I noticed they were carrying Bibles. The Spirit urged me to speak to them: "Hello, what a good surprise to see the Bible." They stopped and inquired, in English, if I knew about the Bible. That opened an avenue of testimony which ended with them inviting me to accompany them. They were going to a gypsy area about 20 miles from Braþov to dedicate a new building for which their Southern Germany church had assisted in raising money. My heart leaped at the opportunity. I hurried to throw my belongings into my small quarters, and the next thing I knew, I was going down a highway to an unknown destination with three men who were strangers. Two of the men were from Germany, the other was a Romanian interpreter from Sibiu. As we traveled, it was apparent that only the driver knew English well enough to carry on conversation. Our talk was centered on the Lord and His work.

It was raining and cold as we reached our destination. I was puzzled as the driver stopped near a building in a small town center and waited. Within a few minutes, two men emerged from around a building and approached the car. They were members of the congregation of gypsies. Since I was a stranger to them, they immediately inquired: "Who is the fellow?" (Not knowing the language, I read their body language.) I am positive that disclaimers where made as the eldest of the two men came close and looked me in the eye. He paused for a minute, then embraced me with a warm hug and a kiss on each cheek. ("Greet the brethren with a holy kiss," took on an added meaning and was very much welcomed.) He reached for my hand and from that point on, guided me through roadways of mud which would have been impossible by car. A colorful wagon passed us being pulled by an ox and I thought, "Lord, this is a wonderful adventure—Thank You."

The church grounds were crowded with people gathered around a white frame building. The time was 11 a.m. Birch wood benches with no backs had been set in rows so close together that about 300 people crowded into a place accommodating 200. All of the guests were seated on a small platform in chairs with arms and backs. What luxury!

The crowd rotated. With several hundred outside listening through open windows, those inside were offered a reprieve from the chilling rain, and every so often, they remembered their brothers and sisters who were still in the chilling rain. The audience was in constant flux. A gypsy concertina rasped out melodies totally unfamiliar to my ear. An aged man prayed, then the children's choir sang a tribute and the service was turned over to the Germans.

The German pastor's opening remarks were not unusual, as he gave an admonition to be as faithful to the Lord, upon receiving this building, as they had been before. (The one German who spoke English was interpreting every word to me quietly.) Then it happened!

The pastor of the gypsy congregation pointed to me and said something in Romanian, which was interpreted to the German, who spoke to his companion, who interpreted to me, "The pastor wants you to say a word. Since I don't know whether you are accustomed to speaking, is this possible.?"

I replied, "I'll try." (If he only knew!)

The Lord said,"Tell them why you came to Romania." I spoke for just a little while and told them the great blessing the Lord was about to give their country. Tears began to flow, and after I stepped down, a fellow rose in the congregation and read a scripture and sang a song. More tears. Then my interpreter rose to speak, and he carried out the theme I had used. I know because later he told me so.

It happened again! No sooner had my friend returned to his seat beside me, than the pastor pointed to me again. "He wants you to speak again." Oh, the anointing! The flow of power that consumed me was very great. I spoke to them about the "living water which Jesus promised would flow from every believer." I encouraged them to take their living water and bring to life every soul they encountered. I spoke to them of Ezekiel and his experience in chapter 47.

Then it happened! Someone in the back fell forward under the power of the Spirit, literally plunging out of his seat. Tears were flowing and hearts were being changed as the Spirit moved. When an altar call was offered, little did I know that no altar calls such as this had ever been given. It was not the custom. Alas, the aisles were so filled that no one could move. They came from outside, inside, and even through the windows. My soul was poured out to the them, and I loved them as much as a father loves his children. Oh! the heart of God that flows through mortal man. The Spirit spoke, "I told you it would begin among the poorest; now watch it spread." "Yes, Lord!, you really did say it."

It was 4:30 p.m. and the Germans wanted to get back to Braþov before dark. On the return trip we were more like brothers than strangers, a companionship spoken of in I John had made us this way, a companionship which cannot be emulated through church bazaars and car washes. After a brief supper, we gathered in the central plaza of the little resort city and prayed and sang, and I blessed the city from a renewed vigor.

(Author's Note: It becomes increasingly evident that the timing of the stair ascent and the timing of the descent was a coordination too meaningful to be coincidental. Lives were at stake and spiritual decisions hinged upon that meeting. A great lesson is learned from this observation—we are to walk in the confidence of His leading, but be sensitive to his leading even down to simple "hello's." The next scenario will prove yet another facet to His direction: it is His attention in detail to our every need.)

BUCHAREST

It was not until I arrived at Bucharest, the capitol, that I would begin to see His hand of provision is often based on our following His lead. There I was with rain spitting against me; I found myself perfectly lost among a maze of buildings. Having followed the directions of a native at the rail station, I was lost and unable to distinguish north from south. It was Sunday morning and no shops were open in the area. I prayed for guidance. The Spirit told me to stop, put my suitcase down, hoist my umbrella, and stand there. After a moment or two, my attention focused on a man several blocks away but headed in my direction. The Spirit said, "I have prepared this man to care for your need. Remain here and when he passes you, then speak to him in English. He will cross the street one block before he reaches you." Just as if he was programmed, the gentleman crossed and walked toward me. When he was near, I asked him in English, "Do you speak English?"

"Yes," was his immediate reply. "I should be able to, I lived in New York for several years—I am an artist." I then queried him as to how I could find my destination. He said, "Well, let me think (he mused as if counting the number of stops), then told me to board the bus which would soon be coming and wait through seven stops."

I confessed, "Sir, I have bought only rail tickets up to now; how do I purchase a bus ticket?"

He looked at me with a funny little smile and said,"I wondered why the Lord told me to put this bus ticket in my pocket this morning. I told Him that I was not going on the bus today, why did I need a bus ticket? He insisted. Here is a bus ticket, be blessed." I was! I boarded that bus with the confidence that He who directs our paths, makes marvelous provision for the trip.

CONSTANTA

(It is not my intent to give every detail of this mission, for length of pages will only allow me to mention the remaining cities. In Constanta (on the Black Sea), two lads were put in my path who were studying for final examinations to be merchant seamen. The Spirit drew us together (at a local pizza restaurant), and within a few days, they trusted Jesus as Lord. We spent some valuable hours together in fellowship in the Lord.

The tears in their eyes as the train pulled away from the station testified to me that the Lord can weld hearts together in a short time. One remarkable aspect of our meeting was that their hometown was the one city the Lord definitely forbade my entry. They were to be the primary witnesses there—not me.

IASI

The very compartment from which I waved goodbye to the young seamen produced an occupant who was to be my guide for the next assigned city. This sea captain little knew who was about to invade his world. Little did I know what revelation I would receive about this provincial city of the Maldavians.

FINALLY, ORADEA

Onward, down to the very last day, the Lord directed and urged, but mainly taught me how important it is to hear His voice—turn right, stand, walk, listen, speak, sit, uncross your leg, look up, smile. This dependence is despised by all except His bride. The Bride knows that oil for the lamp is a provision gleaned by such direction. The Bride wants to hear His Voice, yeah, cannot fathom life without His close companionship. The Bride does not view the loss of self-determination as a sacrifice, but rather gain. Those things that Paul considered dung, ARE!

GOD INTERRUPTS

(Author's Note: This second of two illustrations is a very personal account; therefore, some details will be omitted.)

Sometimes, a person is unaware of the impact of a suggestion or even just a passing word on his or her life. Such was the case when an acquaintance casually said, "You know Oliver, I have a friend in Houston; his name is Dr. Ed Tapscott. If you are ever down there, you ought to look him up. He has a similar background to you and is the academic Dean of the Houston Baptist University." That was in January. No other mention about this suggestion was made again, and nothing more than that one statement was ever discussed or spoken.

The following June, as my wife was preparing for a trip across the state in her capacity as chaplain for her sorority, I decided to visit my sister who lived near Bay City, Texas. Upon returning from delivering my wife to the airport, and as I was gathering a few things in an overnight bag, the Spirit brought the January words vividly to mind. I do not remember having even thought on the subject past the casual word spoken to me.

I found myself reaching for the telephone and calling the University. I had never met this man, Tapscott, nor did not I know the Houston location of the University or even why I was so moved to talk with him. The time was 8 a.m. His secretary made all the usual inquiries. I simply told her a friend had recommended that I contact him. Within a few moments, he was on the line inquiring about our mutual acquaintance and relating that it had been four years since he had conversation with him and was glad to know where he was now living.

I told him my plan for coming through Houston that day and wondered if we might have dinner. He did not hesitate and accepted immediately.

While driving the five hours required to reach my destination, I thought, "Why am I doing this? I really don't know this fellow, and what do we have in common other than knowledge of administration?"

Sparing details, the dinner meal was pleasant and the gentleman was an excellent conversationalist. Our discussions were informative and revealing, but mainly academic. Then it happened!

Around 9 p.m., he asked me, "Have we discussed all the things you were interested in?" Feeling this was a signal to part company, I replied affirmatively and began seeking out the waiter for the cheque. He continued, "Then may we retire to your hotel room, for I have something from the Lord I want to discuss with you." This was an unusual request, but since he had been so accommodating, my answer was positive.

Hotel rooms have a tendency to be similar, and this one was no exception. Sitting on the edge of the bed, while my friend occupied a chair not far away, he began a most interesting discussion. He began by saying that this morning the Lord told him, before he picked up the telephone, to cancel all activities for that evening and be ready to do as He directed. This included calling his wife, whom he was to have met at the airport that evening, and requesting she stay another night in Oklahoma before coming home. I felt very bad about this event and began apologizing for my intrusion. He let me know quickly that it was normal for him to have work from the Lord which required changing his plans and reworking his agenda. I thought how much more obedient he was than I had ever been.

He began to unfold the word of knowledge that he had received about me. It involved his knowing things in my early years of which not even my mother and father had knowledge, little things, things that sometimes affect life unconsciously. My mouth must have gaped open as he pointed out things in my history that no man could have known without the Lord being his informer—matters that needed cleansing, personal stuff that entered into deep emotional spheres where no stranger gets to tread. Psychologist call this one's shadow self.

Ever so kindly, he progressed and encouraged confession, forgiveness, and healing. His words pierced me. It was God speaking and God caring. Tears and humility saturated that room. Spiritual cleansing, of such magnitude that nothing in my life even compared with it, began to take place. This was soul searching by the Spirit which eclipses one's ability to deny or placate or set aside. Every item had to be dealt with NOW.

Unlike house meetings where intimate matters might be touched on and passed aside because of unwillingness or perceived inability to "deal with that issue right now," this was a now thing. Unlike protracted gatherings, where the Spirit might occasion a speaker to touch on personal realms of "Ashtoroth and the darling sin" but for which one has the option of leaving to another time or not, this situation had to be dealt with now. Unlike the magnificent distance which pulpits afford the pew at invitation time, this had to be dealt with now. Unlike the closeted confessional where the discussion gets beyond the penitent's desired comfort zone and a salutary repetition is administered to take care of the problem, this was a now situation. Unlike the "couch and desk" of the professional counselor meting out occasional grunts of recognition with prescriptory regimens of behavior modification, this was a now thing. Unlike the sympathetic, often pathetic, renderings from "heart to hearts" among trusted friends, this was "get down time!"

Every hindrance was viewed and eschewed to the point of cleansing; if something was left unturned, I was not aware of it. Then, he said, "Brother, stand up, for before I leave (It was now 1:30 a.m.), there is one other thing the Lord directed me to do." Whereupon, he laid his hand upon my forehead and said,"Receive you the Holy Ghost in power." A fire came down on my head, charged through my brain, down my chest cavity, down through my loins, down my legs and feet. I fell backward on that bed without being physically pushed. I was totally immersed in a baptism of glory unequal to anything that had happened to me before; I was unable to move as the Spirit of the Lord did a work in my heart that made the cleansing worth it. How long I lay there is unimportant; what is important is that one man listened to God and changed another man's life forever. (I never saw this man again after he departed that morning; I never talked with him again.— I intended to, but the Lord called him home two weeks after this meeting.)

Regardless of the theological ramifications, whether the reader accepts the tenets of sanctification, holiness, or the baptism of the Holy Spirit, one matter prevails: it happened! It happened in a manner which was undeniably from God. No man, regardless of how well trained in therapeutic counseling, could have known what this man knew, nor could he have dealt with my spirit with such deftness, apart from the Spirit of God. From that time forward, the Lord has kept showing me over and again how important it is to bury my personal agenda and yield to His. No man or woman who clings to the selfish resort of self-determinism will know the great excesses of the Spirit. This is no club to be willfully joined by manner of man's invitation or appeal; this is what united an upper room. Its ways are not learned by assistants and its language is not garnered by repetitive teachings. Rhythm and gesture have nothing to do with the pure river that flows from His throne, and no man may enter its waters without invitation from God. Ezekiels must see His glory, and Sauls must see His judgment. I must behold His baptism. Without emptying, there can be no filling. That is what the upper room was all about, and those who remained found out why Pentecost precedes Tabernacles. No one comes to that feast without the fire!

> *The way of the just is uprightness: O Most Upright, you*
> *weigh the path of the just, Yes, in the way of Your judg-*

ments, O Lord, we have waited for You; The desire of our soul is for Your name and for the remembrance of You. With my soul I have desired You in the night, Yes, by my spirit within me I will seek You early; For when Your judgments are in the earth, the inhabitants of the world will learn righteousness. Let grace be shown to the wicked, yet he will not learn righteousness; in the land of uprightness he will deal unjustly, and will not behold the majesty of the Lord.

Isaiah 26:7-10 (NKJV)

CHAPTER EIGHT

Jeremiah's *En Punto* Experience

Jeremiah, like Ezekiel, was a man with specific assignments. God directed him to carry out certain spiritual duties which involved more than just making prophetic pronouncements. The Lord outlined twenty-three specific tasks that were to be carried out in combination with specific words (which came directly from God). These tasks were performed in order to loose certain judgments and forces into the spiritual and natural world, so they could carry out their work on earth. The reflexive result of that loosing caused mighty changes in the social, political, economic, and religious circles of that day. (Much of what Jeremiah did was similar to the binding and loosing which the early saints carried out in their lifetime.) Those changes and the reasons for them constituted the basis for Jeremiah's prophetic words. In other words, the Lord placed twenty-three speed bumps in Israel's path to slow them down as He sought to capture their attention. Twenty-three highway signs were placed in their path in order to say, "Amend Your Ways."

At one point, the Lord sped up "cause and effect" to instantaneous proportions in order to capture the attention of the nation. If the people could see that the time difference between the prophet's word and the completion of those words was short, maybe they would listen more intently:

> The INSTANT I speak concerning a nation and concerning a kingdom, to build and to plant it, If it does evil in My sight so that It does not obey My voice, then I will relent concerning the good with which I said I would benefit it.
>
> Jeremiah 18:9 (NKJV)

Jeremiah reinforced this new criteria for judgment by saying to the nation that God was customizing a disaster especially for them. Upon hearing such, the populous should have fallen on their faces and repented. Instead, they said: "We will walk according to our own plans." God's response to their sin was immediate. Unlike Ezekiel, whose prophecies which involved retrospect as well as present and future implications, Jeremiah dwelled mostly in the present. He lived to see all of his words come to pass. A cogent example is found in Jeremiah 28:15:

> *Then the prophet Jeremiah said to Hananiah the prophet, "Hear now, Hananiah, the LORD has not sent you, but you make this people trust in a lie. Therefore thus says the LORD: 'Behold, I will cast you from the face of the earth, This year you shall die, because you have taught rebellion against the LORD.'" So, Hananiah the prophet died the same year in the seventh month.*

(NKJV)

Again, in the Twenty-first Century, God is speeding up time. (Every aspect of the socio-economic system is accelerated. Instead of years to develop scientific and mechanical devices in business and industry, days are used. The knowledge base of man is doubling, within periods sometimes less than a year, due to computer technology.)

Spiritual forces are also accelerated, pacing things beyond the wildest imagination of man. The instantaneousness of Jeremiah's day looked like time lapse in its relation to current time frames. Therefore, the urgency in the appeal of the prophet Jeremiah to hear the voice of God, and make an immediate response in his day, is surpassed in this present hour. The Last Days demand that those who call themselves by His Name be aware of the importance in not delaying one second, from the sound of His directive—to the installing of that directive in their lives. True believers are increasingly aware that "time is of the essence," their very lives, both mortal and spiritual, depend upon this truth—just as Hananiah's did.

En Punto, more clearly defined, means the carrying out of "The Plan" from His directive—with the expediency of life and death. Not only does it encompass being at the right spot (the place called there), it involves doing the exact will of God without hesitation. Jeremiah was a living example of En Punto, for he, like Ezekiel, did not fail to carry out the exact word given him or fail to appear at the exact place he was directed. Because of this faithfulness and the power of his calling, the Lord revealed to him the future in dramatic proportion. God allowed him to "know" what was taking place and what would take place. Sadly, the prophetic world charms themselves with no such knowledge today. Their conjecture is often pathetic.

When the Lord told Jeremiah, in the first chapter, to look a certain direction, instantly he looked. Whether the Lord was conditioning him for immediate response is immaterial, the fact that from the very first directive he positively responded—that is the focus. He saw an almond tree and with it a word from God. He was redirected to look at a boiling pot and similarly a prophetic word came to him (Jeremiah 1:11-14).

Jeremiah was the living example of the "prophet of the instantaneous." Many prophecies, other than the one concerning Hananiah, were fulfilled within days of their utterance. The sure sign of a true prophet is that his or her words find fulfillment. (**Note**: Between the almond tree and the boiling pot, a graphic review of the history of Israel was shown. Starting with Aaron's authoritative rod and continuing to a place of boiling judgment, there was depicted a journey from doing God's will to facing God's judgment.)

From these first two submissive acts, Jeremiah was ushered into a plethora of truths. Had he rebelled, or failed to respond, he well could have missed his "there" with God. Again, within the first chapter of his book, in verse 17, he was told, "Therefore prepare yourself and rise, and speak to them all that I command you (NKJV)."

Review the progression of these separate acts (Twenty-three speed bumps):

1. *Jeremiah 1:11: Jeremiah, what do you see? (almond tree)*

2. *Jeremiah 1:13: What do you see? (boiling pot)*

3. *Jeremiah 1:17: Prepare yourself and arise.*

4. *Jeremiah 2:2: Go and cry in the hearing of Jerusalem.*

5. *Jeremiah 5:1: Run to and fro through the streets of Jerusalem.*

6. *Jeremiah 7:2: Stand in the gate of the Lord's House and proclaim.*

7. *Jeremiah 11:2: Hear the words of this covenant, and speak to the men of Judah and to the inhabitants of Jerusalem.*

8. *Jeremiah 13:1: Go and get yourself a linen sash and put it around your waist, but do not put it in water...Take the sash that you acquired, which is around your waist, and arise, go to the Euphrates, and hide it there in a hole in the rock...(after many days)..Arise, go to the Euphrates, and*

take from there the sash which I commanded you to hide there.

9. Jeremiah 16:2: *You shall not take a wife, nor shall you have sons or daughters in this place.*

10. Jeremiah 17:19: *Thus the LORD said to me: 'Go and stand in the gate of the children of the people, by which the kings of Judah come in and by which you go out, and in all the gates of Jerusalem.'*

11. Jeremiah 18:2: *Arise and go down to the potter's house, and there I will cause you to hear My words.*

12. Jeremiah 19:1 *Go and get a potter's earthen flask and take some of the elders of the people and some of the elders of the priests. And go out to the valley of the Son of Hinnom, which is by the entry of the Potsherd Gate: and proclaim there the words that I will tell you.*

13. Jeremiah 22:1: *Go down to the house of the king of Judah, and there speak this word.*

14. Jeremiah 24:3: *What do you see, Jeremiah? (Figs, good and bad)*

15. Jeremiah 26:2: *Stand in the court of the LORD'S house, and speak to all the cities of Judah, which come to worship in the LORD'S house, all the word that I command you to speak to them, Do not diminish a word.*

16. Jeremiah 27:2: *Thus says the LORD to me: 'make for yourselves bonds and yokes, and put them on your neck and send them to the king of Edom...'*

17. Jeremiah 30:2: *Thus speaks the LORD God of Israel, saying: 'Write in a book for yourself all the words that I have spoken to you.'*

18. Jeremiah 32:14: *Take these deeds, both this purchase deed which is sealed and this deed which is open, and put them in an earthen vessel, that they may last many days.*

19. Jeremiah 34:2: *Go and speak to Zedekiah king of Judah and tell him.*

20. Jeremiah 35:2: *Go to the house of the Rechabites, speak to*

> *them, and   bring them into the house of the LORD, into*
> *one of the chambers, and give them wine to drink.*

21. *Jeremiah 36:2: Take a scroll of a book and write on it all*
    the words that I have spoken to you against Israel, against
    Judah, and against all the nations, from the day I spoke to
    you from the days of Josiah even to this day...

22. *Jeremiah 36:28: Take another scroll, and write on it all the*
    former words that were in the first scroll which Jehoiakim
    the king of Judah has burned.

23. *Jeremiah 39:16: Go and speak to Ebed-Melech the*
    Ethiopian...

It is interesting to note that although Jeremiah spoke the Lord's words on many occasions, these twenty-three instances constituted direct commands from the Lord. They came from His mouth. (Notice how the Lord used exact commands to direct the prophet.)

Jeremiah was led to focus upon some specific object, or go some particular place, or engage in some specific duty, as he methodically executed each directive. If the reader will concentrate on the prophetic words which follow each of these commands, a great awakening will occur. There was a theme which recurred after each of the twenty-three commands. The nation should have caught the theme. The theme could be paraphrased thusly, "You failed to obey my voice and follow my commands, therefore, a built-in judgment will come to pass."

A principle in the judgment of the Lord was established, a principle that prescribed judgment as being built into the act of disobedience. In other words, disobedience already has its judgment attached—do the act; the judgment follows..

Believers, yes, even whole congregations today, are oblivious to this fact. To fail to obey His leadership and voice today will bring consequences in the future which will cause loss to the kingdom and to the individual. There comes a time, though, in the normal order of events, that God says basically, "enough is enough." Observe the almond tree.

The almond branch, which represented the lamp stand in the Holy Place, was the first object Jeremiah viewed. The word "almond" had a prime meaning of "watching with a readiness to act." Why was God ready to act in the "almond" image and not in the image of the boiling pot? God said, "Because they have forsaken me (1:16)."

Not one person in Jerusalem would have admitted to having forsaken the Lord, but God said they did. The Lord often calls situations differently than man. Multiple times in these prophecies, the Lord judged the people He addressed, as confessing to "having no sin." They stumbled over twenty-three "speed-bumps" and refused to slow their pace to sin and learned little from their experiences.

After each of the twenty-three speed bumps, the Lord, in subsequent verses, mentioned being "forsaken." (After the almond tree and the boiling pot, if you will follow the sequence, you will hear His voice.)

Following the third speed bump, Jeremiah 2:13 declared: "They have forsaken me." "Have you not brought this on yourself, in that you have forsaken the Lord your God. When He led you in the way (highway) (v.17)?" Now look at verse 18, "and now why take the road to Egypt?" (Examine this statement, the "Road to Egypt" was not the Highway of Holiness.) Four separate reasons are offered for going on the Road to Egypt:

(a.) "For they have turned their back to Me and not their face (v.27)."

(b.) "Why do my people say, 'We are lords; we will come no more to You'(v.31)."

(c.) "...and you have not obeyed My voice, says the Lord (3:13.)"

(d.) "...because she has been rebellious against Me, says the Lord (4:17)."

Following the fourth speed bump, God said: "But this people has a defiant and rebellious heart; They have revolted and departed. They do not say in their heart, 'Let us now fear the Lord our God (5:23).'"

After the fifth speed bump, there came: "Behold, I will certainly bring calamity on this people, even the <u>fruit of their thoughts</u>, Because they have not heeded My words, Nor My law, but rejected it (v.19)." (Regardless of modern teaching, thoughts have fruit!)

After the sixth speed bump, the Lord spoke:

(a.) Yet, they did not obey or incline their ear, but walked in the counsels and in the imagination of their evil heart, and went backward and not forward (7:24).

(b.) This is the nation that does not obey the voice of the Lord their God nor receive correction, <u>Truth has perished</u> and has been cut off from their mouth (7:28).

(c.)   And the Lord said, 'Because they have forsaken My law which I set before them, and <u>have not obeyed My voice, nor walked according to it</u> but they have walked according to the imagination of their own heart and after the Baals, which there fathers taught them (9:13-14).'

After the seventh speed bump, the Word was clear: "For I earnestly exhorted your fathers in the day that I brought them up out of the land of Egypt, <u>until this day</u>, rising early and exhorting, saying 'Obey My voice.' YET they did not obey or incline their ear, but everyone walked in the imagination (stubbornness) of his evil heart; there I will bring upon them all the words of this covenant...(11:7,8)."

After the eighth speed bump came these words: "This evil people, who refuse to hear My words, who walk in the imagination of their heart, and walk after other gods to serve them and worship them, shall be just like this sash which is profitable for nothing (13:10)."

After the ninth speed bump, further truth was added: "And you have done worse than your fathers, for behold, each one walks according to the imagination of his own evil heart, <u>so that no one listens to Me</u> (16:12)."

After the tenth speed bump, there was heard:

(a.)   ...because they have forsaken the Lord, the fountain of living waters.(17:13).

(b.)   But they did not obey nor incline their ear, but made their neck stiff, that they might not hear <u>nor receive instruction</u> (17:23).

After the eleventh speed bump, succinctness was used: "Because My people have forgotten Me(18:15)."

After the twelfth speed bump, reasoning fell before truth: "...because they have stiffened their necks that they <u>might not hear</u> My words (19:15)."

After the thirteenth speed bump, a timeframe was added: "I spoke to you in your <u>prosperity</u>, But you said, 'I will not hear.' This has been your manner from your youth, That you did not <u>obey My voice</u> (22:22)."

After the fourteenth speed bump, the image being the good and bad figs, the Lord made this judgment: "...and the bad, very bad, which cannot be eaten, they are so bad (24:3)." Although after this command the Lord did not spell out rebellion, He did show His separation between the good and the bad.

After the fifteenth speed bump, prophecy was increased: "And you shall say to them, 'Thus says the Lord, If you will not listen to Me, to walk in My law which I have set before you, to heed the words of My servants the prophets whom I sent to you, both rising up early and sending them (but you have not heeded), then...(26:4-5).' "

After the sixteenth speed bump, boldness was increased: "Because they have not heeded My words, says the Lord, which I sent to them by My servants the prophets, rising up early and sending them; neither would you heed, says the Lord (29:19)."

After the seventeenth speed bump, God explained: "For I have wounded you with the wound of an enemy...because your sins have increased...because your sins have increased, I have done these things to you (30:14,15)."

After the eighteenth speed bump, Jeremiah added: "...but they have not obeyed Your voice or walked in Your law. They have done NOTHING of all that You commanded them to do; therefore You have caused all this calamity to come upon them (32:23)."

After the nineteenth speed bump, a great fault was discussed: "Therefore thus says the Lord: 'You have not obeyed Me in proclaiming liberty, every one to his brother...who have not performed the words of the covenant which they made before Me (34:17,18).' "

After the twentieth speed bump, God's anger was showing:

(a.)   "Go and tell the men of Judah and the inhabitants of Jerusalem, 'Will you not receive instruction to obey My words,?' says the Lord, But although I have spoken to you, rising early and speaking you did not obey Me (35:14,15).' "

(b.)   "I have pronounced against them; because I have spoken to them but they have not heard, and I have called to them but they have not answered (35:17)."

After the twenty-first speed bump, the Lord revealed: " ...the king cut it [Jeremiah's written prophesy] with the scribe's knife and cast it into the fire that was on the hearth, until all the scroll was consumed in the fire...Yet they were not afraid, nor did they tear their garments, the king nor any of his servants who heard all these words (36:23-24)."

After the twenty-second speed bump, a commentary followed: "...but neither he nor his servants nor the people of the land gave heed to the words of the Lord which He spoke by the prophet Jeremiah(37:2)."

After the twenty-third speed bump, a heart examination revealed the sin:

(a.)   Now the Lord has brought it, and has done just as He said, Because you people have sinned against the Lord, and <u>not obeyed</u> His voice, therefore this thing has come upon you (40:3).

(b.)   For you were <u>hypocrites in your hearts</u> [unlikely text for a message next Sunday] when you sent me to the Lord your God saying, 'Pray for us to the Lord our God, and according to all that the Lord your God says, so declare to us and we will do it.' And I have this day declared it to you, but you have not obeyed the voice of the Lord your God, or anything which He has sent you by me (42:20-21).

The reason these passages are cogent for the present day is because committees meet, boards gather, conclaves congregate (to this very hour) with the same lip service to the voice of God as Israel paid. Their two minute prayers and two hour sessions—where plans, budgets, programs and pillages were discussed—were an abomination to God. Jeremiah said it best:

(a.)   The priests did not say, 'Where is the Lord?' And those who <u>handle the law</u> did not know Me; the rulers also transgressed against Me; The prophets prophesied by Baal, and walked after things that do not profit (2:8)

(b.)   ...among My people are found wicked men (5:26)

(c.)   The priests rule by their own power and My people love to have it so, But what will you do in the end?(5:31)

(d.)   Has this house, which is called by My name, become a den of thieves (7:11)?

(e.)   They are not valiant for the truth on the earth for they proceed from evil to evil, and they do not know Me (9:3)

(f.)   For the shepherds are dull hearted, and have not sought the Lord (10:21) (An unlikely text for the next ministerial alliance meeting)

(g.)   For I have taken away My peace from this people (16:5)

(h.)   <u>Cursed</u> is the man who trusts in man and makes flesh his strength, whose heart departs from the Lord (17:5).

Jeremiah could not speak in the pulpits of this world, today. Just as they sought to kill him then, slander him, and bind him in prison then, so it would be today. His words, centuries ago, were met with closed minds, hearts, and ears. Little did those who listened to him suspect that <u>within</u>

their lifetime, every word spoken by Jeremiah would come to pass. Though he seemed a continuous nuisance to the establishment, in reality his weeping voice and tear stained eyes set him apart from his society: "Many rulers [church rulers, shepherds, pastors—exact translation] have destroyed My vineyard, they have trodden My portions underfoot...the whole land is desolate because NO ONE TAKES IT TO HEART (12:11, NKJV)." Jeremiah took it to heart. God took it to heart. Do you take it to heart?

God is speaking TODAY, but no one can hear Him above the choirs, the stage bands and the programmed details called "a service." God is speaking, but human hearts are too busy with living their individual life to listen; this is why the "secret place of the Most High," has so few occupants. God is speaking, offering counsel which would rearrange priorities, change plans, and reveal the future, but alas, no one is listening. Instead, like the elders of Jeremiah's day, there arises a protest within which says: "Because I am innocent, surely His anger shall turn from me." But God said, "Behold, I will plead My case against you, because you say, 'I have not sinned (2:35, NKJV).'"

Fresh from harlotry (committing oneself to someone or something other than the Lord) the Lord exclaimed: "You have played the harlot with many lovers; Yet return to Me, says the Lord(3:1)." Again the Lord said: "And yet for all this her treacherous sister Judah has not turned to Me with her whole heart, but in pretense (3:10)." Today is a day of pretense, just as in Jeremiah's day!

This was why God portrayed Revelation's seventh church as errant: "Because you say, 'I am rich, have become wealthy, and have need of nothing'—and do not know that you are wretched, miserable, poor, blind, and naked—I counsel you to buy from ME gold refined in the fire, that you may be rich and white garments, that you may be clothed that the shame of your nakedness may not be revealed; and anoint your eyes with eye salve that you my see...therefore be zealous and repent (Revelation 3:17-19, NKJV)."

Many scholars believe the seventh church is the symbolic church of the Last Days. Should this be so, then there is only one remedy coming from the voice of God: "REPENT!" Yes, it is evident that since this is the last word to the churches, it will more than likely be the last thing the churches will do. How long has it been since James 4:9 was used as a Sunday text in your church? (What? Never? Could it be this is the problem?)

Just when the Temple was functioning well according to its leadership, Jeremiah heard God invite the temple worshippers to come to Zion. The power of Jeremiah 3:14 was that they thought they were already in Zion! They equated the temple mount with Zion, but God wanted to show them the real Zion. At the Lord's Mount Zion, they would be able to view true worship and see how different it was (and is), separated from that which was going on. They had allowed man and tradition to determine their definition of worship for so many years they had lost their way; this was why the Lord cried out to them, "Let me show you what I really had in mind." (It is time for every model used in religious circles to be examined with the same scrutiny. The worship model is askew, the ministry model is awry, the clergy model is in disarray; while evangelistic models are lacking, church models are pathetic. When will someone dare to carry these to God and say, "Lord, define again, these areas for us that we may know what you have in mind."

In the twenty-first century, Christendom does not believe they are far from God; no one acknowledges possessing the characteristics of the seventh church of Revelation. No one really seeks after God, for most believe His glory graces their services already and approves their wizardry. (They thought the same way in Jeremiah's time, but listen as God spoke, " Return, O Backsliding children," says the Lord, "for I am married to you. I will take you, one from a city and two from a family, and I will bring you to Zion (3:14).")

Their response was insult, and they took grievous offence because of these words. They considered their worship to be equal to Zion. God wanted to bring them to a place in Him which they could not conceive on their own. God wanted to send them: "...shepherds according to my heart, who will feed you with knowledge and understanding (3:15, NKJV)."

God's shepherds were **unlike** the shepherds they had chosen for themselves. God's shepherds called for different music, different Bible texts, different order, and far different sermons (if they even had sermons). Their order of worship began by seeking Him and ended by abiding in Him. Their altar calls were not to join a group, but to lose some of themselves: "Circumcise YOURSELVES to the Lord, and take away the foreskins of your hearts (4:4, NKJV)." In like manner, Jeremiah 4:14 declared: "O Jerusalem, wash your heart from wickedness, that you may be saved. How long shall your evil thoughts **lodge** within you?" (Remember this message is directed to Jerusalem, the center of worship.)

> *For My people are foolish, They have not known ME, They are silly children, and they have no understanding. They are wise to do evil, but to do good they have no knowledge.*
>
> Jeremiah 4:22 (NKJV)

Separated by over two thousand years, this summation of religion is as true today as it was then. En Punto is a call not only to be where He decides, and to do what He decides, it is a call to know Him. Would you know true worship? Ask Him! Would you seek understanding? Ask Him! What decision in life is too miniscule for His input?

Christendom has arrived at its present state because it has refused to wait upon the Lord and let Him direct its paths—to let Him show them Zion. He is married to us (through His covenant with us). We are in this thing together, or we are not in this thing! (14)

SIX MAJOR TREATISES

THE BLOOD COVENANT:

Jeremiah addressed this issue in one of six great treatises regarding *En Punto*. In the thirty-fourth chapter, the Lord spoke about His covenant. He referred to a blood covenant arrived at by "passing through the halves." (For a study of this ritual covenant see Addendum #2 The Covenant of Blood) Beginning with verse 17, the Lord reiterated that Israel had not obeyed Him:

> *Therefore thus says the LORD: 'You have not obeyed Me in proclaiming liberty, every one to his brother and every one to his neighbor. Behold, I proclaim liberty to you,' says the LORD— (liberty) 'to the sword, to pestilence, and to famine! And I will deliver you to trouble among all the kingdoms of the earth. And I will give the men who have <u>not performed the words of the covenant</u> which they made before Me, when they <u>cut the calf in two and passed between the parts of it</u>— the princes of Judah, the princes of Jerusalem, the eunuchs, the priests, and all the people of the land <u>who passed between the parts</u> of the calf—'*

Jeremiah 34:17ff (NKJV)

Now, I do not know where in history the referenced blood covenant took place, but with Abraham (Genesis 15) such a covenant was made. All children of faith have cut that covenant through and with faithful Abraham. Just as Jacob paid tithes to Melchizedek through the loins of Abraham, you and I have cut the covenant through his loins. That covenant required our redemption through blood, the innocent for the guilty. That covenant required Calvary to free us from the enemy!

THE RECHABITES

While under this same revelation, the Lord commanded Jeremiah to do a strange thing—invite the Rechabites to a "wine" party at the temple.

Jeremiah thirty-five is totally given to the results and the rewards of that invitation. The Rechabites were descendants of Jonadab, the son of Rechab. He had instructed his sons to drink no wine. He also had instructed them thusly:

> *You shall not build a house, sow seed, plant a vineyard, nor have any of these; but all your days you shall dwell in tents, that you may live many days in the land where you are sojourners.*

> Jeremiah 35:7 (NKJV)

Note this picture, the established prophet, Jeremiah, invited them to a gathering in one of the rooms of the main house of worship. This man of God instructed them, "Drink wine." Understand the situation fully—a man of God, who did things and spoke things according the word of the Lord only, said: "Drink wine." If ever in this world a social setting was ripe to change the tradition of a family, this is THE one. What was their answer? "We will drink no wine."

They were quick to explain this was an unwritten ascription in their family. Their father Jonadab had said that his sons and his sons' sons should never drink wine. Verses 8-11 told the story of their faithfulness to Jonadab's wishes. (They could have reasoned, "We live in a different age with different customs, newer ways, more enlightened society; therefore, we can set aside the old man's wishes." They could have excused themselves, this once, by saying, "After all, the prophet instructed us to: "drink wine," and besides that, every other holy man in this temple imbibes." They could have acted like they were drinking wine, but never swallowed it and avoided social castigation.) They could have done any of the things that modern Christians do for an excuse to break covenant, but they did not. Deep inside them, there rose up a protesting voice, long since in the grave— a voice stronger than the urge to change, stronger than circumstances, stronger than the desire to do what they had never done before, stronger than the prophet's bid to indulgence, stronger than the religion of the temple, stronger than the moment—the voice of Jonadab!

The implication splashed across the mind of Jeremiah, "My God, the unspoken covenant of Jonadab is heeded more than the spoken covenant with YOU, Lord." (I know families who have stronger bonds than most believers. I know organizations that are built on stronger covenants than most believers claim to have with the Lord. I know false sects, sacerdotal societies, and pagan religions that have stronger ties to covenant with a false god than Christians claim with Jesus!) Is the voice of Jonadab stronger in his sons than the voice of the Spirit in the Sons of God? This is an En Punto question!

At its core is the strongest question that could be asked today; it is stronger than God's "Adam, where are you?" (Properly translated, Adam means: "Of the Blood." Does this mean we carrying the DNA of God?) The question is the same as in the garden. "Church, where are you? Believer, where are you?" God is saying, "O, my beloved to whom I am married, where are you?" These questions should sound down the halls of every church. En Punto's major question is, "where are you?" Its answer should be, "I am in your Presence, Lord. I am at **There**. I am doing your will. I hear your voice."

> *Thus says the LORD of hosts, the God of Israel: Go and tell the men of Judah and the inhabitants of Jerusalem, 'Will you not receive instruction to obey My words?' says the LORD.*
> *'The words of Jonadab the son of Rechab, which he commanded his sons, not to drink wine, are performed; for to this day they drink none, and obey their father's commandment. But although I have spoken to you, rising early and speaking, you did not obey Me.'*
>
> Jeremiah 35:13-14 (NKJV)

Actions have consequences. God pronounced a blessing upon the sons of Rechab and a curse toward Israel because of this. "Jonadab, the son of Rechab, shall not lack a man to stand before Me forever." This word was not spoken to philandering Israel and it is not spoken to today's church. Better to be a Rechabite than a Baptist. Better to be a Rechaite than a Roman Catholic. Better to be a Rechabite than a Methodist or Presbyterian. Better to be a Rechabite than a Charismatic, regardless of the name in lights on the marquee. Better to be a Rechabite than a non-protesting Protestant or a piteous Pentecostal! No wonder there is judgment on the scene—relenting relativists fill the aisles!

The destruction and deception rampant in all echelons of religious society must be laid at the feet of humanistic relativism. The Rechabite-like voice of Jonadabs has been silenced by committee, board, and brethren (Seeking to pay for the sanctuary, they have compromised its sanctity). Whether in the back room of the Temple or the front room of the church, the voice of the Absolute must be heard!

En Punto demands that His voice have total power to direct. He must be able to say, "Drink this; Don't drink that; Do this; No, move over here." The wine party did not appear to be a "big deal," but had the Rechabites compromised, the blessing of standing before Him forever would never have occurred. So strong is this truth, that history could have been rewritten for many biblical persons—but they understood, "no big deal," was!

THE PROPHET'S MISJUDGMENT

Listen, the man of God in I Kings 13:7-9 would have lived out his days had he not disobeyed the Lord by listening to another voice—even if it was another prophet. Read it:

> *Then the king said to the man of God, 'Come home with me and refresh yourself, and I will give you a reward.' But the man of God said to the king, 'If you were to give me half your house, I would not go in with you; nor would I eat bread nor drink water in this place.' For so it was commanded me by the word of the LORD, saying, 'You shall not eat bread, nor drink water, nor return by the same way you came.'*

> (NKJV)

The "man of God" rehearsed all the Lord told him to do. He obeyed God, up to this point, by refusing the King's hospitality and by going a different route home. Little did he suspect there would be a fellow prophet's house at Bethel (translated: "The House of God"), and for him, it would be the house of ruin.

The "Old Prophet" of Bethel (longing for someone to share with and have sweet fellowship in the Lord) pursued the "man of God" and found him sitting under an oak tree. An invitation to go home with him ensued. The "man of God" rehearsed a second time, the word of the Lord. Twice now, out of his own mouth, he had given an account of the word given him by God. Right out of the mouth of a fellow prophet came the invitation to sin:

> *I too am a prophet as you are, and an <u>angel spoke </u>to me by the word of the LORD, saying, 'Bring him back with you to your house, that he may eat bread and drink water.' <u>But he lied to him</u>. So he went back with him, and ate bread in his house, and drank water. NOW IT HAPPENED, as they sat at the table, that the word or the LORD came to the prophet who had brought him back...*

> I Kings 13:18-20 (NKJV)

The next words were not music to the "man of God." In essence, the lying prophet said that because the visiting prophet had disobeyed God—"your corpse shall not come to the tomb of your fathers."

Is it strange that the Lord would give true prophecy to a lying prophet? It happens all the time. Verse 24 asserts that God did a supernatural thing: "So when He was gone, a lion met him on the road and killed him. And his corpse was thrown on the road, and the donkey stood by it; the lion also stood by the corpse." Men passed by and saw his corpse and informed the lying prophet, whose words were: "It is the man of God who was <u>disobedient to the word</u> of the Lord (v.26)." (How important is it now to do the exact will of the Lord?)

When the old prophet buried him, he cried out: "Alas, my brother!." Is this not my own weeping heart? Is this not the reason for my own tears? "Alas, my brother!," is but a phrase between sobs. When one knows this principle, this unbending truth, it causes him or her to cry out in his or her spirit: "Alas, my brother." A thousand church steps should hear that burden expressed! The sad reunion of a million classmates should hear this broad invective in the land of the free. Just because some great one said it, just because a religious significant declares a vision, just because it seems convenient or the right thing to do, just because it is the expected thing or a prophet says it—or whatever excuse one may have to disobey the voice of God—the end result is the same—enter The Lion! (He really is like a roaring lion seeking whom he may devour.)

"Alas, my brother!," how great is this cry coming up to the throne of God, today. It is the enigma of Saul's Abner, who died like a fool died. His "hands were not tied, his feet were not in chains." Regardless of the locale today, to visit any congregation, to hear any message, to view any convention or walk among brethren elicits the cry, "Alas, my brother!"

The reason Jesus' last word to the last church was "REPENT," is because it is what universally must be done. With the bread of disobedience in our mouths and the wetness of its wine of wrath still on our tongues, we must not think to saddle up and attempt to go on "as if nothing had happened." Actions such as this only invite the Lion!

God only knows what would have happened had the "man of God" repented. God only knows what would have happened had he traveled forward from the oak tree and lived in the world of: "well done thou good and faithful servant." The only road to the world of "well done" is decided at the moment of the king's invitation, the prophet's appealing restive, and at the oak tree of decision. <u>Jehovah's voice is the only voice the "man of God" must obey!</u>

Has the Lord changed? Has His displeasure with disobedience mellowed with time to the point where now He tolerates what man so easily accommodates? A thousand times let the resounding "NO" penetrate the air. "I change not," still falls from His lips. <u>Trusting the lying words of a false prophet has cost the church more dearly than words can tell.</u> The "man of God" trusted in lying words and so have literally millions trusted in rabbi's, priests, prelates, pastors, elders, and error's words to this day.

"Not so!," comes the cry in response to such an accusation flung at the modern church, but lo!, if true intentions were flashed upon the "Power Point screen"—then one would see as God sees. God said, "<u>Thoroughly</u> mend your ways and your doings." The same appeal should be what is Power-pointed on the screens of mega churches instead of the next song or the text of a sermon.

> *Behold, you trust in lying words that cannot profit. Will you steal, murder, commit adultery, swear falsely, burn incense to Baal, and walk after other gods whom you do not know, and THEN come and stand before ME in this house which is called by My name, and say 'WE ARE DELIVERED TO DO ALL THESE ABOMINATIONS?'*
>
> Jeremiah 7:8-10 (NKJV)

Jesus used the next verse in this text for His own sermon almost six hundred years later. Speaking to a similar group while standing on the same temple mount, Jesus said:

> *Has this house, which is called by My name, become a den of thieves in your eyes? Behold, I, even I, have seen it, says the LORD.*

(Go ahead, talk to me about being patient and the prospect of reform. Tell me about the necessity of working within the established church in order to bring change. I will reply, "There comes a time when the word must come forth." The time is NOW!)

In other words, God was saying, "Look at things like I look at them—not through your ultra-forgiving eyes, but through My eyes. (You and I are living in the generation that prompted Jesus' warning about the blind leading the blind.)

It is at this juncture, the Lord refers to another place in history—Shiloh.

SHILOH AND THE TEMPLE

The Lord brought up the subject of His old place of blessing—Shiloh. Shiloh was mentioned to bring an illustration of how the Lord dealt with His people in the past. Shiloh was where the ark of the covenant and the tabernacle dwelled. Shiloh was where Joshua divided the land among the people of Israel. Shiloh, home base to Israel, was like a touchstone which marked the end of the wilderness and the open door to the Holy Land. Shiloh was where decisions were made and judgments were passed down. Shiloh was where the warmth of God's presence was found in the tabernacle. Shiloh was a place that should have been the reflection of the

Genesis usage of the word Shiloh (speaking of Jesus being Shiloh and was translated "He's who it is"). "The scepter shall not depart from Judah, Nor a lawgiver from between his feet Until Shiloh comes; and to Him shall be the obedience of the people (Genesis 49:10, NKJV)."

The Shiloh of Jeremiah, instead, was translated: "to draw out or extract." Eli's Shiloh should have been a place of repentance where the most common of men could come before the Lord and find solace. It should have been a place for "drawing out" the inner man and the extraction of sin. Instead, it was the home of Eli, Hophni, and Phinehas. Although God spoke to Samuel at Shiloh, He did not speak to the High Priest at Shiloh. Filled with fornication and adultery, Shiloh, the blessed touchstone, had become a stinking outpost from which God departed.

Psalm 78:60 (NKJV) says it best:

> *So that He forsook the tabernacle of Shiloh, the tent which*
> *He had placed among men, and delivered His strength into*
> *captivity, And His glory into the enemy's hand.*

Later, David wrote about where the Lord traveled after leaving Shiloh, "But chose the tribe of Judah; Mount Zion which He loved (78:68, NKJV)."

Shiloh, whose last infamy was the death of its priests and the hauling away of the sacred Ark, stood as a desolate example of what it means to be, "God Forsaken." Now God pointed to Shiloh and with the force of its ignominy, He declared:

> *'But go now to My place which was in Shiloh, where I set*
> *My name at the first, and see what I did to it because of the*
> *wickedness of My people Israel. And now, because you*
> *have done all these works says the Lord, and I spoke to*
> *you, rising up early and speaking, but you did not hear, and*
> *I called you, but you did not answer, THEREFORE I*
> *will do to this house which I gave to you and your fathers,*
> *as I have done to Shiloh.'*

> Jeremiah 7:12-14 (NKJV)

The Lord then said He would cast them out of His sight and neither Jeremiah nor anyone was to intercede in prayer for them. He declared that: "My anger and My fury will be poured out on this place—on man and on beast, on the trees of the field and on the fruit of the ground. And it will burn and not be quenched (v. 20, NKJV)."

Why is all this being done? Because the people of Israel did not obey the voice of the Lord. They went their own way; they went backward and not forward. They stiffened their neck and did worse than their fathers did at Shiloh. "They set their abominations in the house which is called by My name, to pollute it (v.30, NKJV)."

God said the real problem was a pollution problem. To this very day, there is a pollution problem within religious structure, a problem of global proportion. World pollution holds no candle to the spiritual pollution that God sees.

Although the world wrestles with greater portents of pollution than ever before, global warming, non-potable water, burgeoning air contamination, and pesticide residue, these are trivial pursuits compared to the spiritual pollution found in this universe. (Natural pollution threatens to drown sea coasts, fry the equator, cause rapid death, produce incurable diseases, and make earth uninhabitable. As one surveys the vast problems facing the new world government which is rapidly being formed, an awareness of a problem which cannot be solved by international courts arises, spiritual pollution.) Think of a greater pollution problem, of the spiritual pollution in the houses of the world which have been dedicated to God. Think of the death of its adherents caused by the unseen exhaust of man's spiritual mechanisms. Think of the vast ramifications of the pesticide residue from false teaching poured regularly over biblical truth in order to eradicate it. Think of the impure stream coming from the polluted wells of theological sycophants. Then, there is the smoke screen of supposed sacredness which causes the congregation to stifle, seeking for one breath of that which is pure. Spiritual pollution has been rampant longer than global exhaust. Spiritual pollution was present in Jeremiah's day and the continued compromise of clergy and class has increased its toll on truth and holiness. These conditions are exponential today! But God, does not change. He, who rained down fire upon the second "place of His dwelling," will not hesitate to do the same today. No, our sacred halls are not God-proofed, although this would seem to be the goal. Our candled cathedrals, convenient auditoriums, and our little chapels in the wildwood are about to hear a rumble of Theocratic proportion.

The God who forsook Shiloh and departed from the Temple will have no hesitancy in judging our temples. Instead of latter day rain and end time raptures, let it be understood that He, who began at the sanctuary in Ezekiel, will not hesitate to bring fire! God remembers Shiloh!

This is why Shiloh is mentioned again by Jeremiah in the twenty-sixth chapter, verses 4-6:

> *If you will not listen to Me, to walk in My Law which I have set before you to heed the words of My servants the prophets whom I sent to you, both rising up early and sending them (but you have not heeded), THEN I will make*

this *house like Shiloh and will make* this *city [Jerusalem]*
a curse to all the nations of the earth.

(NKJV)

Is it any wonder the multitudes who heard this word moved against
Jeremiah with: "You will surely die." (Note where their actions took place:
"And all the people were gathered against Jeremiah in the house of the
Lord (v. 9).")

Elaboration is not needed; the picture is clear to the weakest of minds.
Irrespective of the freshness of the Pentecostal movement throughout the
world, if they or anyone else harbors the likes of Shiloh, then the judgment
of Shiloh lies at their door.

God is asking, "What about me?" Every consideration is made for the
convenience of the paying customers, from pew lighting to pulpit finesse,
while God says, "Where am I in this picture?" These questions are about
to be answered and history will show that those precious sites, where once
you met with Him, will become melted jumbles of judgment! (If somehow
one's "error-conditioned mind" cannot grasp the vastness of error and the
propensity of the judgment upon it, then think upon Shiloh and the Temple
at Jerusalem.)

Shiloh today is no more than a spot on a map; its windswept corridors
house no greatness. If there is a landmark or monument raised to identify
the place of the tabernacle where the living God came down and once
dwelled, no one can point to it. To see the desolate surroundings of Shiloh
today, is to admit, "God's judgment is complete."

THE TEMPLE

Now, turn to the Temple mount at Jerusalem and see the same type of
obliteration. Today, daily battles are fought to preserve a heritage that has
stood in ruins since 70 A.D. Look at the "wailing wall," which was the
foundation of a spiritual centerpiece, where the Prophet Jeremiah stood to
observe a nation's sin. Vast crowds once entered its gates regularly and
the smoke of its sacrifices rose every day and every night. So dear to the
heart of its public was the Temple, they idolized its walls and were consoled by its presence. Look at it now; look at the place that once was filled
with His glory while Solomon prayed at its dedication. Look at it now, the
once proud center of all Judaic promise and see what God did. God had
no hesitancy in bringing down a "man-corrupted organization," which long
before had ceased to search for His face. If His judgment fell against the
Temple, how much more against a profligate body called, "the modern
church."

The fierce wrath of God is about to be loosed in gigantic proportion upon that which man holds most precious: his own handiwork and his freedom.

Two other precious places God has already attacked, Shiloh and the Temple. When Shiloh was not the work of His hands, it became the work of man's pollution. When a place is precious in the eyes of both God and man, that place is truly sacred. When a place is precious only to man, that place cannot be truly hallowed. When the Temple was no longer His Temple, the thieves who occupied it were judged by His Son and the place cleansed by fire. Soon, it will become evident that the congregations of the world have also been judged by the Son, and the cleansing by fire will take them. Because the pollution of Shiloh had found its way to the Temple, the Lord of Shiloh judged the Temple! Because the pollution found in both is now found in modern Christendom, what shall be the result?

Pollution drowned the ministry of Eli, and its awful chemistry eroded the Holy Place. Could not the same be said of today? Could not the passage in Jeremiah 23:14 be spoken accurately again to what exists as a religious cesspool? Alas, who will speak it? Certainly not pulpiteers whose salaries and status depend on popular affections.

> *I have seen a horrible thing in the prophets of Jerusalem;*
> *They commit adultery and walk in lies; They also strengthen*
> *the hands of evildoers, SO that NO ONE TURNS back*
> *from his wickedness... Profaneness [translated POLLU-*
> *TION] has gone out into all the land. Do not listen to the*
> *words of the prophets who prophesy to you, They make you*
> *WORTHLESS.*

(NKJV)

Substitute any leader's name in your congregation, and the same cry becomes credible today. Yes, the systems of religion are filled with pollution. The congregations are made worthless. Their living water has turned to wormwood and verse twenty-three is correct: "In the latter days you will understand it perfectly." We understand. We understand.

THE ORACLE

Part of our understanding must come from the passages concerning the oracle of the Lord, as pointed out by Jeremiah in 23:30ff. This seemingly small portion of scripture carries weight beyond its volume.

The Lord began condemning all the prophets except Jeremiah. The office of prophet, heretofore, had been a major source of traditional venue for hearing from God. As a matter of fact, other than the written word, no other voice was heard but that of the prophet (aside from special angel visitations or the occasional voice of God, Himself). Rarely did the High Priest deliver a message from God. From kings to the common man, most of the people of that day depended on the prophet for direction. Now, according to the Lord, that source had dried up.

One problem prevailed through this period: even though the prophets had not heard a word from the Lord, they continued prophesying. Sadly, the people were still depending on the prophet for reliable information from God. They depended on the prophet to tell them "what the Lord wanted them to do." Grasp the picture? God said the prophets lied every time they opened their mouths. What they declared may have sounded good, but God did not give the message, so it was a lie.

Their logic, reasoning, and biblical accuracy might have been impeccable, but one thing was lacking—God did not direct their words. Their very presence on the religious scene was a lie—because the implication was that God sent the prophets. Their reckless attitude caused them to exhibit reckless action. When the people would ask those prophets (leaders), "What is the oracle (burden) or in other words: What does God want us to do to carry out His will, as the People of God, within a world needing our witness?" They were asking the wrong question of the wrong people. In their spiritual condition, the prophets were NOT the arm of the Lord's witness.

Because the majority depended upon man and never questioned the validity of the false prophets, the people had learned to lean upon lies and deceit to such a point they were incapable of making sound judgment. This very hour, a similar case is true within the modern church.

God's answer was shocking: "Stop asking THOSE questions to THOSE guys!" Three groups were gathered as one in this mandate: the people, the prophet, and the priest. The Lord gave three directions: first, He told Jeremiah what to say to the combined group.

> *So when these people or the prophet or the priest ask you [the real prophet, Jeremiah] 'What is the oracle of the LORD?' you will say 'What oracle?'*

(By repeating their question, Jeremiah was, in essence, saying: "Oh, yes, that supposed oracle. Well, if you really want to know the oracle of God, then I will give the real oracle.") The real oracle of God is:

> *I will even forsake you, says the LORD.*
>
> Jeremiah 23:33 (NKJV)

(Jeremiah was told to give the latest oracle (the latter always supercedes the former) from God, one that can be unequivocally relied upon: "I will even forsake you.")

The Lord's second command was to the combined group:

> *And as for the prophet [false] and the priest and the people who say, 'The oracle of the LORD!' I will punish that man and his house. [Just for saying those words]*
>
> Jeremiah 23:35(NKJV)

Speaking directly to the three "P's," the Lord commanded them not to delight themselves in believing that they had an oracle. If they even said the phrase: "the oracle of God," the Lord's punishment would fall on them. (Has anyone ever told a child, "I don't want to hear you say that again," and within minutes hear those forbidden words? What was the reaction?)

Third, the Lord forbade them from asking the prophet (the false ones) about the oracle of the Lord. "Your neighbors' word and your friends' word would be as reliable as the 'unsent prophet,'" the Lord said.

God advised the populous to seek for themselves the word of the Lord, right from the mouth of God, but they were never to proclaim that word as an oracle. This was an extremely important matter. If someone even used the phrase, "the oracle of the Lord," instant judgment would fall. The Lord said they "perverted the words of the living God, the Lord of Hosts, our God." God was angered at hearing His word perverted. (The perversion of God's word and words is so severe today, that justice and truth lie dead in the streets.) The punishment was spelled out, "I, even I, will utterly forget you and forsake you, and the city that I gave you and your fathers, and will cast you out of My presence, and I will bring an everlasting reproach upon you, and a perpetual shame, which shall not be forgotten (Jeremiah 23:39-40, NKJV)." (When people require an oracle from God, they should brace themselves for real truth.)

Parallels are all over the place with this issue of the "oracle." En Punto requires speaking only the words of the Lord, from a heart clean before the Lord, and at the place of the Lord's choosing. The false prophets missed it in all three arenas. (They are not alone, for thousands of pulpits, prelates, and pastors do exactly the same thing every week. God sends no word, but they speak with the same authority as if He had. The people, seeking to know the Lord's will, are dependant on the veracity of their remarks. The presence of a religious leader in a place presupposes the leader acts for God. Not So!)

The Lord drew the line in these verses and has never redrawn it.

This word stands! The principles put forth in these passages are several: first, there is a common word and common judgment for people, priest, and prophet. Listen carefully, the people were not excused for believing the lying lips of a false prophet, neither are the congregations of today—excused.

Another principle is that every man is responsible to hear from the Lord himself. Yes, there are many carefully cropped messages brokered from crystalline pulpits, but they lack one element—they are often spoken when God did not! The word of the Lord is to be found by the believer—on bended knee-in the "secret place." Thousands of misdirected efforts are undertaken by unsuspecting laborers because some person "at the front" took liberties with the word of the Lord. It is past time to repent! Repentance is a mandate, lest the church become "an everlasting reproach and a perpetual shame."

The word of a true prophet (and that of a true leader) sounds different from those who are not in this category! True words are affirmed in the Spirit and are true renderings. So reliable were the words of the prophet Jeremiah, that the prophet Daniel read his work and found answers for questions that had not risen in Jeremiah's day. In other words, when Jeremiah penned them, he had no inkling he was penning answers for Daniel. Think of it, there were answers in Jeremiah's writings that applied to Daniel's questions! That is how the true word works. Listen to Daniel, a prophet in his own right, read from Jeremiah's words (recall that the Lord had directed Jeremiah to record his prophesies in a book):

> In the first year of Darius the son of Ahasuerus, of the lineage of the Medes, who was made king over the realm of the Chaldeans—in the first year of his reign I, Daniel, understood by the books the number of the years specified by the word of the Lord, given through Jeremiah the prophet, that He would accomplish seventy years in the desolations of Jerusalem.

Daniel 9:1,2 (NKJV)

Daniel's reaction, when he read from Jeremiah, was a great intercessory prayer in sackcloth and ashes. Daniel confessed for himself and then the people—their failures and disobedience. The words of Jeremiah, upon the heart of the man of God today, will elicit the same results. The problem today lies in the fact that God's people have not read Jeremiah—let alone gotten as far as chapter twenty-five, verses 11-12. Observe how Jeremiah's words affected his day.

In 2 Chronicles 36, the Lord placed a synopsis (miniature picture) of the spiritual tenor of Jeremiah's society. The scene focuses upon Zedekiah (v.12): "He also did evil in the sight of the LORD his God, and did not <u>humble</u> himself before Jeremiah the prophet, who spoke from the mouth of the LORD." Chronicles continues:

> *He stiffened his neck and hardened his heart against turning to the Lord God of Israel. Moreover ALL the leaders of the priests and the people transgressed more and more, according to all the abominations of the nations, and defiled the house of the Lord which He had consecrated in Jerusalem. And the Lord God of their fathers sent warning to them by His messengers, rising up early and sending them, because He had compassion on His people and on His dwelling place. BUT they mocked the messengers of God, despised His words, and scoffed at His prophets, until the wrath of the Lord arose against His people, TILL THERE WAS NO REMEDY*
>
> (v.12-16, NKJV).

Name one abomination that was done then which is not done today in the houses called after His Name. Speak up! Silence reigns! Guilty! Guilty, a thousand times over, must be the pronouncement by the teller of truth! The Lord supplied a remedy for Daniel: it was to fall on his face in confession. This remedy is open to the churches of today, but where is that remedy being applied?

While Daniel was searching for an answer for his spiritual puzzle, he found it and also found the need for repentance. Such is the way of the Word of the Lord. If one would know the way to hear from God, start with His word.

[**Author's Note:** The following study is mandatory for the people of God who have an intercessory calling.]

MOSES AND SAMUEL

These great men of the Bible are mentioned by Jeremiah in the fifteenth chapter. This was not the only time in the word of God where great men of the past have been used as examples. Just as Moses and Elijah appeared on the Mount of Transfiguration, standing as representatives of the Law and the Prophets, so these men stood symbolically. There was a difference: Samuel, not Elijah, was chosen to form this twosome. Samuel represented the end of the Eli System and the beginning of a new order. It was a new order based on the person, not the office. The Lord told Eli that He would honor those who honored Him. Instead of honoring the Priesthood as a unit, He made it a matter of individual sanctity.

There is a further difference: both these men were great intercessors. Jeremiah is saying in essence, "even if the great intercessors came before me, I would not change my mind." God specifically said, "I am tired of relenting (Jeremiah 15:6, NKJV)." The Lord had held back His judgment upon this nation while He searched for the righteous. No one like Moses and Samuel could be found among them. Therefore, the Lord began to enumerate the consequences of that lack. (A beautiful study in miniature relating to Moses and his office as intercessor can be found in Psalm 106 [Addendum #3].) In reviewing the Lord's anger with the children of Israel during their wilderness journey, the Psalmist wrote:

> *Therefore He said that He would destroy them, Had not Moses His chosen one stood before Him in the breach, To turn away His wrath, lest He destroy them...*
>
> Psalm 106:23 (NKJV)

Even if the mighty "breacher," Moses, arose in Jeremiah's day, the Lord would not allow him deference.

Listen to the Lord's "I will's:"

> "*I will hand them over to trouble,*"
> "*I will appoint over them four forms of destruction,*"
> "*I will stretch out My Hand against you,*"
> "*I will winnow,*"
> "*I will bereave,*"
> "*I will destroy,*"
> "*I will bring,*"
> "*I will cause anguish and terror.*"

All these things came to pass on the generation of those who thought they were doing the exact will of God. Their religious community was filled with prophetic reassurances, with one exception, Jeremiah. Hark! Observe this carefully: when the sound from pulpit, pew, temple, townhouse, conference, and convent are so similar as to say the same things—look out! The religious world is at this place now!

Turn again to the text passage on Moses and Samuel. In their day, each had their opponents, but they had their God. In both lives, they faced down the vile and stood firm for the sacred. In both cases, their God was their guide and none other. In both careers, character stood above coin, as they refused to make any move without a move of God. Both men knew what the voice of God sounded like; they knew what it was to attend the words of the Lord. Both men stood as gateways to a new direction from God: Moses from Egypt to the new land, Samuel from Shiloh to Jerusalem. These bright lights from Hebrews 11, as powerful as they were, could not change the destiny of judgment on Israel. Israel had gone too far! (Think of how far Christendom has traveled.)

As verse nineteen pointed out, when the sacred is mixed with the vile, the prayer of the intercessor is polluted by its surroundings. The pure sound of a Moses and Samuel, standing in their several offices, failed against such pollution. There is a time when there is no remedy. God said in the last days, we ought to understand this truth! (Having a Moses and a Samuel in our spiritual past does not compensate for having folly in our spiritual present.)

THE SASH (Jeremiah 13)

This passage has been chosen by the Spirit as the fifth correlative to En Punto. The sash was made of linen, which depicts its holy use. Linen clothes were worn when entering into the presence of the Lord. "For as the sash clings to the waist of a man, so I have caused the whole house of Israel and the whole house of Judah to cling to Me," says the Lord, "that they may become My people, for renown, for praise, and for glory; but they would not hear (13:11, NKJV)."

Imagine a nation worn like a sash around the person of the Lord. Displayed for the universe to behold, this nation was to be like the fine linen worn by the priesthood. Israel was to be pure, clean, holy, and emblematic of the personal closeness they enjoyed with God. Spiritual Israel occupied a dignity afforded it by being God's personal choice of adornment. Their usefulness was signified in that they were destined to: "hold things in place, while I did my work." Israel would be "right there with Him as He moved among the peoples of the earth and would function as a beautiful token of how God wants His People to be close."

Instead, they had been put away for their rebellion and hidden away for another time because of their stain. No washing of water was to be upon them, for ritual cleansing was not sufficient. Tucked away from the presence of the Lord, they were subject to all the stains of association with the earth, something that would never have happened had they remained the "chosen sash." The "chosen sash" was marred beyond usefulness and stained beyond cleansing. This is the story of the sash. The symbolic sash of Jeremiah had a spiritual significance beyond that of a mere garment, however. Look at a few of these significances.

It is necessary to point out many of the spiritual parallels between Jeremiah's sash, and Judah and Jerusalem worn as a sash. Jeremiah's sash was one of personal choice, just like their nation was chosen by the Lord. Jeremiah's sash was worn for a short while; God also was only able to wear His sash for a short while. Jeremiah's sash was worn for both utilitarian and emblematic purposes. (A waist sash is worn so close to the body that the body of the wearer scents it.) This nation should have been as a fragrance of the Lord. Jeremiah was to hide his sash in a rock at the river Euphrates. The Euphrates was one of the streams from the garden of God after it left the garden. It was portrayed in this picture as the pure river of God having been contaminated by the world. Its contact with the world had caused it to become like the world.

Jeremiah's sash, instead of being hidden in the secret place of the most high, was tucked away in the world and in contact with the world and its erosive effects. It stayed away from the presence of God long enough to become useless. Hidden away from the constant cleansing that is appropriated to the presence of God, it became an irredeemable object—though it once served a high purpose. It exemplified the sad deterioration of historically significant items cherished for "the place they once occupied."

A rotten painting, a termite eaten chair, and a rotten garment falling apart at the threads through constant exposure to sunlight share the graphic portrayal of the sash. All these items could be mourned not only for their uselessness, but for the fact they are lost to posterity.

The "beloved of God," separated from the source of life, found themselves a scurrilous castaway. No nation can exist on its past usefulness in the hand of the Lord and His kingdom; they must remain in contact—being full of His cleansing. Being brandished as the sad remains of a sash carries no glory. Why did this happen? Jeremiah offers an explanation from God:

> *This evil people [remember they considered themselves to be righteous], who refuse to hear My words, who walk in the imagination of their heart, and walk after other gods to serve them and worship them, shall be just like this sash which is profitable for nothing.*
> *For as the sash clings to the waist of a man, so I have caused the whole house of Israel and the whole house of Judah to cling to Me, says the Lord, that they may become My people, for renown, for praise, and for glory; but they would not hear.*

Jeremiah 13:11 (NKJV)

The Lord spelled out the purpose for wearing Israel and Judah as a sash. It was His intention to make them His people. It was His intent to adorn them with renown, praise, and glory. Then He used those great negating words, which clear from memory everything that has gone before: "BUT they would not hear."

Is this not the sin of every body of believers in this present hour? Who in Christendom believes they are not "O.K." in their frail state? Who, among all those naming the Lord as King and Jesus as Savior, dares cry out; "We are become Useless to Him." Who is it that confesses, "We are become profitable for nothing?" Who acknowledges; "We walk according to whatever comes to mind, and worship in the same manner?" Who, among Christendom, does not act as if they are already in "renown," the progenitor of "praise" or the repository of "His glory." There is a renown (based on the power of money, prestige and numbers). There is a praise that comes from "services" so designed as to raise the emotional or religious level of its participants. There is a glory that emanates from man (but it is a glory diminished by thousands of years of sin.)

No, the sash was not washed, cleansed, or restored (renewed by new cloth or by introducing new thread). There was no talk of its future. Like the summary of an assayer, it was written off as being "profitable for nothing." Such is the indictment of most of what is held dear to Christendom's ranks, the works of their hands, and the pride of their accomplishment. Instead of a sash for every season, God has chosen not to wear emblematically a "body of believers" who refuse to "hear." Jeremiah did not stop with this illustration; he pointed out the role of the assayer.

THE ASSAYER

Jeremiah 6:27 is the sixth focus of En Punto in Jeremiah. Jeremiah was told that he was appointed as an assayer and a fortress. Although the combination does not seem congruent, in reality it is. Given the attitude of those he was addressing, one aspect would seem to follow the other. Actually, in the text, both words are linked. Assayer, "bachan," means "to examine, try, prove or test." Jeremiah was unique in his use of this word. The only other place in the Bible it appears is in Jeremiah 9:7. "Bachun," is a similar word and is the Hebrew word for tower (like a watchtower). Fortress also carries a meaning as "a secure place." In other words, the Lord was saying (paraphrased), "You are going to ascertain the purity of My people, and all the while, you will do this in a secure place where outside influence is not a factor." Jeremiah was to do independent work, uninfluenced by the society, yet dealing with the society.

As assayer, the Lord gave him a grim picture of his duties. Those duties are the same ones He assigned to Himself in Jeremiah 9:7. The assayer was to determine the quality of the metal, the purity of it, the value and worth of it, the highest and best use for it, and the proper care of it. The Lord does not say, "Jeremiah, refine these people." He says in essence, "judge them." God holds the refining job for Himself. The Lord told Jeremiah to know and test their ways (their life and pathway). Some of the work had already been done for Jeremiah because the Lord had already assayed His people as stubborn rebels, walking slanderers, bronze and iron (important aspects), as well as corrupters. He told Jeremiah that even though He had put them in the fire of famine, pestilence, and sword, the wicked were still there.

In Ezekiel 22:18ff, the Lord explained the process He will use to capture and remove the impurities that are mingled in them. He planned to put them in the furnace of tribulation.

> *Son of man, the house of Israel has become dross to Me; they are all* **bronze***, tin,* **iron***, and lead, in the midst of a furnace; they have become dross from silver...As silver is melted in the midst of a furnace, so shall you be melted...*
>
> Ezekiel 22:18,22 (NKJV)

The Lord, through Ezekiel, called His people bronze and iron. This is extremely important to grasp because in this repetition there is a message.

There is a little passage in Leviticus, chapter twenty-six and verse nineteen, which is endemic to this passage in Jeremiah. The Lord explained, to His people, that should they determine not to walk after His command and obey His voice, then they would suffer some consequences. The first rung in the ladder of consequences was judgment at low intensity, however, the second quadrant of consequences would increase the intensity; It was in the second quadrant that iron and bronze were mentioned together. He promised to make their heaven iron and their earth bronze. In other words, He would not answer their prayers, and the fruit of their harvest would not come to pass. Israel knew what iron and bronze meant.(15) To them, it meant that God was going to put them in the seven times furnace. In the intensity of that furnace; all impurity would be evident and removed. Impurity is difficult to see from a surface examination, for without melting the entire metal, one cannot get to the impurity to pull it away. Just as the tares were closely sown in the wheat, so the people had allowed their rebellion to permeate the fiber of their being. Jeremiah was not given the job of furnace keeper, he was given the responsibility of assayer. Beyond determining the significant elements of the object, the task of the assayer was faithful reportage.

The degree of impurity must be reported to the rightful owner, meaning this information was God's alone to know. It was not the duty of the assayer to give anyone information except the party employing him. Thus, he must make his decisions and report back to the Lord. In His reportage, he was liable to be questioned about his accuracy and methodology. He must give a reason for his judgment. In the end, it would become obvious if the assayer and his benefactor agreed.

Oh, There is joy in knowing that your appraisal matches His! In doing His will, we find it is akin to "thinking, doing, and appraising" the universe before you, just as He does. This is why in the latter days, He assigned the saints this wonderful task. In Revelation 20, John says that the office of judge will (already fixed) be given to the saints.

> *And I saw thrones, and they sat on them, and judgment was committed to them.*
>
> Revelation 20:4 (NKJV)

Oh Assayer, what do you find today among those who name the name of Jesus? What will you report to the King of Kings? Do you not know that part of the process of assaying is acknowledging the elements of impurity within oneself? Do you not need the Spirit to point out certain things within the life of the Assayer that must be cleansed and brought under scrutiny? Those that sit on thrones must! Pure casts out the impure!

Author's Note: It was the prospect of that "throne-ship" that moved within the heart of Jesus as He was sent to the earth. It was a constant before Him: "Don't miss the throne!" It must be a constant before us in the last days. Look heavily into the next chapter for a more complete study of this portent.

CHAPTER NINE

Jesus, Epitome of *En Punto*

*I*f you found Jesus in the Temple, it was because He followed the Spirit's prompting to go there. If He laid hands on the sick, or raised the dead, or prayed all night, it was because the Spirit led Him. No turn, no advance, no word was outside the scrutiny and realm of the Spirit. He and His father walked as One, talked as One, worked as One. When He prayed for those who were His, His request was for them to be One in Him—just like He was with the Father.

His Gethsemane prayer of "not My will, but Thine be done," showed proof enough of His obedience to the exact will of the Father. It was His obedience to that will which led Him to Calvary. His obedience to the cross was the gateway to the throne. One must always precede the other.

Calvary was a fixed appointment in time, and everything either moved toward it or flowed from it. Jesus had to be on time, prayed up, walking without sin, following exactly the leadership of the Spirit. There was no room for dalliance, for dalliances thwart destinies. The twenty-first century is a cavalcade of religious dalliance. Its splendorous amusements suck life from its public and demand allegiance on the level with a pagan deity. Ask any believer who can ascertain the truth, "What determines your day?" Then look at the dalliance. Ask Jesus, "Who or what determined your day?" His answer would have been swift, "The Father!" The very same Father holds "the hour of the end," close in His mind. The same Father, carries the "broad picture of redemption" always in the forefront of His heart. Every person, even Jesus, finds his or her place in Him and in His great strategy for salvation. To the religious, history is a puzzle; to Him, it is a portrait. All believers, who follow the example of Jesus, find that they too have a schedule to meet, a schedule which demands they be prayed up, paid up, and postured.

In Isaiah 50, there is a most beautiful portrayal of how Jesus ordered His life; in sublime sentences, the prophet synopsizes Jesus' heart toward the Father.

> *The Lord God has given Me the tongue of the learned, that I should know how to speak a word in season to him who is weary, He awakens Me morning by morning, He awakens My ear to hear as the learned. The Lord God has opened My ear; and I was not rebellious, nor did I turn away.*
>
> Isaiah 50:4,5 (NKJV)

This was how Jesus began His day, walked through His day, and ended His day. When Jesus declared that in His earthly walk, He was not rebellious nor did He turn away, He was saying this was His mode of life. He was the example; that was the regimen! The same regimen that Jesus observed must be our regimen. We must be awakened by His hand and directed by His voice—everyday. We must know His plan for that day. Our tongues must speak words which have been crafted by the Father. His words are the ones which are in season to those who are weary. (Millions in Christendom are weary. They are weary of working in the fields of manmade religious pursuit and being rewarded with a church-defined glory. The psalmist, David, rightly spoke: "You , O Lord, are a shield for me, My **glory** and the One who lifts up my head [Psalms 3:3 NKJV].") It is His words which stir the human heart like no others. His word has the power to quicken ears so they will hear.

According to Isaiah, the Lord is the One who must awaken our ear ("stir up" is another definition for "to awaken"). From "stirred up" ears, our souls are "stirred within us" (did those on the Emmaus Road not say that it was His words which caused their hearts to burn within them?) Without being "stirred up," there is nothing to say. Why does it seem those who have heard the least speak the most? Why are religious leaders so intent to speak from hearts which have not been stirred?

Chronicling the life and ministry of Jesus through the gospels with an eye toward the Isaiah 50:4 passage, reveals some latent truths. Jesus was on God's schedule. Self determination was not His forte. At the age of twelve, He said, "I must be about My Father's business." Note the use of the term "business," (tois, means: affairs of /or things of My Father) rather than ministry. The Father's business demanded discipline and perceptivity. It created a schedule of its own and required diligence. It was based on a plan and the execution of that plan. It, however, was the Father's business; it was also the Father's plan! The Father determined the realms where His business was to take place. He determined who would represent His business and in what domain. The Father is the determinate in all areas of His business. The Son had to learn the business for Himself, so one day the Father could say, in essence, to Him: "Son take over the business." Jesus invested himself in the Father's interests. To learn the Father's business calls for the investment of time, talent, and tenacity. This was an investment; this was an entering into the personal world of the Father. Every believer must know what it is to be about "my Father's business." The equation of "the Father's business" is not equal to the embedded religious concept described as "ministry." Often, "ministry" stands in the way of the "Father's business.

The "Father's business" is not a clandestine enterprise, for He who created all things left no avenue of doubt that His Son is the center of His plan. Prophets heralded things that would take place in the Son's life with such accuracy, that for Jesus, it was an ever unfolding pageant. Similar accuracy is available to every believer. The stumbling, error-prone church needs to spend time on its knees until accuracy returns to its ranks.

Review the gospel accounts and note the times when Jesus went places in order to fulfill biblical prophesy:

1. Matthew 4:13: And leaving Nazareth, He came and dwelt in Capernaum, which is by the sea, in the regions of Zebulun and Naphtali, that it might be <u>fulfilled</u> which was spoken by Isaiah the prophet, saying:

   'The land of Zebulun and the land of Naphtali, The way of the sea, beyond the Jordan, Galilee of the Gentiles: The people who sat in darkness saw a great light, and upon those who sat in the region and shadow of death Light has dawned.'

   Isaiah 9:1,2 (NKJV)

2. Upon entering Peter's house and finding his mother-in-law infirm, Jesus healed her and a multitude of others who came to the house.

   That it might be <u>fulfilled</u> which was spoken by Isaiah the prophet, saying: 'He Himself took our infirmities and bore our sicknesses.'

   Isaiah 53:4 (KJV)

3. Matthew 12:15ff: "But when Jesus knew it, He withdrew from there, and great multitudes followed Him, and He healed them all.

And He warned them not to make Him known, that it might be <u>fulfilled</u> which was spoken by Isaiah the prophet, saying:

> *'Behold, My Servant whom I have chosen, My Beloved in whom My soul is well pleased; I will put My Spirit upon Him, and He will declare justice to the Gentiles. He will not quarrel nor cry out, Nor will anyone hear His voice in the streets. A bruised reed He will not break, and smoking flax He will not quench, Till He sends forth justice to victory. And in His name Gentiles will trust.'*

Isaiah 42:1-4 (NKJV)

4.   Jesus began to speak in <u>parables</u>, and as Matthew 13:14 pointed out, it was in order for scripture to be <u>fulfilled</u>:

> *Hearing you will hear and shall not understand, And seeing you will not perceive; For the heart of this people has grown dull, Their ears are hard of hearing, and their eyes they have closed, Lest they should see with their eyes and hear with their ears, Lest they should understand with their heart and turn, So that I should heal them.*

Isaiah 6:9, Luke 8:10(NKJV)

> *Matthew 13:35: That it might be <u>fulfilled</u> which was spoken by the prophet saying, 'I will open My mouth in <u>parables</u>; I will utter things which have been kept secret from the foundation of the world.'*

5.   Jesus' triumphal entry into Jerusalem was based on fulfilled prophesy. Matthew 21: 4,5: All this was done that it might be <u>fulfilled</u> which was spoken by the prophet, saying,

> *'Tell the daughter of Zion, Behold, your King is coming to you, lowly, and sitting on a donkey, a colt, the foal of a donkey.'*

Zechariah 9:9(NKJV)

6.   When Jesus was talking with His disciples before His arrest, He again met a Divine appointment:

> *Then Jesus said to them, " 'All of you will be made to stumble because of Me this night, for <u>it is written</u>: 'I will strike the Shepherd, and the sheep of the flock will be scattered.'"*

Matthew 26:31; Mark 14:27
Zechariah 13:7 (NKJV)

7. Jesus had His garments divided. "...that it might be <u>fulfilled</u> which was spoken by the prophet:

"They divided My garments among them, and for My clothing they cast lots.

Psalms 22:18 (NKJV)

8. In Luke, there is a passage oft quoted for its compact description of the anointed ministry of Jesus, yet it is the fulfillment of that which was spoken centuries before:

The Spirit of the Lord is upon Me, Because He has anointed Me to preach the gospel to the poor, He has sent Me to heal the brokenhearted, To preach deliverance to the captives And recovery of sight to the blind, To set at liberty those who are oppressed, To preach the acceptable year of the Lord. Then He closed the book, and gave it back to the attendant and sat down... And He began to say to them, 'Today this Scripture is fulfilled in your hearing.'

Luke 4:18-21 (NKJV)

9. Jesus in speaking to his arresting party, affirmed that daily he fulfilled the scripture written about Him.

I was daily with you in the temple teaching , and you did not take Me. <u>But the Scriptures must be fulfilled</u>.

Isaiah 53:7

10. Jesus turned His face to Jerusalem on another occasion with no other purpose than to fulfill the word of God:

Then He took the twelve aside and said to them, 'Behold we are going up to Jerusalem, and all things that are <u>written by the prophets</u> concerning the Son of Man will be accomplished.'

Luke 18:31; Psalms 22 (NKJV)

11. Jesus, in explaining to His disciples the necessity of being defensible, mentioned the following verse:

For I say to you <u>that this which is written must still be accomplished</u> in Me: 'And He was numbered with the transgressors.' For the things concerning Me have an <u>end</u>.

Luke 22:37, Isaiah 53:12 (NKJV)

The great plan of the "Father's business" was extremely detailed for Jesus.

It is impossible to believe that the same accuracy by which these matters materialized in the daily walk of Jesus are not definitive for "His Business" today. NO! The Father has a plan—with "Jesus-like people" in that plan. These must speak the exact word He issues, on the exact day He prompts, in order for that plan to be fulfilled. Yes! The Father has ordained His Sons in the earth to walk in their own destinies—doing exact things, in a certain way, on a certain day, at a certain hour, so the last days will be a fulfillment of those things spoken by the prophets.

With gusto, the pulpits of Christendom proclaim: "God has a plan for your life." However, never in their wildest dreams have they imagined the exactness required to carry out that plan. Marshalling troops to follow some meandering trail of "man-determined" program or plan has been "simple." It required little discipline. The "simple" follow such leadership. Modern congregations have allowed dalliance to replace diligence, and subsequently, the plan of man has been substituted for the plan of God.

Those who consider themselves "Sons of the Living God," have lost contact with the Business of the Father! His plan requires attention to detail. Attention to detail is a vital ingredient in industry but is rarely seen in religious circles. Attention to the details of the Father's Business is well nigh unheard of.

Every day, there must be the fulfillment of God's concerted plan upon the earth. Can you not see this picture? His work constitutes a mighty chain of belief, linking the obedience of one believer to the obedient act of another. God's plan may require a saint in the Ukraine to rise early and pray in order to intercede for power to be upon one of the Lord's children in Africa. Without the prayer in the Ukraine, the soul in Africa is not emboldened. This is an intricate linkage. So vital is this linkage, that prayer warriors have little idea about the power they possess—often moving heaven and earth with their obedient prayers. The church is silent most of the time about this subject because the church as we know it is carnal and far from the purpose of God!

Envision God's dignitary (Defined as a servant who does not rebel against the guidance of the Lord, but rather turns toward Him) scurrying to a task as he or she feels an urgency inside him or herself. He or she is bid to travel across town and speak a word in season to a weary soul. That weary soul, upon hearing the obedient messenger, with the encouragement of his words resounding inside, now is emboldened to speak or do that which the Lord God has commanded him or her to do. From the "Emblazoned Saint" issues a phrase, a treatise, a written score, that, when spoken or written, causes great spiritual upheaval in the camps of darkness. Evil is thwarted; God's power is released. Why? The Divine linkage system has done its exacting (En Punto) work!

Linkage is an important part of the Lord's work, yet few are even conscious of its power. This kind of astuteness is vital, for if one emulates Jesus, no other demeanor will do. Consider the accuracy by which Jesus lived His life, and then realize the Lord has not changed His ways. He, who sent the prophets, will commission those in the latter days who are willing to be sent.

God's plan is not always a plan with no pain, however. It was so for His Son, and it will be so for those who make themselves available to His Plan. Better to die in the midst of carrying out the exact plan of God, than to live carrying out the plans of man. The structures of man will to be destroyed. The Bible is clear in Revelation 6:11:

> And a white robe was given to each of them; and it was said to them that they should rest a little while longer, UNTIL both the number of their fellow servants and their brethren, who <u>WOULD BE</u> KILLED **as they were**, WAS COMPLETED.

> (NKJV)

God has a plan that includes martyrdom such as the world has never known. No wonder power words were used by Paul such as, "stand," "endure," "suffer," and "remain faithful." These words are to be imprinted onto the believer's most inner being.

Stephen's only sermon, his focal witness on earth, came to a conclusion of rocks. Did he have an inkling that the God given message, that came pouring out of his belly like living water, would cause blood to pour from his veins as well? How was he to know, when the first words passed his lips, that the anointing on those words would be life to the hearers and death to him. Stephen's martyrdom stood in the great plan of God. He sacrificed himself, like Jesus, at the exact moment, on the exact day, at the exact hour that Saul of Tarsus was in the crowd. (How important was it for him to be obedient unto death? Once he made the decision to speak, the other followed in course.) Has God's plan for the end of the ages some method of by-pass whereby the modern saint will be excused from such obedience?

Every believer is expected to be in his or her place, moving in the Spirit and carrying out his or her specific duty, in order to be within His master plan. Observe the beauty of such a plan: His plan is not dependant upon our obedience, but our judgment is.

Consider how intricately defined are these last days. Two witnesses appear on the scene in Revelation BEFORE the woman and man-child of chapter twelve. These two witnesses are strong and powerful (Are they not portrayed as prophets with unusual anointing?). At this specific moment, because time is short—somewhere on the earth— a unique calling may well be coursing the spirit of some boy or girl, man or woman, prompting them to stand and be those witnesses. They are being prepared, encouraged, and directed, today. Their appearance on the scene of their "moment of destiny" will play an important part in the prophesied word of John in Revelation 10:11. Their plight is set. Regardless of one's treasured eschatology, these prophets are people of destiny, and wherever they appear on one's chart is immaterial to fact. They will appear at the exact moment known in the heart of God. He has a plan! It is also in His plan for these men to be overcome by Satan. It is His plan to breathe into them life and revive them.

These witnesses will function under the prophet's anointing. They will be like those yielded prophets of the Old Testament (God still has some who are "available to be sent."). Their words will not bend or be compromised, which indicates that the earth has been void of such preachments. Since their message is one of torment to their listener's; is this evidence that the hearers have never heard a strong word from a strong body of believers? Could it be the Laodicean church never repented, never purchased the necessary appointments of Revelation three? (It is to the "over-comers of luke-warmness" that a reward is given.)

No place will be found for those who remain in Laodicea and loll under the teachings of the "Rabbi's of Redefinition." These rabbi's declared wealth when God declared poverty. Laodician rabbi's declared revelation when God declared blindness. These rabbi's declared, "they had need of nothing (they had it all)," while God declared they were miserable, wretched, and naked. If this congregation prevails to the time of the great tribulation, there must certainly be a need for two prophets.

Two early witnesses appeared in history before these "end time" ones. The former witnesses turned fire upon no one; nonetheless, they stood as "absolutes" in a playground of religious relativism. They were Jesus and John, the Baptist.

RABBI'S OF REDEFINITION VERSUS TWO WITNESSES

Jesus walked with John the Baptist, and like the two witnesses of Revelation, they hurled into the religious scene invectives that could not be ignored. The Temple message which was preached in Jesus' day was a message that had been refined by the "Rabbi's of Redefinition." The people were so deceived that a precious few could see the truth and come away from those teachings and traditions. (For the reader to fully understand the degree of deception, imagine darkness being accepted as light. At the beginning of this study, a passage was used in Isaiah 50; it is now appropriate to continue in this prophesy in order to visualize the extent of that deception.)

> *Who among you fears the Lord? Who obeys the voice of*
> *His Servant? Who walks in darkness and has no light?*
> Isaiah 50:10 (NKJV)

Isaiah asked a fair question because no one who walked in obedience; all walked in darkness—since light was inherent in fearing the Lord and obeying His voice. No one feared; no one obeyed. Thus, the prophet pinpointed the difference between man's light and God's Divine Light.

> *Look, all you who kindle a fire, Who encircle yourselves*
> *with sparks; Walk in the light of your fire and in the sparks*
> *you have kindled—This you shall have from My hand:*
> *YOU SHALL LIE DOWN IN TORMENT.*
> Isaiah 50:11(NKJV)

The Lord differentiated between the true flame, which lights the path of man, and the light kindled by man. God's light directs man's path to obedience and the exact plan of God. The difference is the brilliance of the sun, compared to the embers of ashes. The "ember" portion of that difference is where the church is today. Encircled with the embers of a fire kindled by the hands of man, the church rejoices while languishing in ignorance of the true light. God's people, who obey His voice and fear the Lord, walk in a brilliance unknown to and never experienced by them. How can this be? Better yet, the question is now: "how did Laodicea ever become the end-time church?" Could it be they had minister's of redefinition in their pulpits? There are some answers to these issues.

REDEFINED LIGHT: EMBER LIGHT

Isaiah addressed, primarily, a body of believers, who considered themselves enlightened. In reality, they were only lighted by embers. Jesus spoke to a body of believers who considered themselves enlightened as well. The Temple crowd of His day was an "embers crowd." Today, the Spirit speaks to a body of believers who consider themselves enlightened. They, too, are an "embers crowd." Therefore, the judgment of the first lies at the door of the latter.

Yet, the central truth of Isaiah's question was the central truth of Jesus and the Spirit. Ember-light can only exist as true light when those who accept it have redefined what light is. The righteousness of the Scribes and Pharisees was only acceptable in a Temple which embraced the redefinition of righteousness. (The Spirit of God is showing the people of God, that universally, there has been a redefinition of almost every truth in the word of God.) Cultural, sociological, and psychological definitions have redefined righteousness, glory, sanctification, and the work of God. This has been done in order to coincide with man's ember-light. The product of such appeasement is a corporate structure accustomed to the dark. The kind of commitment to the plan and work of the Lord, which was detailed in this chapter of Isaiah, is unheard from pulpit and pew in modern society.

The Lord said (through Isaiah), that it is not possible to walk in Him and not have the true light. It is the absence or presence of His light which is the determining factor of judgment. Light can only be derived from the author of light. His words, "Let there be light," still form universes. It is the same for the soul of man to whom He utters, "Let there be light"—a spiritual universe is opened to him. Spiritual light produces spiritual enlightenment. Enlightenment traditionally has been the foremost quest of mankind. This is especially true in theological circles. If, however, the quest ends in failure, somewhere in the darkness, one can make out the shadow of the modern congregation.

If modern hearts are true and will answer honestly, there is not as much spiritual light as is being claimed. Evangelists speak of it, pastors claim it, prophets proclaim it, but alas, what is called light, in their redefinition of terms, is really modified darkness. Herein is the whole specter of the modern religious world; it is a world of redefined terms. The phantom of redefinition hovers with its shroud seeking to change, minimize, and detoxify the Spirit that fell at Pentecost. It was into a world of theological redefinition that Jesus was born. History gathers itself again to stultify and rename every grace, and every sin, according to its terms and on its conditions.

Jesus is coming again and surprise (to the "supposed" body), He will find the same ethos as He found before. The redefinition attempts made during His earthly walk are resurfacing in modern clothing. In order not to be affected by the teaching of the temple and synagogue in His earthly ministry, it was necessary for Him to keep an open ear to heaven. This was why God specified His modus operandi in Isaiah 50. Is it any wonder that Jesus was awakened by the Father every morning and was given the tongue of the learned, and the ear of the learned.? His ears had to hear different things than the ears of the high priests of redefinition. His tongue had to speak different things than the rabbis of redefinition. Why? Because He received from the Lord. and the Lord still has His wisdom ready for the non rebellious. The question is, "Who will turn their face toward Him."

The key to the ministry of Jesus was not that He had sinless blood flowing through His veins, but that He had a ready ear to the Father. He did not strain the words of the Father through the sieve of redefinition. It is easier to redefine "glory," than to be possessed by the "Spirit of Glory (I Peter 4:14)." It is easier to redefine "miracle," than to abdicate the "throne of my dictation," and allow Him to work one. (Currently, there is such a demand for "miracles," that miracles must occur on a weekly basis or something is deemed wrong with one's ministry or church—who determined that?)

REDEFINING THE MINISTRY OF JESUS

The endless list of the "redefined," seeks to extend itself even to the redefinition of the ministry of Jesus. His ministry and life is being redefined every week, every Sunday (as well as every opportunity men choose for a gathering), whether in conference or convention. What is the result of such redefinition of Jesus and His ministry? There now stands a church, who does not know its founder. It is ironic that those who ushered in the twentieth century were credited with knowing more spiritual truth than those who have ushered in the twenty-first! If this is not so, then, why are those pioneers used as the continual point of reference for credibility?

DEFINITIVE WORK OF JESUS

Jesus set the definition for much of what theologians and churchmen have tried to redefine. The True Light of the world still shines upon human religious effort, and in its spot light restores what has been eaten away.

There can be only one definition of the life and ministry of Jesus. He was the Son of God, who walked by the Spirit of God, and heard the voice of God from which He did not rebel or turn away. He focused His life upon one thing—He must occupy the throne by the right hand of the Father. He must occupy it or redemption, which was to be finished, would have gone unfinished forever.

Herein is the tragedy of the mindless, heartless, godless morass called Christendom—to them there is no picture of Revelation 20, no throne to occupy, no voice to be heard above every voice, no will to be done above every will. There is no sense that if they fail, that which must be finished will forever go unfinished! Alas, the soul not witnessed to is lost! The stronghold not pulled down executes its victim as surely as the hangman! These are spiritual matters which are being dealt with by Christian-humanism. Humanism sees every task as earthly and appropriates nothing to the realm of the Spirit. Paul needed no textbook to understand the idiocy of using human reason to approach spiritual matters; he cast it aside.

Paul challenged believers to run for the prize of the high calling, a portent for which no one in Christendom can now define. Religious spin has made "the High calling," extinct. A mandate that once began, "Go ye into all the world and make disciples," has been modified to mean, "ministry."

Candles, you see, are no substitute for the "high calling," neither are pithy sayings, poured over an excuse of a sermon, related to "His Light."

Lest the reader forget, *En Punto* is that state of being holy on the highway of Holiness. It is Spirit-being mediated through a life of being— "there." It is Man's, "NOW," in harmony with God's, "I Am." It forever remains in the present tense.

While Jesus carried out the exact plan of the Father for His life, He was met with continual opposition from the "refined of the redefined." Their concepts of the good and the holy were antithetical to His teaching about the subject. Review a few of the challenges He encountered, and it will become evident that the "spiritual leaders" had been trained by the rabbi's of redefinition.

Matthew 7:29:   for He taught them as one having authority, and not as the scribes.

Matthew 9:14:   Why do we Pharisees fast often, but Your disciples do not fast?

Matthew 12:2:   Look, Your disciples are doing what is not lawful to do on the Sabbath.

Matthew 13:54:   Where did this Man get this wisdom and these mighty works?

Matthew 15:2:   Why do Your disciples transgress the tradition of the elders?

Matthew 21:   the chief priests and the elders of the people confronted Him as He was teaching, and said, 'By what authority are You doing these things? And who gave You this authority?'

Shallow-spirited churchmen present plenty of opportunity to discuss shallow issues. None of these matters had an ounce of spiritual content, but they represented the total concern of their initiators. Jesus did not use these occasions just to blast the hierarchy; Jesus used these times to reply with the exact word of the Father. It was necessary for Him to be in the presence of these officials in order for certain words to be spoken to them. His words, then, became judgment to them.

In like manner, the Lord wishes His servants today to be ready to render His exact words, so judgment may come. Jesus expected few who heard these words to repent. He was fully aware of His words' import and scope, along with the reason for saying them. Jesus was no "pinball-being" rolling around on God's Game-table. His work was not a chance bumping into this or that occasion, nor was He characterized by rolling down some trough in order to light up a score board of spiritual points.

Jesus awoke by the hand of the Lord, and His day walked out the plan of God for His life. (Perhaps, someone reading this text will discover its truths and begin a purposeful walk in the Lord which will uproot the trees of redefinition and clear the disenchanted forest like a cyclone.)

These are the last days and the Lord is raising up "over comers," "...because it has been given to you to know the mysteries of the kingdom of heaven, but to them [which are not over comers] it has not been given (Matthew 13:11)." To the over comer, it was said, "Have you understood all these things?" Their answer was concomitant with their commitment, "Yes, Lord (Matthew 13:51)!" The formula is forever simple, the voice of the Lord must produce, in the saint, an immediate, "Yes!, Lord!"

Paul cautions not to lose the "simplicity of Christ (II Corinthians 11:3)," and rightfully so. Jesus did what the Father told Him to do. In like manner, He trained His disciples, "So the disciples went and did as Jesus commanded them (Matthew 21:6)." The disciples had listened well to His words in Matthew 12:50: "For whoever does the will of My Father in heaven is My brother and sister and mother." This is called the "formula for immediate response."

This "formula of immediate response" was summarily attacked by those who had not committed their lives to Him. As John 3:16 is the pivot on which redemption stands, so II Peter 3:16 is pivotal to understanding those who seek to circumvent His words:

> *Paul...also in all his epistles, speaking in them of these things, in which are some things hard to understand, which those who are untaught and unstable twist to their own destruction, as they do also the rest of the Scriptures.*
> *You therefore, beloved, since you know these things before-hand, beware lest you also fall from your own steadfastness, being led away with the error of the wicked; but grow in the grace and knowledge of our Lord and Savior Jesus Christ. To Him be the glory both now and forever. Amen.*
> II Peter 3:16-18 (NKJV)

Paul was aware that even those in the early church would have to contend with these "minister's of redefinition." His words of caution still ring true:

> *...such are false apostles, deceitful workers, transforming*

> *themselves into apostles of Christ. And no wonder! For*
> *Satan himself transforms himself into an angel of light.*
> *Therefore it is no great thing if **his ministers** also trans-*
> *form themselves **into ministers of righteousness**, whose*
> *end will be according to their works.*
>
> II Corinthians 11:13-15 (NKJV)

In these accelerated days, close to the end time, how many are listening to one or more of these metamorphic transformations?

> *The coming of the lawless one is according to the working*
> *of Satan, with all power, signs, and lying wonders, and*
> *with all unrighteous deception among those who perish,*
> *because they did not receive <u>the love of the truth</u>, that they*
> *might be saved. And for this reason <u>God will send them</u>*
> *strong delusion, that they should believe the lie, that they all*
> *may be condemned who did not believe the truth but had*
> *pleasure in unrighteousness*
>
> II Thessalonians 2:9-12 (NKJV).

Jesus walked through this tangled maze of satanic confusion with clear revelation. He gave the supreme example for us to follow. As He walked in continuous revelation, so must we all.

Paul spoke of such in Galatians 2:2: "And I went up by revelation and communicated to them the gospel." This is the essence of the walk of Jesus on the earth. The miracles, the wonderful teachings, the marvelous acts of kindness were characterized in His accolade concerning the faith of the Centurion. The Centurion spoke to Jesus about how his servants responded immediately to his command, of —"come" and "go." In like manner, he simply asked the Lord to give a command and he would be convinced a miracle would follow. Jesus knew this man moved as an "authority" under authority. Jesus did the same! So must we!

Author's Note: The next chapter deals with realms of authority.

CHAPTER TEN

Spheres of Authority

C oterminous to the study of *En Punto* is the study about realms of authority. Jesus was the progenitor of this teaching in His dealing with the Centurian. Jesus marveled at the Centurian's faith, thereby laying emphasis upon "authority under authority." The Apostles understood that spheres of authority were given them and they in turn taught others. Paul also knew the boundaries and the blessings related to spheres of authority. He was constantly aware of being assigned certain areas, projects and works, which no other person could accomplish and beyond which he would not reach.

> *For we dare not class ourselves or compare ourselves with those who commend themselves. But they, measuring themselves by themselves, and comparing themselves among themselves, are not wise. [This is one of the great sins among churchmen today.] We, however, will not boast beyond <u>measure</u>, but <u>within</u> the LIMITS OF THE SPHERE WHICH GOD APPOINTED US a sphere which especially includes you.*
> *For we are not extending ourselves beyond our sphere [thus not reaching you], for it was to you that we came with the gospel of Christ; not boasting of things beyond measure, that is, in other men's labors, but having hope, that as your faith is increased, we shall be greatly enlarged by you in our sphere, to preach the gospel in the regions beyond you, and not to boast in another man's sphere of accomplishment.*

> II Corinthians 10:12-16 (NKJV)

Paul introduced the subject with a single comment, "For even if I should boast somewhat more about <u>our</u> <u>authority</u>, which the **Lord gave us** for <u>edification</u> and not for your destruction, I shall not be ashamed (2 Corinthians 10:8,NKJV)." Although the reader is not given details, two things are evident. First, there is a clear distinction between traditional authority vested in man (sociologically speaking, there are certain social roles which have authority built-in them, "tax-collector," "judge," "clergy," "President.") and are different than authority given by God for edification. Second, there are realms of authority which differ in scope within the various spheres of God-given authority.

Spiritual authority occupied a clearly defined role in the lives of the apostle Paul and Jesus. That role was determined in the heavenlies, for it was "other-world" defined. The natural world is structured to place certain persons, by reason of education, political position, or social standing, in places of authority. Society is so arranged to accept, validate, and rarely question, the validity of authoritarian office or the person in an office of authority. The higher the office, the higher the requirements for that office. Varying degrees of expectation are assigned to each level of social authority. As the position rises in power, that position commands a greater degree of expectation. The clearest picture of this was the trichotomy between the power-authority of Rome, the lesser authority of the Jewish religious courts, and the greater spiritual authority of Jesus. That trichotomy is still apparent.

Spiritual authority is not derived by any of the means on which social authority is based. Yet, there is evidence aplenty, those who occupy religious position today have gotten to those stations by the same methods and through the same machinations as their worldly counterparts. Paul and Jesus would have none of it.

(In the study of power, there are many forms and methods used in power structures. The most common is the "rational-legal" authority which is bestowed by society to bureaucratic entities through enacted rules and regulations. Bureaucracy in religious circles is arrived at in the same manner. Charismatic authority is another, arrived at through extraordinary personal abilities while inspiring devotion and obedience; it follows as a close second. In religious circles, this is the most popular form of invested power. None of these authorities approximate what Jesus and Paul taught as spiritual power.)

Paul pitted himself against those who operate in man-delegated or socio-hierarchical power in spiritual matters. He also clarified his stance by acknowledging that there are others, beside himself, who occupy spiritually assigned places. Paul refused to compare himself with those who were so spiritually assigned. The reason he refused to compare himself with these "spiritual-others" was simple—every assignment is unique and carries with it the necessary spiritual tools to carry it out. These tools equip the person with supernatural assets which are not inherent in that person. Neither the assignment nor the tools are matters for personal boasting. If there is glory to be gained from carrying out the assigned spiritual role, let the Lord receive the glory—and let the accolades of a job well done come from Him. These lessons form the initial criteria for operating in Spirit-determined authority.

Within Paul's framework system of authority, there are few examples which can be pointed to in modern religious organization, not because the Lord has ceased to assign spiritual authority, but because those who occupy God-appointed positions may not be "surface-apparent." Many of those who claim spiritual positions on the surface do not possess those positions by the Spirit. Hence, Paul's teaching does not include many areas of power which are in operation within Christendom today.

With traditionalized power comes title and rank; this is why Paul did not scurry to be called, "Bishop," "The Right Reverend," "His Eminence," "Superintendent," or "Missionary Evangelist, Paul." What relationship have these titles and their respective offices to the real task? Most of these positions are engaged in carrying out the works of man.

Paul differentiated between those who occupied "invested" hierarchy and himself. They gained their right to boast based on a comparison test that amounted to "one-upmanship" or at the least, "horizontal acceptance within man's tolerance levels." It was against such that Jesus struggled on a daily basis. By whatever name the synagogues of today are called, whether church, cathedral, or assembly hall, their staff is as fully exemplary of spiritual incapacity as their counterparts in Jesus' day (High Priests, Pharisees, Sadducees and Rabbi's [this group, not the shepherds, missed the hour of His Birth]). Religious hierarchy approximates the corporate structure of business.

What society views today is a religious corporate ladder and that is why society accepts it so easily, condescends to it, and is satisfied with such arrangement. These religious offices have nothing to do with spiritual authority.

Spiritual authority is often known only to the Lord and the person to whom it is assigned. God is the sole authority above this kind of assigned authority. God alone judges whether or not spiritual authority has been executed to its fullest or not.

And all the churches shall know that I am He who searches

> *the minds and hearts. And I will give to each one of you*
> *according to your works.*
>
> Revelation 2:23 (NKJV)

Since there is no standard measure given man to determine who receives an assignment, or how broad the scope of the assignment, little is known about the whole nature of the office of spiritual authority. Paul offered insight, however, into this delicate area.

Serious concerns surround study of authority because much deception flows around this subject. This is especially true when man seeks to substitute traditional religious office for spiritual authority.

Since the Lord did not empower Adam to dominate Eve or, for that matter, to have dominion over other men, spiritual authority, necessarily, must have a different nature than that which is exercised within the framework of religion. (The only examples of religious authority within view of the average congregation is that which has been gained by worldly principles.) The majority of church members are only acquainted with vested authority; they have never seen spiritual authority, born-of-God, in operation. It was so in the time of Jesus; it is the same today!

The elder who dictates who must marry whom looks strangely like a Pope handing down edicts, rather than one occupying true spiritual authority. Neither Pope nor elder exercises true spiritual authority in these issues or, for that matter, any other matter. Both elder and Pope derive their position through legalistic processes; therefore, a principle can be derived from viewing their ranks: the weaker the spiritual authority, the stronger the dependence on legal authority. Spiritual authority does not operate in legalism.

Spiritual offices occupy themselves with different interests than vested offices. Spiritual authority is not interested in "coverings" or "convention." Spiritual authority is intricately tied to the "work" of the Lord. Its primary assumption is focused on doing the "work" of His kingdom.

In the life of Jesus, two words took prominence: "work" and "things" of the Lord. John, more than the other gospel writers, stressed these two venues. Spiritual authority was based on "assigned work" given by the Father to benefit His kingdom. The Lord empowers those who are to carry out, "His assigned work." It is His work which stands. It is His work which acts as the standard for all judgment. Those who do His work will hear, "Well done thy good and faithful servant." Those who do good works which are not His assigned work, will find piles of ashes as their reward (works tried by fire).

Jesus repeatedly, through His words and example, pointed out these differences. His indictment of the scribes, Pharisees, Sadducees, and Levites was based on this premise. Not one of them would have been accused of not doing "good works," but all of them would be accused on not doing the "Lord's work." They were constantly in the Temple; they were associated with every detail of worship and praise. They tithed; they gave of their time and their talent to the works of the Temple. They prayed, fasted, read the Torah, and observed carefully every sacred day.

Few of them recognized the true "work of the Lord," as was evidenced by their inability to recognize the Son of God. Jesus and His disciples were the only ones doing "the work of the Lord (Anna, Simeon and John, the Baptizer, were the exceptions)."Jesus possessed the spiritual power for the tasks given Him. His assignment was clearly to do nothing apart from that "work" given Him by the Father. Spiritual power and authority ONLY COMES in relation to "that work."

The most serious indictment against the modern church is that it cannot differentiate between the work of the Lord and the work of man. Therefore, it cannot discern spiritual authority. Hosea addressed frontally the issues, which read like a contemporary commentary, in his book written nearly three thousand years ago. Blinded by their iniquity, the prophet proclaimed to them:

> *And Ephraim said, 'Surely I have become rich, I have found wealth for myself; in all <u>my labors</u> They shall find in me no iniquity that is sin.'*

Hosea 12:8 (NKJV)

Their self-appraisal indicated the depth of their sin, for in vindicating their life style, they became transparent and revealed their heart. They used the phrase, "My Labors." To this, God said (paraphrased), "I have given them symbols through the witness of the prophets." Prophetic words hung over their society like drapes of judgment over broken windows of robbery. The words of Jesus to His generation assumed the same character. How difficult is it to see that "doing My labors" is different than the Lord's Work?

In *En Punto*, Chapter Nine, there was a discussion about the exactness of Jesus' ministry which took Him from place to place and person to person. If the reader will take the Gospel of John and pull out the physical movement of the Lord from beginning to conclusion, a wonderful revelation will take place. (Take the time to seriously look at all the places Jesus went and the sequence of them. John did a masterful job in portraying this truth. The physical territories acted as spheres of authority, where specific deeds and words took their special place.)

In order to study the passages in John related to this subject, it is necessary to look back to the focal scripture in 2 Corinthians 10:13:

> *We, however, will not boast beyond measure, but <u>within</u> the LIMITS OF THE SPHERE WHICH GOD AP-POINTED US, a sphere which especially includes you.*
>
> (NKJV)

The word "sphere," is elemental to this study. Derived from the Greek word "kanon," it refers to "a cane (kane)," "a measure, rule;" in the N.T., it means "a prescribed range of action or duty."(16)

A reference in the gospels to John the Baptist spoke of him as being a "broken reed (or cane)" (Matthew 11:7;12:20) in the eyes of his contemporaries. In the eyes of the Lord, he was one with great spiritual authority. No one (other than Jesus) had greater spiritual authority in the annals of spiritual history than John. John's measure of authority was tremendous.

Authority is given by measure. The Holy Ghost, who bestowes it, is without measure (a significant truth). Spiritual authority is a separate entity. Spiritual authority may be limited, expanded, changed, or removed by the One authorizing it.

Spirit-given authority has time and space delineations. There are prophetic utterances which eclipse the life span of the "utterer," while other words are within the framework of one day. That means Ezekiel's prophecies have spiritual authority down to the end of time.

Jesus' words have authority beyond the framework of time. Jesus did the "work" and "things" of the Lord, hence was never without power. He operated within the "sphere" God gave Him. It affected His every move and His every deed. When one understands this arrangement, then Jesus' words about "greater works will you do," take on added meaning. (Many rest from their own works, but to rest from "His work," is significantly different!)

John 4:34: "Jesus said to them, 'My food is to do the will of Him who sent Me, and to finish <u>His work</u>.' "

John 5:26-27,30: "For as the Father has life in Himself, so He has granted the Son to have life in Himself [any spiritual authority is part and parcel of Jesus' authority], and has given Him authority to execute judgment also, because He is the Son of Man.....I can of Myself do nothing [different from the humanistic teaching of the current church], As (in the continuous state of hearing) I hear, I judge; and My judgment is righteous, because I do not seek My own will but the will of the Father who sent Me."

Earlier in John 5, Jesus said: "Most assuredly, I say to you, the Son can do nothing of Himself, but what He sees the Father do; for whatever He does, the Son also does IN LIKE MANNER." (The exercise of spiritual authority is based on the premise of "in like manner.")

Later in John 5, Jesus declared: "But I have a greater witness than John's; for the *works* which the Father has given Me to finish—the very works that I do—bear witness of Me, that the Father has sent Me." Jesus declared plainly, that the works He did were assigned works. (What about the myriad number of works set before the body today as the "work of the Lord?" In reality, they are the works of man, designed for the glory of man, and clearly have no authority in them for spiritual consequences. Thousands are deceived into believing they are doing the "good works of the Lord," when, in actuality there is none of the Lord in those works [Be careful Mr. T.V. projectionist, Ms.Usher!].)

Just after Jesus fed the multitudes (a work of God), He taught the multitudes: "Do not labor for the food which perishes, but for the food which endures to everlasting life, which the Son of Man will give you, because God the Father has SET HIS SEAL on Him...This is the work of God, that you believe in Him whom He sent." (Jesus' teaching was clear, the spiritual work based in Him will produce that which does not perish.)

John 6:37-39: "All that the Father GIVES Me will come to Me, and the one who comes to Me I will by no means cast out. For I have come down from heaven, not to do My own will, but the will of Him who sent Me. This is the will of the Father who sent Me, that of all He has given Me I should lose nothing, but should raise it up at the last day." (This coincides with Paul's statements about the inclusion of the Corinthians in his sphere of authority. Spiritually, the Lord gave the Corinthians to Paul and He did not forsake them; he ministered to them, and their abundant work within that sphere would produce the total crop. Not one would be lost! The sphere would expand.)

John 8:16: "...I am not alone, but I am WITH the Father who sent Me." (He meant that His spiritual connectivity was a constant in His life.)

John 8:23: Speaking to the Pharisees, the most believing bunch in the whole religious realm (they believed in angels, the resurrection, divine healing, exorcism, and everything connected to miracles—they were the conservatives, the fundamentalists, the orthodox), he said, "You are from beneath; I am from above, You are of this world; I am not of this world."

John 8:26: "I speak to the world THOSE THINGS which I heard from Him." "Things" are both word and deed. Listen, those "things" are the words which must be spoken and the deeds that must be done in order to loose the captives, open the eyes of the blind, bring down spiritual barriers, and loose on the earth those spiritual elements which will change the universe. There are words which MUST be spoken in this generation.

There are "things" the Lord wants said today. There are "deeds" which He wants done today for the same reasons as in Jesus' day. They have life in themselves and when released upon the earth, produce manifestations beyond the significance that man places on them.

In Revelation 8, the prayers of the saints were mingled with spiritual incense and, upon being combined with spiritual fire from the altar of God, were cast upon the earth which caused "noises, thundering, lightening, and an earthquake (v.5)." Note the result of Jesus' speaking, "AS HE SPOKE these words, many believed in Him." It is not in the multiplicity of words that kingdoms are shaken, but in THE words given from above. (Oh!, when believers assemble, what would occur if they could hear THAT word?!)

It was just after this teaching that Jesus defined who a disciple was. John 8:31: "Then Jesus said to those Jews who believed Him, 'If you abide in My word, you are My disciples indeed.' " (Much of what is taught as "discipleship" today has no inkling of the teaching exposed in this chapter. To be a disciple, one must abide in His word just as He was faithful to abide in the Father's word. Just as He derived spiritual authority from His connectivity, He enjoins those who will be His disciples to do the same.)

In John 9:1-2: Jesus was coming out of the Temple, where judgment-words had to be spoken, and the reaction to those words was: "they took up stones to throw at Him." Jesus had to go outside the establishment to accomplish the work of His Father. (Sadly today, in order to do His Work, it may require going outside the establishment.)

OUTSIDE THE TEMPLE, the assigned sovereign work of God had to be done for a witness against them. A blind man needed healing and Jesus healed him—outside the Temple. There were two reasons for His action—to give sight to the blind and to establish further proof of blindness in those coming from the Temple. John 9:4: "I must work the WORKS of Him who sent Me while it is day, the night is coming when no one can WORK." Jesus, later on, said: "For judgment I have come into this world, that those who do not see may see, and that those who see may be made blind." (Listen, He did certain things because those acts were spiritual acts meant not just for the person, but to set in motion spiritual consequences—blindness in some, sight in others. Those with spiritual authority do the same.)

John 10:32: Many good works I have shown you from My Father. For which of those works do you stone Me?

If I do not do the <u>works</u> of My Father, do not believe Me; but if I do, though you do not believe Me, believe the WORKS, that you may know and believe that the Father is in Me, and I in Him (John 10:37-38).

The WORKS of the Father were done to produce faith in the observer. (How different these are from "random acts of kindness.") Faith producing works have results because power is released from them as was seen in John 10: 42, "And Many believed in Him there."

John 12:48-50: "He who rejects Me, and does not receive My words, has that which judges him—the WORD that I have spoken will judge him in the last day. For I have not spoken on My own authority; but the Father who sent Me GAVE ME A COMMAND, what I should <u>say</u> and what I should <u>speak</u>. And I know that His command is everlasting life. Therefore, whatever I speak, just as the Father has told Me, so I speak." (These words were spoken just after He centered on the prophetic words of Isaiah. The Pharisees did not believe Him, even though these were heavenly dictums.) John 10:42: "Nevertheless even among the rulers many believed in Him, but <u>because of the Pharisees</u> they did not confess Him, LEST THEY SHOULD BE PUT OUT OF THE SYNAGOGUE; for they loved the praise of men MORE than the praise of God." (This is the reason religious leaders do not repent and turn away from the fruitless systems they operate in this very hour. Listen to their jargon: "Brother, how many did you have in attendance today?" or "What size budget do you project for the new year?" These concerns have nothing to do with what Jesus was talking about.)

John 14:10-12: Do you not believe that I am IN the Father, and the Father IN Me? The words that I speak to you I do not speak on My own Authority; but the Father who <u>dwells in me</u> does the works. (This is a key passage, for the works are not generated with man nor carried out in man's power.) "Believe Me that I am in the Father and the Father in Me, or else believe Me for the sake of the works themselves. Most assuredly, I say to you, he who believes in Me, the works that I do he will do also; and greater works than these he will do, because I go to My Father.

(This verse and the next have been used many times to launch man's works and man's programs. Strutting these verses across the stage of man's performance was never the Lord's intention. The "greater works" are to be done in the same manner as the works done in Jesus and through Jesus. It is the Father who determines the work and does the work through us. Many a building program would falter if this truth were known, for there would be no financial resources to complete them.)

Jesus promises great authority and power to assist the believer in the task of speaking <u>His words</u> and doing <u>His deeds</u>. The Holy Spirit will assist and Jesus will answer whatever we ask in His Name, and then v. 23 will come to pass:

> *If anyone loves Me, he will keep My word; and My Father will love him, and* <u>WE</u> *WILL COME to him and Make* <u>OUR</u> *HOME with him.*

Jesus emphasized that these are not His words, but the Father's words, to them (14:24). He reiterated the source of His actions and words in verse 31:

> *But that the world may know that I love the Father, and as the Father GAVE Me commandments, so I do.*

> (NKJV)

Spiritual authority comes from the force of the originator of those words and deeds. John 15:14: "You are My friends **IF** you DO WHATEVER I COMMAND YOU."

Spiritual authority is not based on an office. It is not assumed through officialdom. Spiritual authority comes from heaven alone. John 15:15 ff, indicates that Jesus considered those who bear this authority to be "insiders." They are no longer servants but friends. He said that spiritual authority comes from His choosing, appointing, and protecting those so endowed.

Spiritual words and deeds must have a central producer, that producer is Jesus. Sometimes He simply says, "Speak Thus and Thus," for His command carries weight. Regardless of our opinion of those words, those are the ones which must be spoken. In like manner, Jesus often spoke things given directly to Him by the Father. He said them because the Father judged the occasion: "If I had not come and spoken to them, they would have no sin, but now they have no excuse for their sin... If I had not done among them the works which no one else did, they would have no sin; but now they have seen and also hated both Me and My Father (John 15:22,24)."

John 17:4: "I have glorified You on the earth. I have finished the WORK which You have given Me to do." (Jesus spoke it, Paul spoke it, and it is possible for the believer of this age to speak these words—"I have finished the WORK you gave me to do.")

John 17:18: "As You sent Me into the world, I also have sent them into the world." (Believers are sent out LIKE Jesus was sent out. They are to do the "Works," the "Things" of word and deed, that the generation around them may hear and see. The "things" from the Father and His Son must have vent upon the earth through our lips and hands. We are not sent out at random, to a world at random, saying random things and doing random deeds. Confused multitudes long to hear the clear sound of the Living God and to see the pure acts of His Hand.)

Jesus' words on the cross take on a different meaning in light of all that John has written. John 19:30: " So when Jesus had received the sour wine, He said, 'It is finished!' and bowing His head, He gave up His spirit." Jesus was referring to more than just Calvary when He spoke those words. He meant that His life had culminated by accomplishing every word and deed at the exact behest of the Father. Every word and deed was on time and in time. Paul said similar words but another way: "I have finished my course, I have kept the faith (II Timothy 4:7)." Jesus and Paul understood the framework that surrounds the spheres of spiritual authority.

Paul understood that, within the perimeters set by the Father and the Son, there were words that must be spoken and deeds which must be accomplished in order for judgment to stand complete. God has ordained this to be. Rocks will speak, if man refuses!

Spiritual authority does not rest in traditional power such as the bishopric, the pastor, the deacon, the elder, but in the specific spiritual "sphere" given by God for edification. Paul cautioned Timothy: "And they will turn their ears away from the truth, and be turned aside to fables, but you be watchful in all things (II Timothy 4:4-5a)." There are thousands who attempt to take the scriptures and bend them until they apply to almost all areas of "church life." These are the same people who seek to legitimize man's works and draw favor from their constituents. Because the words of the Bible have spiritual authority which remains to the present, great judgment will fall on these false teachers. Yet, they persist!

Another group, however, give themselves to pure renderings from the Lord and are aware that by doing so, they offend those who do not. They do this, in the face of a clear teaching that the real work (words and deeds done within the "sphere") may well cause castigation and death. However, it is in the "limits of the sphere," where great authority can be applied because the source of that authority is God. (The church has rarely seen God-assigned spiritual authority at work. There is no model for them to turn to as an example. This is about to change!)

God has assigned and still assigns "sphere's" today. I know of one man who was assigned a whole city as his sphere. He was given that assignment while residing in a distant town, far from the assignment city. While praying in the Spirit, the Lord revealed His work. The Spirit gave the man a vision of the entire city area. The vision took the man out of his body (so to speak) and carried him on a Spirit-tour of the area. The Spirit showed briefly where pockets of resistance to the work of the Lord had formed. He showed him inside governmental offices and revealed scenes of theft and corruption. He carried him from one side of the city to the other, pointing out family units under darkness and why no spiritual-awakening had taken place within its boundaries (though it was a very old community). Then the Spirit directed him to sell his personal property, in a place where he had resided for twenty-five years, and go and build a house in that city, so that he actually owned a part of his mission. The man was obedient. While building his house, every laborer, with the exception of two men, made a commitment to give their lives to Jesus. Even truck drivers delivering materials fell under the power and influence of the Spirit.

After the house was built, the man was led by the Spirit on different occasions to go to certain places in the city and walk the streets proclaiming, "Jesus is Lord over this street and these houses."

In three years, that man and his wife walked every street in a city of sixty-seven thousand. They distributed thousands of tracts and ministered to many hundreds of people. They witnessed to many of the city officials and had influence with union leaders and tradesmen. They mixed with professionals and business leaders, many of whom would cross their path while they was carrying out a God-assigned task.

Often the Lord would have the man stand on the deck of his home and shout into the wind, "Thus saith the Lord God—corruption and defilement will depart this city government." Sometimes, the Spirit showed him the offices to be affected. In a short while, discovery of graft came to light. Newspapers reported over thirty people had been indicted for crimes in various places of responsibility within three years. The city went from being in the red financially, to being in the black during this time.

Many times, the man was directed to walk along ocean docks and pray that those places which had been virtually silent for ten years would come to life and bless the economy. Within one year, a major company located there. Within two years, a multi-million dollar agreement was signed, putting the wharves back in operation. Today, steamship companies and new port facilities (along with several other commercial enterprises) are alive on its docks. The city manager claimed that for the next ten years, millions in income were already contracted for.

The man of God was shown to approach every church, synagogue, and meeting house (several were store front churches) and pray for the pastor and the congregation to have a new experience with the Lord. Laying hands on the physical buildings created a point of contact to release the exact words to be spoken over them. Recently, a major evangelist has decided to concentrate on this city as a project for revival.

No one in council chambers or commerce halls would acknowledge this God-called man had anything to do with the favorable effects on that city, but this man was sent by God and given spiritual authority in many realms. True transformation can only occur when God-assigned men and women carry out those assignments specifically. Who can judge the work? Who knows the disasters avoided, the tragedies missed? Who can surmise what blessings yet lay ahead because of His faithfulness in word and deed? Spiritual authority (limits of sphere's) can and do require one quality: "What the Lord says do—must be done."

God is currently stationing His people in strategic places. There currently are massive changes going on in the realm of the Spirit. There are people who never would have dreamed that the Lord would give them a city, who are receiving cities. These are their cities to pray over, labor in, love and weep over. They must become like Jesus, who wept over Jerusalem. He spoke Divine words over His city: "O Jerusalem, Jerusalem, how oft would I have gathered you like a hen doth her brood."

There are men and women of God who are being given "sphere's" in neighborhoods, communities, territories, principalities, and even countries.

People are migrating from their native lands to occupy places of spiritual authority in places all over the world, some permanently, some temporarily. Two examples come to mind, one in the Ukraine and another in Colombia.

A young man in the U.S. felt a strong urge to go to Kiev and pray. The Spirit led him to a central place in that city near a statue of a Communist leader (it has since been removed). By faith, he prayed what the Spirit led him to pray. For several weeks he maintained his vigil, listening as the clock in a central tower "bonged" the passing hours. Sensing in the Spirit that his assignment was nearing an end and not having seen one change in anything or anyone around him, he asked God to show him whether or not to continue. The Lord allowed him one more day and very clearly revealed he must leave and with urgency. What transpired?. Chernobyl! This is an example of a specific sphere of authority during a specific time, but on a temporary basis. Spheres vary in time and duration.

In Colombia, there is a missionary family who occupies a place of more permanent authority. Although Colombia is characterized by terrible instability, the authority of this family increases as instability increases. Their prayers in the Spirit have protected millions from harm and danger. They have poured out their lives as Paul, "for I am already being poured out as a drink offering [which cannot be gathered back to them]." They, and their father and mother before them, are living examples of spiritual authority given by God over a sphere of a country.

As large groups of missionaries and others abandon the nation, the sphere of these faithful witnesses increases. They have had impact in the government and in the general society among indigenous natives and among cosmopolitans. Vast opportunities open to them due to the empowering of the Holy Spirit. It is evident that the life of the son will increase, above the father, in scope and in spiritual impact, as his generation continues to hear the voice of God. Daily, they are called into new arenas to carry out responsibilities of supplying spiritual materials to the nation's military, reaching into prisons, and even testifying to guerilla forces. Their radio broadcasts reach those incarcerated in prisons and those in the countryside who are incarcerated by guerilla activity. They do not take lightly their task, which has extracted extreme prices for their commitment. They have experienced captivity by communists resurgents. Life threats have been made on their children and themselves. They are constantly being bombarded by forces of darkness across the spectrum of their work—but God!

This family is an example of the positioning of thousands into places of spiritual authority. Not just missionaries, but business people, military families, teachers, oil related workers, computer technicians, and scores of professional and non-professional personnel are being placed strategically, by God, throughout the world.

There well may be more than one person or persons exercising their assignments simultaneously within a given area. The Lord alone is the One who guides these activities. No one is in competition with another. No one compares his or her work with another, for many times he or she is unknown to the other. Spiritual authority is not based on glorifying man; it is sourced in the One who must receive glory.

I have seen "wheelchair grannies" with such power that spiritual and physical doors burst open by themselves for them. "Well done, good and faithful servant" is not the reward for "doing good things;" it is a reward for "doing His thing—well."

Jesus spoke to this issue in Matthew 7:21ff:

> *Not everyone who says to Me, 'Lord, Lord,' shall enter the kingdom of heaven, but he who DOES THE WILL OF MY FATHER IN HEAVEN. **Many** will say to Me in that day, 'Lord, Lord, have we not prophesied in Your name, cast out demons in Your name, and done many wonders in Your name?' AND THEN I will declare to them, 'I never knew you; depart from Me, you who <u>practice</u> lawlessness!'*

> (NKJV)

Notice several factors in this passage: first, the double use of the name, Lord. If Jesus was their Lord, they would have been busy at "His work." Lordship is dominion. Working within the sphere of His dominion is primal to His Lordship. (Many work in religious activities which neither reflect His dominion or are under His dominion.) Second, is the use of the word MANY. "Many" means just what it says. Dominions and powers belong to Him and He uses the word, "many." (Could this mean countless thousands?) Third, is an accounting of various religious practices. Whatever wonderful exercise of religious prowess it may seem to be, which emanates from man and not God (even by those who are deemed most spiritual), it is sin to Him. Prophecy, exorcism, and wonders are mentioned specifically in this passage because of their proximity to genuine acts of the Father. These acts become deceptive in the hands of deception. Countless deeds of flesh are referred to by man as the "work of the Lord," when in reality, they have no hint of God in them. Alas, the blinded church cannot tell the difference; therefore, it faces the judgment which will come from following deception. Evil has its shareholders.

> *If anyone comes to you and does not bring this doctrine, do not receive him into your house nor greet him; For he who greets him SHARES in his evil deeds.*
>
> 2 John 10-11(NKJV)

Just as evil shares with evil, the same is true of the righteous sharing with the righteous. Nothing proves this point as much as Hebrews eleven.

Hebrews eleven is a showcase of sharing spiritual authority. Its membership includes slaves, kings, the illiterate, the educated, the fragile, the timid, the strong, and the weak. Often, their names are not included; some of their mighty deeds are. They, along with the multitudes in white, who stand in awe of His Throne, are those who have exercised spiritual authority within the "sphere of their appointment." The lineup in Hebrews has few counterparts in the modern church. What causes this lack?

What seems to be lacking in the realm of the religious is true spiritual authority. The insipid, fraudulent acts of power displayed daily in counseling chambers, pastoral advisory forums, committee activities, and study groups has nothing to do with the spiritual power exerted under God's authority. No congregation is accustomed to an Elisha calling for bears, or a Simon confronting Annanias, or Nathan's pointed finger. Just as the pillar of fire and the cloud is absent, so is the true glory. Christendom has settled for spiritual deception beyond the proportion of the Old Testament prophets' day. They had no New Testament, no printed book they could carry with them. Greater judgment must befall a body who has both the Bible and the ease of one's own copy.

Though the church cries loudly, "We know the Lord," they should remind themselves that they have repeated the wayward word of errant Israel in Hosea's day:

> *And they do not know the Lord, The pride of Israel testifies to his face; therefore Israel and Ephraim stumble in their iniquity; Judah also stumbles with them... (5:4)*

> *...They have begotten pagan children... (5:7b)*

> *...are like those who remove a landmark [so no one knows the boundary between God appointment and man's votive] (5:10).*

> *...Ephraim is oppressed and broken in judgment because he willingly walked by human precept... (5:1 l)*

> *...I will return again to My place till they acknowledge their offense... (5:15)*

> *...I will chastise them according to what their congregation has heard (7:12)*

> *...I have written for him the great things of My law, but they were considered a strange thing (8:12)*

> *...For Israel has forgotten his Maker, and has built temples (8:14)*

> *...the prophet is a fool, the spiritual man is insane (9:7)*

> *...the prophet is...enmity in the house of His God (9:8)*

> *...They became an abomination like the thing they loved (9:10b)*

> *...Yes, woe to them when I depart from them (9:12)*

> *...My God will cast them away because they did not obey Him. (9:17)*

What is the remedy? Real spiritual authority needs to return to the house of the Lord and to His people. This kind of authority often rests on those "outside" the camp because those "inside" the camp are blind to their ways (even as Ephraim, Judah and Israel).

Spiritual authority **is** coming upon the earth in these last days! Enhanced by visions of where spiritual strongholds lie, God-sent words will once again be heard from authoritarian lips. Fiercely armed with a knowledge of Him that surpasses the supposed wisdom of the "enlightened," these saints will call down fire and resist to the face those who betray the kingdom. They will speak to mountains, trees, open fields, buildings, walls, and fortified bastions without judging it to be foolishness. They will be unafraid of man and man's furtive judgments, for they will operate only in the realm of the Spirit. The modern church will fear them! Governments will fear them! The ungodly will be in terror before them!

These are they who, being in their exact places, at the exact time, will utter exact words and do the exact deeds necessary to bring closure to "THY KINGDOM COME, THY WILL BE DONE ON EARTH AS IT IS IN HEAVEN."

Author's Note: The next chapter will continue the theme found in this one. It will extend the ramifications of being exactly in the place the Lord defines. One thing is for sure, as the Lord's great day approaches:

It is time to judge, it is time to repent, it is time to be—EN PUNTO!

CHAPTER ELEVEN

The Place Called "THERE"

DEFINING "THERE"

"There" is a real place. It goes beyond the theological concept of "the perfect will of God," not because "there" is superior to that concept, but because "there" is more concrete than a concept. With a concept comes the ethereal confluence which allows for places like: "just a little outside the perfect will of God," or "living in the permissive will of God," or that wonderful place called,"the secondary will of God." Those places don't even come close to "there."

Within "there," either you live in its confines or you do not—it has definite limits. One knows when one abides at "there." "There" is a spiritual state within a physical surrounding. It is possible to live on earth in a mortal body and live in the place called "there" at the same time. The spiritual and the physical aspects of "there" are not antithetical; they are harmonious.

Actually, there is a highway leading to "there," but few there are that find it. Many temporary places seem like "there," but they are not "there." The confusion comes because there are many temporary places which are the real "there" for today, but are not the "there" for tomorrow. Being "there" is a daily matter. The children of Israel experienced this while in the wilderness. They camped everyday at "there" and waited for the cloud to move or the fire to move to the next place called "there." Sometimes the cloud did not move; sometimes it lingered a long while. The children of Israel learned one thing: The blessing, protection and provision of God was wherever "there" was. Abraham chose to live in tents and be wherever "there" was for him rather than return to his country and rather than mess up and live in places like Sodom. Being "there," for Abraham, was wherever the Lord led him. "There" is the same place for us. The Scriptures tell us that Abraham sought a city whose builder and maker was God. We seek the same place. Scripture says we are pilgrims and wanderers. Most believers have no concept of the magnitude of this issue. We fit God into OUR schedule rather than have no schedule but HIS. It is easy to settle in like Lot. Then there is the need for being rescued.

Once someone settles into a temporary "there," the real "there" moves. The temporary "theres" are stations along the way to the real "there." The real "there" is fluid; it is a progressive state of being where "He is." If one settles into a temporary "there," one has a choice, when it moves, to either move or stay at "here," which is where "there" was before it moved. Don't get confused. This is a spiritual matter as well as a territorial matter. Many people have decided to camp at the last outpouring.

"Here" is a nice place; it is sometimes very comfortable as individuals have more control in the place called "here" than the place called "there." This, of course, is the basic difference between "here" and "there"—the matter of control. HE is in control of "there." "Here" has its history; "there" has its future."

It doesn't take long being around people who have settled in at "here," before it shows. They talk about different things than those who dwell at "there." Their interests are different; their time is spent differently; things that really matter to them are not the same as citizens of "there." "There people" sometimes don't talk as much as "here people," because they have observed the"here people's" reactions when they do. "Here people" are constantly explaining why they are not "there." (To walk in the Spirit is to be "there," and no excuse will suffice for living at "here.")

CITIZENS OF "THERE"

Every generation has had its citizens of "there." Abraham said he sought "there," but he described it as a city whose builder and maker was God. Enoch lived in "there," and it no longer mattered whether he was on earth or in heaven, for there was no difference between the two to him. Paul revealed the same truth when he said that it did not matter whether he lived or didn't live on earth, it was the same. Paul lived at "there." For him, "there" was not always amicable—sometimes it was filled with the opposition.

I Corinthians 16:8-9 says:

But I will tarry in Ephesus until Pentecost. For a great and effective door has opened to me, and there are many adversaries

(NKJV)

"There" for Paul was defined as being in the exact place God wanted Him to be for as long as He wanted him to be there. It is the same for all true believers. Effective doors open to those God knows will be willing to walk through them. This is why the fearful and unbelieving have no part in the kingdom.

Lest the reader fail in trying to understand this concept, thinking that "double" speak is being used in this chapter, let his or her attention be drawn to a passage in the *Song of Solomon*. Solomon's use of the word, "there" in his Song was indicative of a special place known to two lovers. Lovers sacrifice their own wishes to please each other.

I am my beloved's, and his desire is toward me. Come, my beloved, Let us go forth to the field Let us lodge in the villages, Let us get up early to the vineyards; Let us see if the vine has budded, Whether the grape blossoms are open, and the pomegranates are in bloom.

THERE *I will give you my love, The mandrakes give off a fragrance, and at our gates are pleasant fruits, all manner, new and old, Which I have laid up for you, my beloved.*

Song of Solomon 7:10-13 (KJNV)

(**Author's Note:** See Bibliography No.12. The text cited is a commentary on the *Song of Solomon* entitled, *Solomon's Secret*.)

Solomon literally filled this passage with teaching about the place called "There." In this passage, the Shulamite (symbolic of the Bride of Christ) had come to full maturity in her walk with the King. By the time "there" was introduced, the issues which would have kept her out of the place called "there" had already been resolved. Numerous spiritual milestones had been passed prior to her introduction to this special place. She had abandoned the delicacies of the banquet hall (place, provision, security by familiarity, where wonderful provision had been made for her every comfort). Her comfort was not an issue anymore. Her attempts to make the banquet hall her "there" were met with His words,"Come away with me, my love."

The special place, toward which He was beckoning her, lay beyond her vision. Once His vision became her vision, she abandoned her earthly ways. (Earthly ways can produce a "strong-hold" in the lives of those who consider themselves identified with the Bride.)

She had to make the decision whether place or person was the object of her life. Would it be His way or her way? She soon proved her choice. She relinquished her desire to integrate Him into her cultural "heritage." (Up until now, she had insisted on her terms for their being together by seeking to bring him to her mother's chambers.) The Church seeks to bring Him into their earthly realm rather than seeking His "there."

Each abandonment of her ways was met with a deeper manifestation of His glory. To embrace Him on His terms was better than to remain lonely and longing for His touch. In the city, the Watchmen were charged to protect her, but they were not needed when she walked and lived with Him. The protection of His presence was better than the patchy covering of an errant watchmen! His closeness was more to be desired than any communion the world afforded. The discovery that she knew Him better than those who just knew about Him was a life-changing revelation. She knew Him and wanted to be near Him, for where He dwells is always in the place called "there." He dwelled at "there" His whole ministry, for He communed in harmony with the Father. He ministered powerfully from "there." (The question of why His ministry covered certain territories and not others is answered.)

A confident power pervaded their relationship when she finally recognized her place was WITH Him. His repeated appeals to,"Come away," were actually invitations to come to the place called "there." She began to recognize His heart dwelled in "there." At last, her heart sought to dwell at "there," too.

When the final invitation came, she did not hesitate but gladly walked the fields of "there" with Him. She viewed those fields as He viewed them. She traversed the villages and beheld His ministry and saw how different His definition of ministry was. Her former understanding of the term was marred by misconception. His ministry, His way of being and doing, superceded all pulpit definitions she had ever heard. Ministry at "there" was different from all other aspects of what the world had defined as "ministry." Ministering from the place called "there" is a different ministry. It has all the power of His Presence. Being "there" is the sole prerequisite for ministry.

Other benefits issue from being "there" as well, for prosperity and true harvest emanate from its courts. None of the false, accommodative religious bragging will be heard in its streets. The Imperial Palace of His Kingdom operates fully in the realm called, "there."

"**There** I will give you my loves," were words that introduced the Bride to a place where she could receive His love in unparalleled terms. He lavished His love upon her at the place called, "There."

"There" was and is a state of being, where proximity to Him and His love is never diminished. To be "there" was to share with Him in Spirit without measure. To be "there" offered a quality of living which surpassed the "heaven" defined by religion. (It is not the Nirvana of the East Indian sects, nor is it the works-oriented "heaven" of the Muslims or the ill defined "glory land" of old time religions, or the cross-keyed domain of a Catholic hierarchy. All those domains are from identical patterns--which purport some far away place. All of them conceptualize someplace almost unattainable—a place where certain qualities are demanded and whose guarded entry doors exclude the uninitiated.) The real "there" is greater than that. "There" is a place filled with "knowing Him," based on one premise: intimacy with the "Most High."

"There" is an attainable place. Jesus occupied the place called "there" while He was on earth. He cried out, "Me and My Father are One." He said He did nothing except what the Father told Him to do and said nothing but what He heard from heaven. A revelation of how He ordered His life around the Father is found in Isaiah 50:4-5:

> *He awakens Me morning by morning,*
> *He awakens My ear To hear as the learned.*
> *The Lord God has opened My ear;*
> *And I was not rebellious,*
> *Nor did I turn away...*

(NKJV)

According to this passage, Jesus lived every moment of His life in the place called "there." Isaiah said, every morning when He opened His eyes, He looked the Father in the face. It was His Father who woke him daily. His dependency on the close proximity of the Father is to be our example as well.

He did not turn a deaf ear to the Father. He did not turn His back on the Father. Jesus prayed that we, who follow Him, might be just like He and the heavenly Father were—ONE. Jesus knew great blessing accompanied such proximity, blessings as rich as those found in treasure chests. Solomon said those treasure chests were to open to us in the place called "there."

"There," according to the *Song of Solomon,* (7:13) was where spiritual and physical treasures were laid up. The king offered the Shulamite entry to the treasure-chamber of God, for it resides at "there." (v.13). The new and old treasures spoken of in those passages were specially fitted to adorn the ones who came to "there."

Until now, the journey of the Bride had been filled with temptations, distractions and halting. Her journey was also bounded with those who were encouragers, who asserted invitations to go on to greater heights spiritually. Finally, she acted as He acted. She determined to live in the constant flow of revelation about herself and her lover. Such knowledge poured from the well of understanding at the place called "there." The Lord wanted His Bride to come to the place where she would enjoy all that He enjoyed.

"There" is a place of activity. It has fields, villages, farms, and folks. It has fragrances, blooms, and food. It is also filled with discovery about the Kingdom, but mainly, it is where He dwells. "There" is filled with Him, His glory, His power, His unfolding adventure into realms which are incomprehensible to a religious mind. "There" has its Ethiopian Eunuchs, its river Chebars, its High and Lifted Ups. "Theres" boundary begins with "Yes" and continues until it hears,"Amen (so be it)." "Amen" to all He says, wills, and wishes is the great response of its citizenry. His deepest assurances, His great buoying faith, and His greatest joys, are to found at "there." "The fear of the Lord," His greatest treasure, is shared with His people at "there."

Isaiah 33:6 declares:

> *Wisdom and knowledge will be the stability of your times, and the strength of salvation; The fear of the Lord is His treasure.*

> (NKJV)

Reverential confidence pervades "theres" streets, confidence that all He has said and all that He has done was done for His Bride. To possess the treasures of "there" is to own the "pearl of great price."

"There" has its music. Its music is the constant harmony between lovers; its anthems pour from two hearts made one; together their voices blend in singing, "Holy is the Lord."

"There" is the place where prayer is met with action: "You can ask what you will and it shall be done unto you." When one is "there," all the quandary as to proper words, appropriate order, and the acceptability of one's requests vanishes. The minds of its populous are at perfect peace with His mind. They have carried out the command of the Apostle Paul: to "set your affections on things above." "There" is the secret place of the Most High," spoken of in the Psalms.

David spoke of a place under the "shadow of His wings," and the worldly church surmised that he was speaking of an unattainable spiritual state where only a select few have been predestined.

Through valiant feats, heroic achievements, horrendous mistakes, and sinful indulgences, David forged forward with one destiny in mind—He desired to be in the place called "there." His testimony was rife with this understanding:

> *Psalm 5:12: For You , O Lord, will bless the righteous: With favor You will surround him as with a shield.*

> *Psalm 17:14-15: Deliver my life...from men of the world who have their portion in this life...As for me, I will see Your face in righteousness; I will be satisfied when I awake in Your likeness.*

> *Psalm 24:3-6: Who may ascend into the hill of the Lord? Or who may stand in His holy place? He who has clean hands and a pure heart, who has not lifted up his soul to an idol, Nor sworn deceitfully, He shall receive blessing from the Lord, and righteousness from the God of his salvation [To David, holiness preceded imputed righteousness].*

> *Psalm 26:8: I will wash my hands in innocence; So I will go about Your altar, O Lord, That I may proclaim with the voice of thanksgiving, and tell of all Your wondrous works. Lord, I have LOVED the habitation of your house, and the PLACE where Your Glory dwells.*

> *Psalm 27:5: He shall hide me in HIS PAVILION; In the SECRET PLACE of His Tabernacle He shall hide me.*

> *Psalms 31:19-20: Oh, how great is Your goodness, Which You have laid up for those who fear You, Which You have prepared for those who trust in You IN THE PRESENCE OF THE SONS OF MEN [on this earth, there is a place called "there."] You will hide them in the secret place of your presence from the plots of man; You shall keep them secretly in a pavilion from the strife of tongues.*

> *Psalm 56:13: Have You not delivered my feet from falling, That I may WALK before God in the Light of the living.*

Psalm 61:2: *Lead me to the Rock that is higher than I. For You have been a shelter for me, and a strong tower from the enemy. I will ABIDE in Your Tabernacle forever; I will trust in the SHELTER of Your wings.*

Psalm 63:6: *When I remember You on my bed, I meditate on You in the night watches. Because You have been my help, therefore in the <u>shadow of Your</u> wings I will rejoice. My soul follows CLOSE behind YOU; Your right hand upholds me.*

Psalm 71: *Be my strong <u>habitation</u>, To which I may **resort <u>continually</u>**...*

Psalm 73: *Nevertheless I am CONTINUALLY with You; You hold me by my right hand, You will guide me with Your counsel, and afterward receive me to glory ["There," to David, was a compendium which stretched from THE IMMEDIATE all the way to ETERNITY.]*

Psalm 84:10: *For <u>a day in Your courts</u> is better than a thousand. I would rather be the doorkeeper in the house of my God than dwell in the tents of wickedness. For the Lord is a sun and shield; The Lord will give grace and glory: No good thing will He withhold from those who walk uprightly.*

Psalm 91 *is the very epitome of "there." [It's verses began with secret places and the abiding under the shadow of the Almighty. Every blessing is afforded from that position. Nothing is withheld; every aspect of Divine Favor adorns its pages.] Why? "Because you have made the Lord, who is my refuge Even the Most High your <u>habitation</u>. (v.9)*

Psalm 101 *is a declaration of who shall dwell at the place called "there:" My eyes shall be on the faithful of the land, That they may <u>dwell with me</u>; He who walks in a perfect [blameless] way, He shall serve me. He who works deceit SHALL NOT <u>dwell within my house</u>; He who tells lies shall not continue [be established] in my presence. Early I will destroy all the wicked of the land, That I may cut off all the evildoers from the CITY of the Lord.*

Psalm 118: *Open to me the <u>gates of righteousness</u>; I will go through them, and I will praise the Lord. <u>This is the gate</u>*

of the Lord, Through which the righteous shall enter. [The gates of righteousness afford the only entrance to "there."]

Psalm 119: Blessed are the undefiled in the way, Who walk in the law of the Lord! Blessed are those who keep His testimonies, Who SEEK HIM with the Whole heart! They also do no iniquity; They walk in His ways.

Psalm 119:62: At midnight I will rise to give thanks to You, Because of Your righteous judgments, I am a COMPANION of all those who fear You, and of those who keep Your precepts. [David declared his companionship with all who stand in the place called "There."]

Psalm 121:5: The Lord is your keeper; The Lord is your shade at your right hand. [Close, personal, and intimate are adjectives which can only suffice for such proximity as is described here. Close enough for Him to cast a shadow over you is His attentive attendance in the place called "There."]

Psalm 132: 4: I will not give sleep to my eyes or slumber to my eyelids, UNTIL I find a place for the Lord, a dwelling place for the Mighty God of Jacob.

[Yes, David is speaking specifically of the temple to come, but oh!, the temple of the heart. Here, private, intimate promises and words come from the Lord.] The Lord has sworn in truth to David; HE will not turn from it (v. 11).

Psalm 139:5-6: You have hedged me behind and before, and laid Your hand upon me. Such knowledge is too wonderful for me; It is high, I cannot attain it.

Where can I go from Your Spirit? [David then names every conceivable distant place and concludes, "You are There."] If I make my bed in hell, behold, You are THERE. ["There" is only where He is.]

Psalm 145:18: The Lord is NEAR to all who call upon Him, To all who call upon Him in truth.

Passage after passage poured out from the soul of David about the preciousness of the place which can only be described as "there."

THE MOUNTAIN OF THE LORD

From the vantage of "there," the world looks different, news sounds different, actions are judged differently, and knowledge abounds. David called God's "There," a mountain:

> *This is the mountain which God desires to dwell in... The Lord is among them as in Sinai, in the Holy Place. You have ascended on high, You have led captivity captive; You have received gifts among men, even among the rebellious, That the Lord God might dwell THERE.*

Psalm 68:16,18 (NKJV)

(Author's Note: because of the delicacy of the forthcoming subject, I wish to clearly state that there is no attempt at this juncture to create a new theology. However, there is clearly a need to reveal the difference between Zion and Sion. In the Old Testament, the word Zion is referred to 153 times, with 2 times referring to Sion. In the New Testament, all references to Zion are really Sion [7 times]. The following study will embrace these facts.)

David places the Lord in His Holy mountain at the time of the Sinai experience (Psalm 68). The holy mountain is Mount Sion, or Mt. Herman (symbolic of the secret place of the Most High). Symbolically, Sion is like "there." It cannot be approached except through Holiness. The pathways to it are a highway to those who are lead by the Lord. To those who live in unholiness, its paths are obscured. This mountain is separate from Mount Zion which refers to Jerusalem and, consequently, is coupled with worship there. Mount Zion symbolically stands for an intermediary place between Egypt and God's presence. Mt. Sion is the ultimate goal of all who worship in Mt. Zion.

In Ezekiel, as the Lord withdrew from Mt. Zion to His holy mountain (Mt. Sion) and finally into the "there" of heaven, a graphic portrayal of the believer's ascent to His Holy Hill was given. Coming out of the style and ritual of the Temple system, the presence of the Lord returned to His original place in Sion. He dwelled there during the Sinai experience. If the reader can now visualize the difference between Jerusalem, the earthly and the heavenly Jerusalem, then it becomes easier to visualize the difference between Zion and Sion (both of God's mountains).

Isaiah explained this dichotomy in Isaiah 49. The prophet addressed the Lord's mountains (plural) on the earth. He said, first, the Lord has a mission in earth and that mission is "to restore the preserved ones." (Such restoration is open to all who make Him Lord and Savior. He is a light to the Gentiles, a Redeemer of Israel, a Servant of God, and a King in His own right.) He will preserve His people along "the roads," where He will "pasture them on all desolate <u>heights</u>," and will guide and lead them. Now, Isaiah begins to talk about both mountains:

> *I will make each of MY mountains a road, and MY high-ways shall be elevated.*
>
> Isaiah 49:11 (NKJV)

Then, Isaiah deliberated between the two mountains by saying, "BUT ZION said, 'The Lord has forsaken me, and my Lord has forgotten me (Isaiah 49:14).'" To one mountain he ascribes doubt, but to Mount Sion—He ascribes the opposite. In His mountain, there is no room for saying, " The Lord has forsaken me."

Each of His mountains are roads, roads which are on a continuum of commitment. If one stops at Mt. Zion without understanding its relation to Mt. Sion, then "here (Mt. Zion)" will be the "there" of yesterday. The dwellers in Mt. Zion often refuse to move to Mt. Sion. Because of their refusal, inevitably the words of doubt and fear will be heard. "The Lord has forgotten me," is not a sentence heard by the dwellers in Mt. Sion.

Look at the main difference between the two. When one approaches the Holy hill of Mt. Zion, it is through a need for redemption and forgive-ness. It is to worship Him in the fact that the blood of the Lamb (slain before the foundation of the world) is applied to him or her. It is to receive reconciliation.

There lies a road to repentance that goes directly to Mt. Zion. It de-mands a life change which leads to worship of the Lord and sacrifice to self. It demands the living sacrifice of Romans 12:1,2. From its lofty heights of praise and worship, there can be seen another road which leads to Mt. Sion. It is a highway of holiness. From the heights of Mt. Zion, a frontier looms ahead for the believer. (A famous Bible teacher said it succinctly: "the last frontier for the believer is Holiness.")

Holiness has been de-emphasized by the Mt. Zion crowd, who wished to frolic in the laughter of imputed righteousness, having none of their own. However, the gates of righteousness are only entered at the end of the path of holiness. Yes, the Lord imputes His righteousness to us, much as He does salvation. It is given to the whole world before the fact. We are carried by His grace to a place called Mt. Zion until we are able to lay down our lives along with His Son. Then we are again graced with righ-teousness until we walk the road of holiness to enter into Mt. Sion. There, we enter the Gate of Righteousness; there, we enter into His Righteous-ness. No one can stay in Zion and be in the will of God. The Lord's desire is the same desire He manifested at Sinai. He wishes to speak directly to us (His people). The tabernacle was never meant to supplant a "restored" child's place in the presence of the Father. This is why every reference to Mt. Zion in the New Testament should read Mt. Sion (not Zion), for it truly is the place called "there."* "There" is now viewed as a physical place (like Phillip ministering to the Ethiopian), a spiritual place (where communion is with the Lamb and the Father), and a positional place (where imputed righteousness is given until His Righteousness can be manifested as our own). Righteousness, like saving grace, is a planted seed which grows until it occupies the place of beauty it is destined to possess. Salvation begins with imputed, unmerited favor which must grow until we "work out our own salvation in fear and trembling." We must make "our calling and election" sure!

A STUDY IN HEBREWS

The writer of Hebrews extends this truth by recording a mighty appeal to higher ground in the twelfth chapter. After calling the people of God to "make straight paths for their feet," and "Pursue...holiness, without which no one will see the Lord," He turns the spotlight on the true destination of every believer, Mt. Sion. He compares Mt. Sinai and Mt. Sion by saying that Mt. Sinai had the character of judgment, like the schoolmaster—who disciplines with legalism. God took Moses into the womb of His presence and in the glow of intimate contact and revealed the Ten Commandments (the Law). This is the manner in which the Father reveals Himself today, in the intimacy of His mountain.

> And so terrifying was the sight that Moses said, "I am exceedingly afraid and trembling." But **you** have come to Mount Sion and to the city of the living God, the heavenly Jerusalem, to an innumerable company of angels, to the general assembly [festal gathering] and church of the first-born who are <u>registered</u> in heaven, to God the Judge of all, to the spirits of just men made perfect, to Jesus the Mediator of the new covenant, and to the blood of sprinkling that speaks better things than that of Abel. See that you do not refuse HIM who speaks.
>
> Hebrews12:21-25a (NKJV)

Do not be confused, review this passage again and again until you come

---

* The Greek text of the NT uses *sigma* instead of *zeta* even when quoting directly from OT references to Zion.

away shouting. There is a difference between the Mt. Zion at Jerusalem and the Mt. Sion (or Zion) of heaven. There is a difference between Mt. Sinai and the Mt. Sion of heaven. Sinai leads first to Mt. Zion. The law takes the hand of its follower and walks him (or her) to Mt. Zion (Symbolic of redemption) in Jerusalem. There, they are taught the forgiving atonement of a merciful God; neither place (Sinai or Zion) based its authority on close intimacy with the Lord God. Both places were necessary, though, as a starting point but only that, a starting point. The guilty sinner observes the Law and weeps before God for forgiveness and help. The blood is then applied. Standing now in the righteousness of God, he or she is encouraged to seek the higher ground of the "secret place of the Most High." That secret place is the equivalent of Mt. Sion.

For the unredeemed and unransomed, Mt. Sion is hidden by Mts. Sinai and Zion. The soul of man, however, reaches higher because God causes him to thirst for more. Once redeemed, his quest is: "What lies beyond?" As soon as he recognizes this need, there looms the presence of God in Mt. Sion. Loosing himself from man's glory, he seeks to live in God's Glory. The quest of the believer on earth is from glory to glory. The glory is on these two mountains because of the Lord. Zion opens the way to Sion, which is David's "secret place." The Sion we embrace on earth (our "there") is the gateway to the true city of God (the ultimate "there") in heaven. Our fellowship with Him in intimacy, while bound by flesh, can approximate the intimacy enjoyed by those in heaven. "He has made us walk in heavenly places," is not a cliche.

Further into chapter thirteen, the author of Hebrews clarifies this journey. He cites the most basic premise of his discussion is that he is not concerned with earthly deeds or work (v.9), only spiritual matters. He climbs higher in seeking to finish his treatise; he calls his reader to hurry to verse 10:

> *WE have an altar from which those who serve the tabernacle have no right to eat.*

Listen! The WE of this verse is given to earthlings. We bring our sacrifices to Sion, while those of Sinai and Zion content themselves with something less. We are not satisfied until we see His face. Just as Jesus would not be sacrificed inside the gates of religion but was carried "outside the gate," so we must follow Him "outside" that gate. The gate of religion is not the gate of righteousness. The gate of religion catches a glimpse of Mt. Zion, but never sees Mt. Sion. The gate of religion has a pathway leading to it which does not require holiness. The gate of righteousness is arrived at only by the highway of holiness.

Earthly Mt. Zion emphasizes the intermediation of blood and goats (those sacrifices man may bring), while Mt. Sion emphasizes the ultimate sacrifice of anything which stands between us and God. Just as Jesus bore the reproach of religion, so must we! Just as He was judged to be "unfit to live," so we also, in these last days, shall be thus judged. To enter Sion requires a commitment, but to be able to "abide under the shadow of the Almighty," makes the commitment worth it. The Lord is requiring this commitment to take priority in our lives during the last days.

FROM JEREMIAH

Time has changed. Just as Hebrews declared that Jesus changed the focus from Sinai to God's eternal Zion, so the prophet stands as a sentinel in Jeremiah 23 and 30 to declare a change. In these passages, Jeremiah assails the false prophets, who had captured the hearts of the people of God with false promises and assurances:

> *Do not listen to the words of the prophets who prophesy to you. They make you <u>worthless</u>; They speak a vision of their own heart.*
>
> Jeremiah 23:16 (NKJV)

How many today are made worthless by hearing the false teachings of the modern church? Consider it. While people are heading up committees entrusted with designing and building greater edifices to house countless thousands, the leadership of God goes unheeded! Those edifices will face the judgment of fire at God's appearing and be deemed Worthless! The people who did not heed the leadership of the Lord have themselves garnered the same judgment, Worthless!

Jeremiah said it correctly:

> *In the latter days you will understand it perfectly.*
>
> Jeremiah 23:20 (NKJV)

In another place, he uttered a word to be considered. That place is Jeremiah 30:21-22, 24. It is a word laying emphasis upon approaching God:

> *'For who is this who pledged his heart to approach Me?' says the Lord. 'You shall be My people, and I will be Your God'....In the latter days you will consider it.*
>
> (NKJV)

Time truly has changed—these are the latter days. Zion must fade before Sion! No one who names the name of Jesus can be satisfied to dwell in the sacrilege surrounding him or her. Hearts yearn for Mt. Sion and will be satisfied with no other place. Alas, there is no other place! It is the place called "there."

From "there," strongholds are torn down; from "there," the prayers of heaven are gathered and kept; from "there," revelation, words of wisdom and knowledge, come forth; from "there," intercession is made and prison doors open even by themselves. We who follow Him must dwell at "there (Sion)."

Consider this, if the end of salvation is only the fellowship found on a sabbath day, there is no need for Sion. However, if the end of salvation is to be restored to the presence of the living God, then let us loose ourselves from that which holds us to Sinai and move to Sion!

FROM ISAIAH

Mt. Sion is a place where yoga disciplines can never take one, where tantric monotones are never heard, where "bonding" chants are foreign, where mysticism cannot be found. Those who practice such idolatry will not be found in its borders. Those who seek Him tell a different story; it is about a highway which opens to them.

> *A highway shall be THERE, and a road, And it shall be called the **Highway of Holiness**. The unclean shall not pass over it, but it shall be for others. Whoever walks the road, although a fool, shall not go astray. No lion shall be there, nor shall any ravenous beast go up on it: but the <u>redeemed</u> shall walk there, and the <u>ransomed</u> of the Lord shall return, [after being "there"] and come to Zion, with singing, with everlasting joy on their heads, They shall obtain joy and gladness, and sorrow and sighing shall flee away.*

Isaiah 35:8-10 (NKJV)

Can you see it? A highway of holiness which leads to the gate of righteousness which opens to a place called "there (Sion)." Notice, it is a highway of Holiness. Holiness means; "set apart to the service of the Lord." It carries the significance of being "unique," something which is "absolutely different from any other thing that exists." (Every believer had best judge himself along the lines of holiness rather than championing his ability to "blend" into the masses.)

This kind of holiness demands a sanctification which is unpreached, unknown and unheard of in modern religious society. Churches are silent because, against its light, even the steps up to its sanctuaries are defiled by their unholy congregation. It is the difference between Jesus and the Temple.

It is the difference between a humanistic young Moses, having been tainted by the halls of political intrigue (fleeing his assailants), and the "burning bush Moses." The burning bush required him to divest himself of the shoes of his former walk, which was the death principle, and remove them before entering the walk of the Life Principle. Moses did not obtain redemption at the burning bush, he obtained sanctification. He no longer walked as one "who believes," but one who "knows." Walking into the presence of the Most High changes one's perspective and adds its own special assurances. This is the highway of holiness.

Look at who Isaiah said would walk on this highway: The redeemed and the ransomed can travel on it. This highway is not fraught with obstacles of evil or beasts of prey. Since the Lord is the only One who can lead a person to that highway, those who do not "know" Him cannot find the "on ramp." This is the reason it has no "ravenous beast" or "lion (roaring or otherwise)."

This is a HIGH way, not a low road. All through the word of the Lord, there are scriptures which tell about the road to "there." Passionless Pastors, Puffing Prophets, and Piteous Prelates can tell no one how to enter its course; however, the redeemed and the ransomed will never be denied.

Isaiah utilizes two words which English versions render "highway." These, however, are very different words and have variant meanings. The Living Bible separates these words through manipulating them in a way to show their importance: "And a main road will go through that once-deserted land; it will be named 'The Holy Highway.' " The two Hebrew words are *Maslul* and *derek*. *Maslul* is most commonly translated highway, but *derek* takes on a different flavor. It has the hidden meaning of "being a way toward a specific place." It has elements of a "course" or "road to a specific destination."

Solomon addressed this kind of highway, with a Hebrew word *salal* (An elevated, lifted up, piled-up road, like a fully graded road where the low spots are filled, the high spots are leveled, and proper drainage is engineered in order for one not to get mired). "The way of the slothful man is like a hedge of thorns, but the way of the upright is a highway (Proverbs 15:19)." He continues with this venue in Proverbs 16:17: "The Highway of the upright is to depart from evil; He who keeps his way preserves his soul."

The Lord has always used the highway plan to get his children to "there (Sion)." When the children of Israel left Egypt, they were ofttimes unaware that the Lord had a path for them through the wilderness. God could see it when they could not. Deuteronomy 1:31 says: "and in the wilderness where you saw how the Lord your God carried you as a man carries his son, in all the way that you went until you came to this place...who went before you to search out a place for you to pitch your tents, to show you the way you should go, in the fire by night, and in the cloud by day."

The highway of the wilderness was predicated on moving **with** the Lord. When the cloud lifted, the alarm sounded—and the children of Israel gathered up their belongings and headed where the cloud went. The fire by night hovered over the "tent of meeting," where they were obliged to come with their trespasses and get forgiveness. It **must be** the same today, for we are obliged to follow His path. All the self-determined paths that religion offers lead to the "land of confusion." ONLY the moving, hovering Fire of the Holy Spirit will get the sojourner to his place of destiny. Nehemiah's praise to the Lord captured and capsulated how God dealt with Israel:

> *Yet in your manifold mercies You did not forsake them in the wilderness. The Pillar of the cloud did not depart from them by day, To lead them on the road; Nor the pillar of fire by night, To show show them light, and the WAY THEY SHOULD GO, You also gave Your good Spirit to instruct them, and did not withhold Your manna from their mouth, and gave them water for their thirst. Forty years You sustained them in the wilderness, So that they lacked nothing.*
>
> Nehemiah 9:19-21a (NKJV)

Moses pointed the way to the highway of God, but did not stop there. He added Deuteronomy 11: 28 to vent a curse on those who turned from the "way" (the same word as highway in the other biblical passages).

> *and the curse , if you do not obey the commandments of the Lord Your God, but turn aside from the way (highway) which I command you today...*
>
> (NKJV)

David added his affirmation to Moses in Psalm 125:5: "as for such as turn aside to their crooked ways [their crooked highway], the Lord shall lead them away with the workers of iniquity."

Jeremiah stated clearly those who follow religious prescription will wander in their own ways and miss the presence of the Lord.

> *Thus says the Lord to this people: 'Thus they have loved to wander; They have not restrained their feet. Therefore the Lord does not accept them; He will remember their iniquity now, and punish their sins.' Then the Lord said to*

me, 'Do not pray for this people , for their good.'
Jeremiah 14:10 (NKJV)

Jeremiah added to this invective another element of truth: "God will show His back and not His face." Because the leadership of the religious community, when being called to repentance, refused the appeal, Jeremiah gave them (and the modern congregation) something to chew on.

And they said, 'That is hopeless [speaking of God's way].
So we will walk according to our own plans and we will
every one do the imagination of his evil heart.'
Jeremiah 18:12 (NKJV)

To this, the Lord responded, "Because My people have for-
gotten Me, They have burned incense to worthless idols
[like many church projects]. And they have caused them-
selves to stumble in their ways, from the ancient paths [lit-
erally, a way made smooth by the train {royal robe} of the
one going before], to walk in pathways and not on a
highway...I will show them the back and not the face in the
day of their calamity."
Jeremiah 18:15,17b (NKJV)

The paths of man's determination is not the Highway of Holiness; it is a pathway which leads to straying and disobedience or as Jeremiah says: "walking after things that do not profit (Jeremiah 2:8)."

The highway of Holiness is an Emmaus road where fellowship makes the road easier and spiritual hearts burn from the inside because of the communion. Those who walked the Emmaus road felt as if they were treading an ancient path. The ancient paths are paths where the Lord has gone ahead of us. It is a place of tender care, where He has already confronted evil and commanded it to leave.

David said in Psalms 85:13: "Righteousness will go before Him, and shall make His footsteps our pathway." Nothing could be clearer to the follower of Jesus than this statement. The highway of Holiness is reached by making HIS FOOTSTEPS our pathway. Our place is to follow Him, but alas, so many seek to lead! He wants us to get to the Highway of Holiness and stay on it.

So important is this highway that the Lord himself used the words of Isaiah 40:3ff as the text for His introduction into earthly ministry. John, the "baptizer," announced Jesus as the TRUE and LIVING WAY. These were the same words used in Old Testament prophesy about the Messiah, who was to be the Truth and the Way. "The voice of one crying in the wilderness: Prepare the way of the Lord; Make straight in the desert a HIGH-WAY for our God (Luke 3:46)."

Isaiah spoke of the direct intervention of God in the society of men in order to bring His chosen to His Highway.

> *...I will bring the blind by a WAY [highway] they did not know; I will lead them in paths they have not known, I will make darkness light before them, and crooked places straight.*
> Isaiah 42:16 (NKJV)

> *Hear, you deaf; and look, you blind, that you may see. Who is blind but My servant, or deaf as My messenger whom I send: <u>Who is blind as he who is PERFECT and blind as the Lord's servant?</u>*
> Isaiah 42:18-19 (NKJV)

(The Only work of the church is to bring believers to the Highway of Holiness. I know of just a few who seek to do this.) Bless our God, He will not stand idly by watching the "blind leading the blind." He is right now intervening and calling His true servants to the HIGHWAY (The highway, which He alone knows the way to and on.) A few verses farther down, God said his people have been robbed, plundered, snared in holes and hidden in prison houses. He added that they had become a prey and no one delivered them or cried, "Restore." There is One voice, however, which sounds like the rush of many waters, crying: "RESTORE!" God himself is restoring His people, having rescued them from the robbers and the plunderers (Often rescuing them from the ranks of religion and twisted theology). He cries "restore," and no snare (or lair), no prison house door can keep them from Him.

Read on, you who are blessed of God, read on until your eyes fall on those passages in Isaiah 43:l: "Fear not, for I have redeemed you; I have called you by your name; YOU are MINE, <u>When</u> you pass through the waters, I will be with you; And <u>through</u> the rivers, they shall not overflow you. <u>When</u> you walk through the fire, you shall not be burned, nor shall the flame scorch you [Savanarolla, Huss]. For I am the Lord your God, The Holy One of Israel, your savior." His "beloved" is not cast on the highway with no protection along the way; God is the protection.

Feast your eyes on Isaiah 43:4: "...you were precious in My sight, You have been honored, and I have loved you."

Oh!, look at verse 8, "Bring out the blind people who <u>have</u> eyes, and the deaf who <u>have</u> ears, let all the nations be gathered together, and let the people be assembled...'You are my witnesses,' says the Lord, 'and My servant whom I have chosen, that you MAY KNOW AND BELIEVE ME, and understand that I am He, Before Me there was no God formed, Nor shall there be after Me. I, even I, am the Lord, and besides Me there is no savior...I work and who will **reverse** it(v.13).' "

Then, bless the Lord, read slowly and drink from these waters: "Thus says the Lord, who makes a WAY [highway, same word] in the sea and a path through the mighty waters (v. 16)... 'Do not remember the former things, nor consider the things of old. Behold, I will do a new thing, Now it shall spring forth; Shall you not know it? I will even make a road in the wilderness and rivers in the desert.' " In these last days when so much is being said ABOUT Jesus and so little is being said TO Jesus, believer's need a highway.

Listen, time has changed. No, times are not changing—they HAVE changed. In the realm of the Spirit, an eclipse of time has taken place as significant as the difference between B.C. and A.D. During Jesus' ministry, the temple was unyielded to the hand and will of the Lord. During this time, God's method and remedy for such a condition was to move past them into a realm of higher spiritual order. Those who experienced this transition did not understand the significance of God's move—they were left behind to experience the odious demise of it all in 70 A.D. (Notice, it is designated—A.D.) Now a similar situation has arisen, not with the Jews but with the Christians.

The church has lost its responsiveness to God's Spirit, and like then, His method of dealing with the situation is to move to a higher spiritual dimension. History will not record this eclipse in its journals—while looking back to a smoldering, defiled, macabre scene of desecrated church buildings; it is too late in God's time-line.

History is closing and the Highway beckons! Do not be afraid to get on the highway now, for no lions and ravenous beast will befall those who embark on their journey. "There," which dwells within the believers hearts, will tell them they are on the correct road. When they come to the "righteous gate," as it opens, they will find all the others so "sealed." They shall see all those others who have come to the place called, "The Lord is There." Every soul in heaven will have arrived in the same manner!

The great surprise of glory will be the fact that through a series of "being there," we have arrived at "there (Sion)." Revelation 7:17: "For the Lamb who is in the midst of the throne will shepherd them and lead them to living fountains of waters." These are they who have no condemnation for they "walk after the Spirit and not after the Flesh (Romans 8:1)!" The issue has always been, "My way or His Highway."

"Set up the sign posts, make landmarks; Set your heart toward the highway (Jeremiah 31:21)." The societies of Christendom have tainted their people to the extent that there are no signposts within their gates pointing to the Highway of Holiness. Humanism and traditionalism have both obliterated the ancient paths. Sociologists say that culture and social peerage are the most powerful forces in the lives of today's populous.

It is true that ministers are constantly battling with the social acceptability (politically correctness) of certain issues, all the while claiming freedom from such. The society which determines those criteria is corrupt and unholy; therefore, logic would cause the observer to cry "unholy" toward pulpit and pew. Not until both pulpit and pew resolve, through repentance, to hear only from God will this change. Somebody has to set signposts and the landmarks other than the society. It should have been the church, but if holiness is not within the ranks of the church, where will it be? The answer is found in the believer standing in his or her "there."

Every edict of grace, every plan for life, every avenue of blessing comes from the place called "there." The secret place of the Most High is command central. A clear voice comes from a pure altar and its origin is Sion. New revelation, specific direction, words of wisdom and knowledge, all emanate from this intimate realm where thrones and dominions belong to Him and no other. His work with His people has not changed. Just as Moses stood in His presence to obtain Divine command, so must we all. Sion is not an option; Sion is an absolute requirement. Sion offers no platform for performance, no forum for rebellion, no place for senseless prattle so often associated with prayer and pulpit. The secret place is a territory as intimate as that occupied by a bride and groom (so says the prophet Solomon in his Song). The secret place is not a special occasion resort, but a daily base which gives meaning to all that is outside it. Without its pleasures, no man can know life.

> *You will show me the path of life; In Your presence is fullness of joy; At Your right hand are pleasures forevermore.*
>
> Psalm 16:11 (NKJV)

CHAPTER TWELVE

Every Man in Position

*I*n the eleventh chapter of Hebrews there lies as familiar a passage as can be found in the Scripture. It has been hailed as the "Faith Hall of Fame." It has been viewed, turned, and conjectured about in almost every conceivable manner for hundreds of years. Mighty sermons have emanated from almost every verse, as has much personal faith been gendered by reading its text. My father read that chapter every week of his life after becoming a Christian. He memorized the passage and quoted it often in conversation. Naturally, the appeal of this chapter is very strong in my heart. However, there is an element of *En Punto* in that chapter which is often missed.

If one will view these verses apart from the theme of faith found in them, a surprising manifestation takes place. Tied to this manifestation is a truth so strong, it may even be considered as a sub-theme as great as the main emphasis. That manifestation is more apparent as one recognizes the chapter is not just about faith. The passage is about taking a look at spiritual history from the eyes of the Lord and viewing history as a continual series of men and women standing for Him in their assigned places. Assignation does not have to produce a rigid pre-destination doctrine, instead, it can inculcate the broader scope of "being in the will of the Lord."

The chapter begins with the "will of the Lord" expressed in creation. God established the universe by faith, using His Words which were the outward expression of His inward will. He created a stable universe, operating on sound principles so solid that it can bear scrutiny from the most scientific of inquirers.

View this as God calling things into their places, where they have stood

· since their inception and have resisted all the ills and sins of men throughout history. If, perchance, this theme is carried out into the human specter with equal acumen, then men were created to exercise faith-will and stand by that faith against a faithless world. Just as every part of this universe was positioned by Him and will maintain that position until released, so no man was made without regard to position and place.

If Hebrews 11 is viewed as a look down a continuum of men and women, who stood as markers in strategic historical spiritual events, then a remarkable truth emerges. Those persons occupied themselves with one goal: "Being where God wanted them to be." Faith cannot be released from a heart of disobedience. As tempting as it is for scholars to focus on Chapter Eleven as a separate entity, it is tied to the other chapters found in Hebrews. Chapter Ten declares the will of God as tantamount:

> *Then I said, 'Behold, I have come—*
> *In the volume of the   book it is written of Me—*
> *To do Your will, O God.'*

Hebrews 10:7 (NKJV)

The author further says, "By THAT will we have been sanctified (Hebrews 10:10)." Look at the admonition: "let us hold fast the confession of our hope without wavering (10:24)." Revel in the words: "For you have need of endurance, so that **after** you have done the *will of God*, you may receive the promise (10:36)." Notice the cautions which are intermingled with these admonitions have to do with failing to stand, failing to endure, falling away, capitulating to the world, and ceasing to do the will of God. Also intermingled with this truth is the passage: "you became companions of those who were so treated (10:33)." Here is the format for the eleventh chapter: Being companions to those who stood in the will of God. In the last verse of this chapter, the author states this premise plainly:

> *God having provided something better for us, that they should*
> *not be made perfect apart from us.*

Hebrews 11:40 (NKJV)

The last words of the chapter cannot be separated from the "therefore" challenge in Hebrews 12:1.

Every soul mentioned in Chapter Eleven is in the "cloud of witnesses" found in Chapter 12:1. The faith that began with God standing and declaring His Will in the Universe becomes our faith to stand and declare His Will in our universe. Hall of Fame members utilized the same faith as God.

Several "catch phrases" describe those who were highlighted in the eleventh chapter. Of Abel it was spoken, "He was righteous." Of Enoch, the chapter declared, "he pleased God." Acting on that theme, it further underscores, "He is a rewarder of those who DILIGENTLY SEEK HIM (11:6)."

Abel became synonymous with righteousness. Enoch was, in every respect, a God-pleaser. It was the same for Noah. Righteousness was indelibly linked to obedience in the description of Noah. Look at the descriptors used for Noah, "moved with godly fear," "prepared," "became heir of the righteousness which is according to faith." Faith moves, prepares, and becomes. What was true of Noah was true of Abraham.

Abraham obeyed. Wouldn't that look good if the reader's name was substituted? That epitaph of two words is enough to fill history. He obeyed so meticulously that it could be said, "he went out, not knowing where he was going(11:8)." Obeying the Lord and embracing promises from His lips formed a platform for Abraham's life. His place in history was manifold, but simply put, it was based on his standing in the place which was his alone. Get this lesson. Had Abraham failed to stand in His appointed and anointed place in history and time, faith's chain would have been broken and God's plan hindered.

There should be no need for the Lord to say: "Who will stand in the gap and make a hedge," if every man and woman who declares him or herself recipients of salvation would stand in the territory given them. Faith hears the assignment, locks into that assignment, and stands within that assignment until His Will is done on earth as it is in heaven. Each person listed in the Hall of Fame was aware of his or her connection to the great plan of God.

Isaac's blessing was based on future position. Jacob's blessing was premised on the same. Joseph's instructions declared his continuance with Jacob's blessing.

Moses' birth mother stood against kings and man's odds and was not afraid. (Fear not only blocks faith, it signals no quality decision to stand until death has been made.) Is it any wonder Moses stood against kings and priests, wizards and wandering as he "endured (11:27)?" There is no domino effect in the kingdom of our God. The true kingdom is ONLY populated with those who stand. Pillars stand. Perhaps this is why they are referred to as "pillars" in the book of Revelation.

Hebrews does not hesitate to include all types of resoluteness; it was "doing" the will of God which is emphasized in Joshua. It is the resolute stand on the promise of the people of God which is commended in Rahab.

Hebrews ceases naming names and begins to emphasize the "unnamed."

Their acts of faith were characterized in their resoluteness in the face of death and mistreatment.

Unfortunately, sermonizers and biblical teachers tend to summarize the remainder of Chapter Eleven by lumping all the unnamed saints in one category—as faceless martyrs. Look at the action words spoken of them, "subdued," "worked," "obtained," "stopped (aggressors)," "quenched," "escaped," "were made," "became," "turned to flight," "received."

Other words also describe them, "tortured," "trail of mockings and scourgings," "chains and imprisonment," "stoned," "sawn in two," "tempted," "slain," "wandered about," "destitute, afflicted tormented." (Not many sermonizers spend much time with these words, as they hurry to the place: "not made perfect without us." They tend to leave out, that being a companion with these Hall of Fame folks, ofttimes requires the same treatment.)

Standing in the "will of the Father," means declaring that no matter what comes to us, "we will be faithful unto death." Christianity is not "every man for himself," but rather, "every man faithful to every other unto death." (Read this until it becomes clear.)

Words such as, "shall **we** not much more readily be in subjection to the Father of spirits and live (12:9)?" are indicators of the direction of the author's intent. The words "consider Him," "you have not resisted unto death," "endure chastening," "Strengthen the hands which hang down," "make straight paths for your feet," are not placed there as suggestions; they are commands. To live in His holiness and partake of it, we must be obedient to His Will and Word. (Falling short, letting the roots of bitterness grow, and becoming defiled are just a few of the things that cause man to fall and not stand.)

As the book of Hebrews continues the eleventh chapter into the twelfth chapter, one will find that Chapter Twelve, verse twenty-five refocuses upon the seminal truth surrounding every aspect of standing and doing by faith, "See that you do not refuse Him who speaks." He is the one who set the bounds of our habitation. He is the one who places His people in spheres of authority and places of faith. He, alone, is the sole owner of History and has the right to put His people in position around the globe.

GLOBAL POSITIONING

In the Twenty-First Century, much as been written and verbalized about the importance of global positioning. Apart from the technological aspects of being able to determine the location of an auto or person at any given time or place, there is another dimension of crucial importance. Economists and national leaders tend to be more aware of this dimension than those invested with spiritual leadership. When economists use the term "global positioning," they are speaking of rank as it relates to future economic trade. To them, it is important to have presence in the right nations, using protectionary and visionary machinations to insure future growth and expansion in one's business. When national leaders use the term, they often are making considerations regarding power.

Global positioning has its spiritual aspects and always will. Hebrews Eleven, in essence, is about this subject. Had one of those Hall of Fame saints failed, spiritual history would have been written differently. They were globally positioned. They were important, not just as examples, but because they were men and women yielded to God and carrying out His Divine Command. They occupied a position in time, locale, and spiritual history which could be filled by no one else but them. Every believer, who truly is one, has a similar position in spiritual history.

Author's Note: One evening about three weeks ago, the Spirit of the Lord came upon me and a wonderful vision ensued. Up to this point, I thought the book was complete in the previous chapter. That evening changed things. The Lord showed me a wonderful vision of the end time. He pointed out that as the end approaches, those who truly follow Him will be perfectly aligned in His Will. They will be globally positioned.

Each person may not know the logistics of any other person in the great plan. He or she may only be able to attest to his or her personal stand. Many will be unaware that across the globe other true believers will be standing exactly where they should be, full of faith, and listening intently to the voice of God. Global positioning, under this definition, will mean: "Everyone in position around the Globe."

REVELATION 22:20

I saw, in this vision, the force of that awesome specter acting like a great magnet drawing upon the heart of the Lord Jesus. Visualize the result of every man and woman, standing in his or her place of authority, standing faithful to God and crying out: "Lord, Now!"

Gideon and his men surrounded the camp of the enemy, each man standing in his appointed place was a similar specter. Each man equipped with sword, lamp, and shout knew the value of being in his appointed place when the battle became the Lord's. Without this faithfulness, there would have been no victory for Israel.

It is easy now to say, "En Punto" is real!

Bibliography/ Site Page

1. Bevington, C.G., *Miracles*, Bridge Publishing, Inc., South Plainfield, N.J, 1992. (Chapter 2 page 44)

2. Peterim Sorokin, Sociologist

3. Havner, Vance: Message on Revival, 1956

4. Federowe, Rabbi, Clear Lake Congregation, Tex., Lectures on Jewish Philosophy, Galveston College, 1999.

5. Solomon, Robert C., *Introducing Philosophy*, 6th Edition, Harcourt Brace College Publishers, Ft. Worth, 1997, pages 521-522 ("On Ethical Relativism," by Walter Stace.)

6. Ibid, page 518, (discussion of the Philosophy of Immanuel Kant)

7. **Authors Note:** the living creatures had the same four faces as were affixed to banners which were posted on the four corners of the tabernacle of Moses. These banners presented the faces of a lion, a man, an ox and an eagle. Present at Moses' tabernacle was the cloud by day and the fire by night, which was the glory of God. Note that the four living creatures also accompany the glory in Ezekiel's vision.

8. Frishknecht, Donna, National Jeweler, September 15, 2000, Editorial on conditions surrounding the Oppenheimer organization and their DeBeers decisions.

9. Oliver, C.R., *The Sons of Zadok*, Zechariah and the filthy garments, Ransom Press, Florida, 2000.

10. Houston Chronicle, Sept. 6, 2000, declaration of the papal authorities. See addendum 2.

10a. Graham, Jack, Southern Baptist Convention, New Orleans, June, 2001. Article from Houston Chronicle section 3E, Saturday, June, 16, 2001.

11. See: Addendum 3: Notes

12. Oliver, C.R. , *Solomon's Secret*, Ransom Press, 1999.

13. Stendal, Russell, "Treatise On Zion versus Sion," April, 2000

14. Author's note: Understanding He is married to us is the whole construct of *Song of Solomon*.

15. (Please note Psalm 107:16, "For He has broken the gates of bronze, and cut the bars of iron in two." This Psalm is speaking of those "bound in affliction and irons." Note also how they got into this predicament: "because they rebelled against the words of God.")

16. *The Analytical Greek Lexicon* , Harper and Brothers, New York, Twenty-Second edition (undated), page 212.

17. Stendal, Russell, "Treatise on Zion versus Sion," April, 2000.

The Story Of Ann Hall, Ex-nun

T his Addendum is a reproduction of the personal testimony of Ann Hall, my neighbor and friend.

A 60 YEAR SEARCH FOR GOD
This testimony shows
How stronghold can hold one captive
How the Father's love pursues us
How the Holy Spirit guides and teaches us

My Testimony, by Ann Hall

All of us come from different backgrounds, different families, and different locations. These differences have an impact on our lives, which mold us and make us unique.

I was born in 1921 into a very religious family. My sisters and brothers and I were born into a Roman Catholic family. Both of our parents came from Poland. Mother was born in Kiszkowa (near Cracow). Father was born in Dorlowa, Russian State, Poland, where freedom to worship god was forbidden and taken away. However, the Polish people worshipped "in secret."

My parents came to America where they met and along with several other couples started the "Our Lady Queen of Apostles" Polish, Catholic Church and a Catholic School in Hamtramck, Michigan, in 1920. I mention this because it indicates the depth of their Catholic faith, their convictions and the atmosphere in which I along with my sisters and brothers were raised.

We attended " Our Lady Queen of Apostles" school where we were taught by Polish nuns. (Our curriculum was : reading [in Polish and English], math, spelling, handwriting, grammar, geography and Catechism.)

From the moment we awoke, to the moment we retired, we were in a Polish Catholic atmosphere. In school and at home we spoke to each other only in Polish.

As a small child I would get up early (5:30 a.m.)   and go outside to watch the sunrise. I remember on a particular morning when I was about five years old. I stood on the back lawn, the birds (two bluebirds) were beginning to chirp just before sunrise. Something within me called out to God:

"God, I want to **know** you!"

True, my parents taught me about God, about Jesus, about Mary, about the Saints. To know about someone is not the same as knowing that person.

The call of my heart was to know God. I needed to know what I must DO to come to know God personally. And I was willing to do all that was required of me.

In school I studies the Catechism, and I knew it very well. I made my First Holy Communion at the age of 8.

By the time I was 12, the desire to know God had increased.

"May I enter the convent?" I asked my mother when I came home from school one day. Mother was at the stove, cooking supper.

"May I?"

Mother was silent. I saw her raise a corner of her apron as she wiped a tear.

That evening my parents discussed with me my desire to enter a convent. My parents were concerned that I was only 12 1/2 and had not yet fully completed the 7th grade. They did look into the matter and my teacher indicated that I would be able to complete the 8th grade during the summer, in the convent. After some deliberation, my parents approved.

I entered the convent in June of 1934 at the age of 12 1/2. I remember that day very well. It was time to say, "Good bye," to my family. It was most painful to say, "Good bye," to my older sister. I loved her dearly. We always got into mischief together. She is a year older. My brother Tom (8yrs) and my younger sister Esther (5) each gave me a hug, in silence. Mother stayed home with my brother Cass, who was an infant at the time. We said our Good-bye in the kitchen. Mother held me close and wept. The most tearful moment was when my father embraced me and gave me his blessing. He drove me to the convent.

I knew that convent life would be tough, but I was ready and determined to do whatever was required so that "some day I will come to know God."

(A word about convents. Convents do not all have the same rules. They are not all alike. To begin with, some orders are under the jurisdiction of the local Bishop, and others are under the jurisdiction of the Pope. Those under a Bishop's jurisdiction have somewhat more lenient rules to live by. For example; a nun could travel alone; she would wear a lighter habit and veil in the summer and a warm, suitable garb in the winter; she could visit her family and even spend vacations with them. If any rule needed to be changed or added, they could consult the local Bishop. Access to the Bishop was simple.

But not so with those who are under the jurisdiction of the Pope. I entered a convent which was under the Pope's jurisdiction. Our rules were very rigid and remained so until the Second Vatican Council. For example:

* We were never to be alone

* We had to be with a companion nun even when we were in the convent itself.

* We were allowed to have visitors for one hour on the first Sunday of each month, but not during Lent.

* We did not visit our parents in their home.

* We begged in the community for most of the food and ate whatever we were given.

* We flogged ourselves with a chain once a week, more often during Lent.

* We attended Mass every day, twice on Sunday.

* We were obligated to say the rosary every day.

* We prayed in Latin with the exception of morning and evening prayers, which were said in Polish.

* We chanted the breviary our prayer book, three times each day, in Latin.

* Each day we were obligated to spend a half hour in meditation and a half hour in spiritual reading. We read books prescribed by the sister superior, and only those books that have the Archbishop's approval. Three Latin words found in the beginning of the book the NIHIL OBSTAT and IMPRIMATUR.

  (Nothing objectionable with the Catholic Doctrines and permission granted.)

* Our habit was brown in color, made of heavy wool. The headgear was heavily starched. The veil was black wool. We wore the same habit in winter and summer. (I was uncomfortable in summer.)

* We took vows of poverty, chastity, obedience, and silence.

* We were not allowed to keep any money, nor gifts, nor make any purchases.

I was taught that the more physical pain I suffer, the more discomfort I inflict on myself, the more suffering I experience, the more GRACE I will earn.

The Catholic Church taught me that I must earn God's grace—that I must merit grace by doing good works. Convent life re-enforced this teaching! That doctrine had a STRONGHOLD on me!

How much grace is enough to make me pleasing in God's eyes? Actually, the church tells us that you don't know because the state of one's soul is judged at the hour of death.

As the years went by, I found it difficult to understand why I don't know God! In fact, I felt more and more distant from Him. I realized that I had been more receptive and at peace with God when I was a young child. So, after twenty years of being a nun I knew that I had to leave the convent so that I could search for my God! For 20 years I did all I knew to DO and yet I found myself to be judgmental, unforgiving, and angry.

No one saw the condition of my heart, but God did! Oh, I kept all the rules but there was a battle in my heart. The world saw me as "holy" because they looked at the garb, but my heart was hiding behind that garb and my heart was like that of a Pharisee.

In order to leave, I needed to receive a special dispensation from the Pope! Otherwise, I would face excommunication.

To a Catholic, excommunication is serious business. It means you are "cut off" from the Catholic Church. It means you are "cut off" from receiving grace. It means you have lost your salvation. It means you are condemned. I did not want condemnation, I want to KNOW God!

The procedure of obtaining dispensation took several months. I did not inform my superiors of the process because they would have stopped the proceedings. When I received my dispensation I was free to leave. I left that same day. I was 32 years old.

The day I left the convent I had only the garb I wore. I had no money, no knowledge of how to handle money, no knowledge of how to dress, how to buy food.

The day I left the convent I was alone for the first time. I was walking down the main street in Detroit, Woodward Avenue. In the distance I heard organ music coming from the nearby Cathedral. I walked into the Cathedral and for the first time in 20 years I was free to select the pew I wanted.

I knelt down and said, "God, where are You? I don't know You, but if I have to go to every church in the world, I'll find You."

My family found it especially difficult to accept me, so I stayed with a Catholic family I had met through the church. The mother, whose name was Rose, helped me adjust to the world. She also helped me get a teaching position in the public schools.

My mother found it especially difficult to accept me. She never asked me, why I left the convent, all I could say to her was, "Mom, I did receive a dispensation from the Pope. Mom I am not excommunicated."

But mother took it hard. I would come to visit her when it was dark and I left when it was dark. I made a number of visits to see her. That year, my mother died.

I also found it interesting that none of my brothers and sisters to this day ever asked me why I left the convent I had doors slammed in my face by family members.

Rose helped me get situated close to the school where I was to teach. I had decided that during the spring break I would take a Greyhound bus trip no place in particular, so that I could see the world, observe people, see how they behave, and listen to their conversations. When I told Rose about my plan, she suggested that instead, I should fly to San Francisco and spend the week with her daughter, Bobbie, who worked for the American Broadcasting Company (KGO). Fabulous!

Bobbie had advised me that she could not meet me at the airport in person due to her work schedule that day but, that she had a fellow employee, a man named John, an engineer at KGO, who would meet me.

As I walked up the ramp at the San Francisco airport and saw my escort I said to myself, " This man knows the Lord. He will help me to know Him, too."

I was a memorable week. Sunday of that week was Easter Sunday. We went to a Baptist Church. John sang in the choir. This was my first visit to a church other than Catholic.

John and I began our acquaintance that week. We were married that same year.

John left broadcasting for aerospace engineering and his work assignments took us to many states for the next 28 years. We attended numerous churches: Baptist, Lutheran, Community Methodist, Christian, Church of God, Presbyterian, Latter Day Saints and even Catholic.

John was, always, very willing to go to a church I suggested. I thank the Lord many times for John. John has helped me in my search for God, even though he didn't know I was still searching.

During all those years I had never confided to John about the "hunger" in my heart. He had no idea that I was not receiving the Word. I believe this silence was due to my convent training.

Question: Why wasn't I hearing the message in the churches we attended?

Why was I doubting?

The answer is simple: I had a strong FEAR of the Bible!

"Why" Because Catholics were forbidden to read the Bible, under fear that they might misunderstand something and fall into heresy which would lead to excommunication. This ban was lifted by the Second Vatican Council in 1958.

But now, Catholics are encouraged to read the Bible daily. IN fact, the church states that a "faithful" who reads the Bible daily for at least 15 minutes as spiritual reading is granted an indulgence of three years.

I left the convent four years before this ban was lifted.

Never in my life had I been allowed to read the Bible. I had never even opened the Bible, much less read from one! That is why I feared the Bible and teachings of its meaning.

That fear—FEAR OF THE BIBLE—had a very strong hold on me. Fear of the Bible would not permit me to accept any teaching except the Cathohlic doctrines presented in the Catechism. The only standard against which I was able to measure truth was the Catechism!

I didn't know how to help myself. In 1981 I became very ill. According to the evaluation of the top doctors in Ann Arbor I was diagnosed with lupus and given three months to live. My desire to know God began to fade. That year I turned 60. I feared death.

On January 30, 1982, John and our daughter, Dorothy, wanted me to hear one more preacher. My reply was: "I've heard them all, they're all alike. NO! I will not listen to another preacher!"

They persuaded me. We drove the 80 miles from Peck, Michigan, to Detroit, not to a church but to a State Fairgrounds and a utility building used in cattle auctions. I was amazed at the beautiful expressions on the faces of the people going in. They were joyous and peaceful, "I want that peace and joy, too."

The Lord remembered what I had said about not listening to the preacher. The preacher did not preach. He sang. He sang songs glorifying God and the Name of Jesus. During that hour the Holy Spirit opened my ears and I began to understand that I, too, can fellowship with my Lord and come to know Him! All I had to do was believe His Word, receive His Love, and trust in Jesus completely.

And, then, the preacher preached for three hours and I hung on every word. Our Heavenly Father sure has a sense of humor!

At 11:15 that evening I asked Jesus to come into my heart, to a "let's get acquainted, Lord"—time.

I went forward and accepted Jesus to be my Lord and Savior. Then a miracle happened! As the minister prayed for me; he placed his hands on my shoulders and ended the prayer with "In the Name of Jesus." On that Name, the Name of Jesus, my FEAR of the Bible was suddenly gone. I had, instead a deep hunger for the Bible! I could hardly wait to get home to begin reading the Bible.

That night I opened the Bible for the very first time. It fell open to John 14 and my eyes looked on verses 26-27, where Jesus says:

> "...the Helper, the Holy Spirit, whom the Father will send
> in My Name. <u>He will teach you all things</u>, and bring to
> your remembrance all that I have said to you. My peace
> I give you. Do not let your heart be troubled, <u>nor let it be
> fearful</u>."

That night the Holy Spirit and I had our first Bible Study together!

It was several days later that I became aware that I was not sick anymore. The Lord had healed me! I had no use for the medication so I discarded it.

From that day forward I read God's Word. I read slowly. Everything was so new to me, and so alive! I was spending about three to four hours daily in reading the Bible. I shed many tears of joy.

I realized that I needed to know how to pray. So far, I've been praying to Mary and to the Saints. So, since the Bible says: "The Comforter, the Holy Spirit , will teach you..." I asked the Holy Spirit to teach me to pray, and He did! (Jn 14:26,27)

This is how I was led to pray and to fellowship with Jesus. An example: Luke 7:11-16.

I read the passage to myself then I read it to Jesus and we talked about the matters at hand.

To this day the Holy Spirit and I read the Word together. To me, it is a simple time of fellowshipping with Jesus, while, at the same time I am getting to know my Lord—more and more.

I was excited when I read in Luke 11:9-13, "ask and you shall receive, seek and you shall find, knock and the door shall be opened"....that was for everyone.

This is Jesus speaking to me, not the Pope, not the priest, and not the Mother Superior.!

As I was growing in God's Word I knew that I had to deal with the teachings of the Catholic Church. I had to know. Did I misunderstand what the Church taught me and what I had been teaching to hundreds of children? Just what does the Catechism say about Mass, Mary, Eucharist, indulgences, scapular, the Bible, Sacraments, grace purgatory, the Pope? I had to find out. So, I went to a Catholic Bookstore and purchased the latest edition of the New Baltimore Catechism and the latest books about devotion to Mary and about the scapular.

I read the entire Catechism. I found that I had not misunderstood the teachings of the Catholic Church; that what I taught was exactly what the Church is teaching today. I also wanted to purchase the Documents of the Second Vatican Council, but the Bookstore had none.

However, a friend who was with me in the convent, Sister Irene, gave me copy of those documents. I did not know that she was in Rome during the proceedings of the Second Vatican Council and served as secretary to one of the Cardinals of that Council. I saw her seven years ago. We talked about the proceedings and in particular about he changes the Vatican Council proposed for the nuns. Evidently, the changes were quite drastic. General Mother Superior of the convent I was in did not cooperate with all the proposals of the Vatican Council. She decided not to change. As a result, the nuns were given an option to stay or to leave—and many left! Sister Irene left. She started a new order known as Servants of Jesus.

Obtaining the documents was, indeed, an eye opener to me. I found that NONE of the Catholic doctrines were changed! Except for one, they remain unchanged except for the manner in which the Sacraments are administered, and the Mass is offered. Devotion to Mary is encouraged more than ever before. Mary is to be venerated by the Catholic Church as god's Mother, as the co-mediator, as co-redemptrix. The only doctrine that was chanted was the doctrine of the reading the Bible. Catholics are allowed and even encouraged to read the Bible. That is a big Praise the Lord!

Let me explain something that took place when John and I were visiting my older sister and brother in law in 1982. My sister (Dorothy) was excited about something. She said,

" Oh, Ann, let me tell you about something that happened this past week. Chester and I made our final payment on a cemetery plot. The man in charge offers gifts of either a color TV or a Bible to people when they make their final payment. So he asked, " do you want a color TV or a Bible?" I was thinking that Chester will probably want the color TV. Ours broke the previous week, so I quickly said, " I never had a Bible. I want the Bible." I want to show it you, Ann."

She brought it out. It was a big Family Bible. She had it wrapped in her finest linen. And it was still sealed with a plastic wrapper. She handled it with great respect.

She remove the wrappings. Then she asked, " Ann, is this a good Bible?" So I asked her, " Do you remember what the church taught us about checking out spiritual books" Do you remember the word, IMPRIMTUR and NIHIM OBSTAT?

"Oh, yes!"

"Well, let's see," I said. In the meantime, Chester went to the kitchen. He wanted to pop some popcorn, but he couldn't find the popcorn, so yelled from the kitchen for Dorothy. When she left, I quickly said, "Lord Jesus, what did I get myself into? Help me, please. What do I do, now?" I saw a pen on the table I grabbed it and as I opened the Bible, I saw that it was an American Standard Bible. It was just great, so I wrote IMPRIMATUR and NIHIL OBSTAT and wrote the Cardinal's name below IMPRIMATUR in a scribbly sort of way. I closed the Bible and put the pen away just where I found it.

Dorothy cme back to the room and sat down, " Now, let's see if this a good Bible," she said.

She opened her Bible and looked, "Oh, it is a good Bible!"

She was SO happy. And I said to her, " You know, Dorothy, actually no imprimatur is necessary in a Bible. The Bible is God's Word. She agreed. Her next question was, "Did Blessed Mother have other children?" "Oh, yes!" and I found it for her in the Gospel of Mark. She read it. She was a little puzzled, but she said, " But this is God's Word, so it is true. Jesus had brothers and sisters."

And now, I want to touch on the very NERVE of the Roman Catholic Church, namely the worship of Mary. I found dthat when speaking of Mary as NOT being the co-mediator, NOT being co-redemptrix, the channel of all graces, would always bring an explosion of feelings and words.

Devotion to Mary is based on tradition and appearances of Mary and the supposed promises Mary gives to those who wear a medal, say the rosary, wear a scapular and totally consecrate themselves to Mary.

As I reviewed the Catechism and the latest books on Mary, I realized that I was actually worshipping Mary. How did I know that?

Throughout the years I couldn't part with the rosary and the scapular.

I knew that I must get rid of the rosary. I tried to throw it away but I had a most difficult time—I just couldn't. I asked myself if it had become an idol to me. I asked the Holy Spirit to help me. I searched the Bible for scriptures on "idols." Isaiah 42:8 say s, " I am the Lord, that is MY Name. I will not give my Glory to another. Nor my praise to graven images."

I repented before my Lord and I knew that I had to physically throw away the rosary. I repeated this verse as I put the rosary into the garbage can. And I had Peace!

Would you believe that throwing away the scapular was even more difficult?

Whenever God dealt with the graven images and the idols, He always commanded them to "burn them in the fire." So, I took a bucket outside, shredded some paper and started the fire. Then I threw the scapular into the fire and it "burned in the fire."

Satan is a deceiver. Just look at Genesis 3:15.

The Catholic church changed the pronoun, and so, changed the message. Even now Satan is deceiving many by drawing the attention away from Jesus and focusing on Mary and the saints.

I want to read one line from a book I received from a nun (who is trying to convert me.) It is a biography of Mother Angela, the founder of the order I was in. She lived to be 74 years of age. Toward the end of her life she said, " What must I DO to find god? I call to Him, I search for Him...in vain."

Oh, I KNOW HIM.

My testimony does not end here. The Holy Spirit is constantly guiding me, helping me, and teaching me.

Ann Hall, Conroe, Texas

The Blood Covenant:

*E*ver grateful for the teaching of the blood Covenant in the 1970's, its truth has not been received universally. Simply stated as an assumption within the word of the Lord rather than a direct delineation, it has caused skepticism to abound. However, there are elements of great value to be gleaned from this teaching and with its attendant lessons which will assist a believer to understand Covenant with God.

Although an addendum can only serve as a brief overview of the attributes of blood covenant, its essential elements will be condensed to outline form. Fleshing out this study will depend on the amount of interest the reader possesses.

There are elements of the blood covenant in David's dealings with Jonathan, God's dealings with Abraham and it carries these facets into the New Testament especially in Romans and Hebrews.

I am indebted to an itinerate evangelist who took the time to reveal these truth to me personally and to expose their elements for my own perusal. He synopsized them for me and his method shall serve as the method of deployment in this treatise.

Based on Nomadic necessity for mutual protection of families and their goods, this type of socio-religious methodology surfaced as a method widely exercised in the Middle East. Supposing two heads of families with large followings of human extended family members and all their goods and animals, some mutual pact would serve them in their preservation.

These two family heads would come together to solidify a "pact" between their consenting families to provide resources for binding the covenant. Several symbolic duties were required of each participant. (A review of Genesis 15 will be a good preface, here Abraham enters into a Covenant with God. God instructs him to cut in half various animals and prepare them for the Covenant bonding.)

ELEMENTS OF THE COVENANT

1. Elements outside the halves:

    a. Exchange of coats: the coats symbolized the character and honor of the person wearing it. (Ie: Joseph's Coat of Many Colors) Here is the exchange of person symbolized. "Put on Christ, like a garment" is the New Testament correlation.

    b. Exchange of swords or weaponry: The hilt of the Nomadic dagger was in crested with family precious jewels and symbolized the status and wealth of the family. To carry another's sword was to pledge that the one possessing it would protect the rightful owner's family in the same manner and reliability as his own. Each pierced the palms of his hands and introduced a darkening agent to the wound in order that whenever those hands are raised, they remind the   world that a piercing has bonded a covenant of blood, their own blood. Each participant clasps the others hands and their mutual blood flows symbolically between them. "As we clasp our hands in mutual bonding, we declare to the world that we are brothers of choice." What a wonderful thing to carry these marks in one's hands, for should an invader appear and notice the pierced hands, he will not know the number and size of those covenanted with. Only one thing is for sure, there would be someone, perhaps many someone's, who unidentified as they were but pledged to rain down vengeance upon them in retaliation for the attack. (Let that sink into your person when you observe Calvary.)

    c. Exchange of names: The infusion of another's name into the name-set of the signatory of the other was a major item. It meant each time a signature was required, the "other" name of the person covenanted with would appear as part of your own name. Imprinting such as this was a significant move, for it meant never making a decision that did not include a thought of the other person. After all, their name became part of your name. (Look at Abraham in Genesis, when God endowed Him with part of His own name. Abram was changed forever to Abraham.)

d. Walking through the Halves: Certain birds and animals were ceremonially cut in half and some larger animals were hung parallel to each other forming an aisle or walkway between them. The animal blood dropped and stained the roadway. Though sounding gruesome in its import, this was one of the key elements found in Genesis 15, when God walked through the halves to consummate His covenant with Abraham. Hence, the covenant is known by the blood. Among the two family heads, they were to walk toward one another in the midst of the halves and pass saying, "as these have lost their lives because of this covenant, so I am willing to lose my life and shed the blood of myself and family in defense of your family." Such a precious spilling of blood was symbolic of a great pact between these two adults. Such a covenant was not taken lightly.

e. The exchange of Information:

Usually taking place as a witness to both families, this portion was performed before everyone involved. The extended family was joining the action.

1. Accounting of wealth: an accurate accounting of the wealth of each participant was given for public display. All accounts, assets, liabilities, everything was disclosed. The purpose of this was to reveal that even non-equals as to wealth need not be ashamed, but could join without hesitation to another. The greater could covenant with the lesser. Nonetheless, the pledge that followed was very significant.

2. A pledge from each, guaranteeing the other mutual possession of the other's wealth was fundamental. To draw upon these resources required no further documents; simply give a call to the covenant partner and say, " I need such and such." "Agreed."

3. Since the extended was included in the possessions of an individual, human wealth was also guaranteed. Labor was also available for each other's projects through this profound act.

f. Final Witness: bread and the wine.

As a final act of covenant, the two parties, before the witnesses of the extended families, partook of a symbolic meal. Each broke bread and gave to the other as a token they were willing to break their bodies in defense of the other.

Wine was shared as a token that their blood would be willingly shed for each other. (Note: A powerful meal is this Lord's

Supper, which will not be taken again with Jesus until the con-summation of the covenant.)

Various and sundry aspects other than these appear from time to time which are relegated to the Covenant of Blood; I have sought to include only the basic aspects which my research has concluded. There may be other elements which are valid, but these are what I feel comfortable with as the prime ones for the Blood Covenant.

One outcrop of this study is that if one party breaks covenant, it does not release the other from the duties of the initial covenant. Only a future covenant added to the old one can supercede the original. The new one does not negate the original only adds features not covered in the first.

So powerful is this relationship through covenant that generations be-yond the original parties find children and grandchildren benefiting from its ties.

The Lord is in covenant with his people and the promises of the Bible reveal the strength and tenacity of our binding relationship to Him. He cannot fail. He cannot fail. His resources are ours for the asking; His fidelity can be depended upon. He defends us against all enemies, but gave his own Son as satisfaction for the covenant—not shedding the blood of bulls and goats but His own precious blood. He has given us HIS NAME. He has shared family secrets with us and engaged us like sons and daughters. He has sworn his allegiance to us and given every assur-ance of working for our benefit. What more can He say than was said by Jesus, "Take, eat, this my body broken for you." "This is the blood of the New Covenant, drink ye all of it." We put Him on as a garment, we have the Sword of His Spirit, and the world (our enemy) sees His nail pierced Hands.

Study of Psalm 106

Briefly, look at the elements surrounding the children of Israel as they left Egypt heading to the Promised Land. Just walk through these scriptures and jot down the various things God said they did.

1. Fathers in Egypt did not understand Your wonders 106:7

2. Rebelled by the sea. v.7

3. Soon forgot His works; they did not wait for His counsel v.13

4. Lusted exceedingly in the wilderness and tested God in the desert. v.14

5. Envied Moses in the camp and Aaron the saint of the Lord. v.16

6. Made a calf in Horeb. v.19

7. Changed their glory into the image of an ox. v.29

8. They forgot God their Savior v.21

9. They despised the pleasant land v.24

10. They did not believe His word, but murmured in their tents, and did not heed the voice of the Lord. v.24

11. They joined themselves also to Baal of Peor. v.28

12. Provoked Him to anger with their deeds. v.29

13. Angered Him also at the waters of strife. v.32

14. Rebelled against His Spirit (and caused Moses to speak rashly "with his lips.")

15. Did not destroy the peoples (God commanded this be done.) v.34

16. They mingled with the Gentiles (nations without God) v.35 Learned their works, idols.

17. They sacrificed their sons and daughters v.38 (look out, to the great Idol , "wealth", have we not done the same?)

18. Played the harlot by their own deeds v.39

19. They rebelled against Him by their counsel and were brought low by their iniquity. v.43

Which of these sins cannot be not found among us today? Even those who claim to be "different," and bolster no church or denomination, have these same sins in their ranks. The Psalmist rightly said that after some great act of God, people might believe for a while, but they soon forgot His works. Natural man chooses his own will above God's will.

The greatest sin of them all is this self-determination. "They did not wait for His counsel." That sin caused them to lust after things that would not profit them, even as the Lord gave them their request. (Listen, this is the case often) He "sent leanness" into (notice it was a matter of imputation) their soul.

In the hour of great "techno-church," with television as its main media, there is a greater leanness of soul than can be measured. Does this leanness approach the dark ages of religious authority? YES! People are shouting rapturously, as the ministry struts its "hour upon the stage," and returns to their former ways without possessing anything from the Lord. God does not desire a herd; He had that in the wilderness. God desires the heart, the soul, and the mind, whether individual or corporate.

The distance between "believing His words," "singing His praise" and "forgetting His works," is a short distance. The distance between Moses' interdiction and "They did not believe His word," is one half a verse! There is a short distance between the words "murmuring in the tents" and "did not heed the voice of the Lord!"

"Murmuring in the tents" is greater among Christians today than among the Israelites in David's day. (There are more Christians today than Israelites then.) *Not heeding the voice of the Lord*, was pointed to as the prime reason for such behavior. It is the same today. One great difference is that the "murmuring" has broken out in the streets. It has broken out into the public arena. It has broken out into the courts. It has broken out into politics. It has broken out into almost every aspect of modern life.

Look at the response of the Lord:

1. Saved them for His name's sake

2. Rebuked the Red Sea

3. He led them through the depths

4. He saved them from the hand of him who hated them

5. Redeemed them from the hand of the enemy

6. He gave them their request.

7. He sent them leanness into their souls

8. He opened the earth up and swallowed Dathan

9. Fire and flame burned up the wicked

10. He lifted up His hand in an oath against them

11. Sent a plague among them

12. His wrath was kindled against His people, so He abhorred His own inheritance

13. He gave them to the Gentiles

14. Many times He delivered them

15. He regarded their affliction

16. He remembered His covenant and relented according to the multitude of His mercies.

17. He made them be pitied by their adversaries

This is a catalogue of a great and forgiving Savior, as well as a God of powerful judgments. One thing is to be remembered, it is not a variance from all other times in History. God blesses after judgment. When the people repented and returned, He was there for them. It will be the same now. The basic difference lies in the time frame—after this final judgment, there will be no time of repentance, for there will be no more time!

ADDENDUM # 4

Liz Manning and the Cake

This is a brief account of obedience by Liz Manning of Broken Arrow, Okla.

Glenn and Liz Manning moved into a new neighborhood last year and attempted to be neighborly to the families occupying the houses surrounding them. The lady next door seemingly made a point of avoiding any courtesies even to the point of never returning a normal greeting of , "Good Morning." Weeks past into months with the same results, until finally a resolve was made by the Mannings not to pursue anymore niceties. It was shortly after this the Holy Spirit told Liz, "Make a cake and take it next door." She questioned this prompting, but in obedience baked the cake and went next door to present it to the unfriendly lady. It was received without even an invitation to come in and was met with evident coolness. Liz returned home confident she had done the will of God but questioning the purpose.

In a few days upon returning from an outing, as Glenn was putting the car in the garage, the lady next door came striding across the yard with her baby in her arms. She was crying. She asked Liz if she would pray for her child as its fever was very high. Immediately Liz began praying in the Spirit and the child's fever abated. This miracle would not have taken place without "cake obedience."

It is necessary to follow the Spirit specifically and down to the last detail.

Mattie Pearson 🖋

I include this addendum to familiarize the readers with Ms. Mattie Pearson. Mattie listened to the Holy Spirit. She read the Word and was in daily prayer for many things the Spirit would show her. She prophesied and often had a word of knowledge about various people. Often, Mattie would go on "special trips." It was not uncommon for her to tell Henry, her husband, "I have to go on a couple of days journey to such and such a place and wait for the Lord to show me the person I saw in a dream." Sure enough, things would be just as she saw them and God would bring a soul into the kingdom because of her obedience. Church folks often did not understand this peculiar saint of God because the wave length she was operating from was different than theirs.

Once, when she was in her early 70's, Mattie felt the Lord calling her to Korea. She had never been on a plane; she had never been out of the country. Obedient to the Spirit she began packing for a long trip and buying travel books about Korea. Finally, she mustered up enough courage to tell Henry. He had long ago learned not to try to deter Mattie, because she was used of the Lord. He thought strangely used sometimes. She asked the Spirit when she must go, how long she must stay and all the things normal for a trip. The Lord told her to plan to stay for a month, that He would direct her in every detail. That was nice, but no further words came. She boarded the plane to Seoul and planned to sit in Kempo airport until He directed her. On the plane she sat next to a Korean businessman. During the long flight, she led him to know Jesus. He invited her to stay at his large and ample home. She was requested to tell the members of his family and extended family about Jesus. The businessman manufactured musical instruments. After three weeks had passed, all the members of his family but one had accepted Jesus as Savior. Mattie was a missionary now in the Biblical sense. Her stay with the family caused many others to come to Christ. When a month was almost full, she took one final tour of the manufacturing facilities to discover that the name on the new organs was "Pearson." The businessman wanted to honor her for bringing him to Christ and being faithful even when she did not know all the details.

Mattie Pearson is one of God's dignitaries spoken of in Jude and evil spoken of in the last days. Religious folks just don't understand her kind, but God does. He calls them "faithful unto death."

Quotable Quotes

While (many) believers are focused on rapturing out, God is focused on divine appointments where people on deserted roads can be apprehended by Spirit-led people of God—who know answers! Chapter 2, page 9

Supernatural living includes supernatural adventures. chapter 2 page 10

We know the False Prophet will attempt to deceive many through trickery and false miracles (feigning the supernatural), but when the Lord shows up, Jehovah will change the definition of "supernatural" for this old world. 2:11

Alas, there is breaking upon the earth a new message about a Kingdom almost unheard of in the kingdomless systems of religion. This is the Kingdom of God and His Chirst. Its gospel sounds vastly different than the diatribe associated with Sunday services. It is unafraid of the crowd and not based on any criteria short of the glory of God. It is the message from a heart "filled with the Spirit," wielding the "sword of the Spirit."

Caught between the demand of the people to hear something and the savage results of saying something "incorrect," ten-forty-five on Sunday morning finds its messenger frustrated and its congregation lost. 2:15

The hardest of rocks are thrown by the religious crowds, the cruelest of dictums fall from prelates lips.2:16

In Paul's day, the decrees of Caesar meant less than the road to Damascus. 3:25

Presently, pious prelates prescribe popular potients patented in Pablum-labs poured out as pitiful placebos to impoverished parishoners. 3:7:

When God spoke, they moved. When the stirring of their spirits by the Holy Spirit came forth, they arose. Better to go at the first stirring than to be churned in turmoil fearing the stirring is over! 3:15

Religious spin has early roots! 4:9

It matters who hold the "steering wheel" to your life.6:2

(Having a Moses and a Samuel in our spiritual past, does not compensate for having folly in our spiritual now.)8:34?

There is a THERE for every individual who resides in the Lord Jesus. Chap 6

Chapter 7: As the world deteriorates, the necessity to hear from the Lord accelerates.

Chapter 8 Churches will comprise those precious sites, where once you met with Him, they will become melted jumbles of judgment!

Chapter 8, page 32 En Punto requires speaking only the words of the Lord, from a heart clean before the Lord, and at the place of the Lord's choosing. The false prophets (of the time of Jeremiah) missed in all three arenas.

Chapter 9 There was no room for dalliance, for dalliances thwart destinies. The twenty-first century is a cavalcade of religious dalliance.

Chapter 10 Prophetic words hung over their society like drapes of judgment over broken windows of robbery.

It is as if all the error of the Hebrew Temple, during Jesus' day, had suddenly found itself in Christendom (chapter 1 page 17)

Biographic Data/Authors

*D*r. Cosby R. Oliver, PhD, is an adjunct professor in the MACE division of Montgomery College, part of the North Harris Community College system. He is a retired professor of Philosophy and Behavioral Science. Dr. Oliver is also an ordained minister. During his 40 years as minister and college professor, Dr. Oliver has acquired an understanding of the Bible from a mission's perspective. Having served in 54 countries and extensively in Latin America, his life experiences allow him to draw upon a large frame of international reference. As President of OEA, Intl., a non-profit missions organization, he is in contact with missionary enterprises world wide. He is the author of *Solomon's Secret*, a commentary on the *Song of Solomon* (1999), *Sons of Zadok* (2000) and *En Punto* (2002). He is married to Betty A. Oliver, a career professor of English at Montgomery College.

① Ernie & Gwen Hall